CLOSE TO MY [...]
SNAPPED . . .

My eyes flew open. Cautiously, I turned my head. A straw sandal was poised inches from my face. Its mate came down beside it, followed by a rifle butt and a flurry of guttural speech. The Japanese!

Out of the corner of my eye I could see Weng with his hand clamped over his brother's mouth. Chien's eyes were wide with fear.

Only a thin screen of branches separated us from the enemy. I sat motionless, not even breathing, and waited for the end.

The sandals moved an inch to the right, and were joined by another pair. A volley of harsh voices ricocheted around the little clearing. It sounded like five or six different men. . . . Certainly there were too many to be overpowered by one blood-caked pilot and two young boys.

I could hear the exhalation and inhalation of every breath those soldiers took, see each fiber in their worn sandals. I could even smell them, a curious musty scent of rice and fish.

The rifle butt in front of me swung up and out of my line of sight. Its muzzle pierced our pine needle screen. A khaki sleeve brushed against a branch. I willed myself invisible. . . .

CHINA THROUGH THE EYES OF A TIGER

ROLAND SPERRY
with
TERRYL C. BOODMAN

POCKET BOOKS

New York   London   Toronto   Sydney   Tokyo

An *Original* Publication of POCKET BOOKS

 POCKET BOOKS, a division of Simon & Schuster Inc.
1230 Avenue of the Americas, New York, NY 10020

ISBN: 0-671-66942-7

First Pocket Books printing January 1990

10 9 8 7 6 5 4 3 2 1

POCKET and colophon are trademarks of
Simon & Schuster Inc.

Printed in the U.S.A.

Acknowledgments

I would like to gratefully thank the following people, who are and have been of tremendous importance to me.

My wife, Enola, for praying for my safe flights
and thereby making them safe

My three precious children, Diane, Ron and Kathy

My mom and dad, for letting me fly in the first place

My brothers, J.D. and Odell

Bob Huffman, for being a true friend
and an ace photographer

Dan Mortensen, my pal

Philo Hatch, for making me believe in myself

And God, for getting me through Hell and back.

—Roland Sperry

A thousand thanks to my family—my beacons in the night.
And to Philo—you're the top.

—Terryl C. Boodman

Foreword

Flying Tiger. During World War II that phrase conjured up an image of a tough, heroic fighter pilot, a flying ace all guts and glory, leaving a trail of downed enemies across the face of China.

The Flying Tigers was the brainchild of Claire Lee Chennault, a U.S. Army Air Corps general who was resigned from active service in 1937 due to partial deafness.

At this same time, China found itself plunged into war with the Japanese. Almost totally defenseless from the air, the country desperately needed help. Chiang Kai-shek, its political and military leader, appealed to General Chennault, offering him a post as Chief of Staff of the Chinese Air Force in exchange for his expertise. Chennault accepted and began to put together his elite group of American fighter pilots.

A deal was struck with the U.S. Army Air Corps. Any pilot chosen by Chennault could resign his commission, go to China in the service of the AVG (American Volunteer Group), and regain his commission upon his return to the U.S.

Chennault was a brilliant tactician, an innovative pilot and a born teacher. He devised methods of flying, diving and dogfighting that made his pilots aces unparalleled in Asian skies. By the time America joined the war in 1941 and incorporated the AVG into the Army Air Corps, the Flying Tigers, so-called because of the fierce tiger shark faces painted on the nose of each plane, were legendary.

While General Chennault was starting his volunteer group, I was finishing up at the University of Texas, where I was something of a track star, and going on to become a flight instructor in Hawthorne, California.

I have been in love with airplanes and flying since the days of my youth, when I watched, open-mouthed, as our local bootlegger soared over the scrub-covered hills, his shadow winging effortlessly over river, rocks and trees.

I received my private pilot's license on my seventeenth birthday, my commercial pilot's license on my eighteenth birthday, and my flight instructor's license only a few months after that. But I never dreamed, back then, that I'd end up a Flying Tiger.

Time is a strange substance. The events I have set forth in this book happened forty-four years ago, more than half a lifetime earlier. Looking back is like passing through a mirror—some things are reflected with startling clarity, as if they were even now unfolding before my eyes. Others are murky, or blurred, as if viewed through an old glass in which the silver has faded and tarnished. In places the two views merge into one, so that a moment within an hour, or an hour within a day leaps into brilliant focus, leaving the balance suspended, dimly visible, in the deep well of time.

Perhaps that isn't time but memory. Or perhaps they are one and the same.

I have attempted to write this story exactly as it happened, dipping back into time to the thoughts and feelings and knowledge I had *then*. Except for the first few pages, a foreshadowing of the future, I have set out events as I perceived them at the time. In 1941 we didn't know when the war would end, or how, or why. In 1944 we knew nothing of space travel, nuclear disarmament, VCRs or even TV. The elusive fabric of time was different, the memories not yet formed; the past was still the present.

And to recapture it, all I have to do is remember . . .

CHAPTER ONE

Shot Down over
Hong Kong

A full moon hung low over Kweilin, China, throwing into sharp relief the jagged, incisor-like mountains which surrounded the town and covering the rice paddies with a silver sheen. Beyond the rice paddies it picked out the wide swath of runway leading into the American air base and cast deep shadows into the rammed-earth revetments where the planes stood in three A.M. silence, tiger sharks' teeth bared in readiness for the next battle.

In the barracks at the north end of the base, a sliver of moonlight pierced the burlap over the windows and stole into the bay I shared with eleven other pilots. As Duty Officer for the coming day, I had the semi-private end of the room to myself. Sleep, heavy as a drug, hung thickly in the still air, and I turned my face into it greedily. The last verse of "I'll Be Seeing You" drifted endlessly through my mind and the inescapable, indefinable smell of spices and incense, damp earth and human fertilizer that was China insinuated itself into my senses as strongly as when I was awake.

Three hundred miles to the southeast, the Kowloon

docks of Hong Kong slumbered under the same bright moon glinting off the gunmetal gray of Japanese warships at anchor.

Across the harbor, Chinese sampans bobbed with the tides, and in Kweilin I too flowed along on a tide of sleep, unaware that within hours I would be shot down over that same waterscape and my life would be entirely in the hands of Kuan Yin, the Chinese goddess of mercy. But I didn't know, and so I dozed on under the scratchy regulation blanket until the jangle of the telephone woke me with a start.

I jumped up at once to answer it, my heart pounding as it always did when it was my turn as Duty Officer, and grabbed it on the second ring.

"Hostel Number One, Captain Sperry speaking, sir."

Captain Gentry's low voice echoed dully in my ear. "Have your men report to the mess hall immediately. I want them in the briefing room by 0500 hours."

"Yes, sir."

I put down the phone and looked at my watch. Four-thirty A.M. An ungodly hour to be awake, much less to have to wake anyone else. There's something unnerving about being jarred into consciousness in the small hours of the morning, some inner timeclock that tells you something is very wrong.

And of course, something was wrong. We were in the dark heart of World War II, October 1944, and this call was either because the enemy was headed our way or because we would soon be headed theirs. In either case, fear was in the air. You could smell it mixed in with the fertilizer wafting in from the fields and the coal smoke pouring out of the hostel stove and the leather of the bomber jackets slung on pegs on the walls.

But I was twenty-four years old, a pilot with the

famous Flying Tigers, and very serious about my responsibilities. I preferred to think of that undercurrent in the air as danger rather than fear, and to believe that, despite the cliche, danger was my business. It made it easier to believe I was going to make it.

I lit a candle and went around shaking everybody awake, feeling like a cross between a camp counselor and somebody's mother. It gave my heart an odd thump to see these guys, so peaceful in sleep, and think that I could very well be waking them to a day of pain or terror or eternal sleep. That kind of thinking made me move gently as I put my hand to a shoulder or shook a foot poking out from under a blanket; but then the guys would get up groaning about the earliness of the hour or complaining that I had woken them from a dream of a particularly luscious girl, and then they were just ordinary guys with ordinary lives and I was just one of them.

Back at my locker, I pulled on my regulation khaki slacks and shirt and the leather jacket called an A-2, and stepped out into the autumn chill. I didn't feel like joking with the guys this morning; I wanted to be outside, to get matters under way and over with.

The moon, waning into pre-dawn, was still bright, illuminating the dirt path to the mess hall. The cooks had been up for hours already, slaving over vats of powdered eggs and gluey oatmeal, but there was no way to know that from out here. No welcoming light spilled from the building, for the Japanese had taken to night-bombing our bases and we were operating under blackout conditions.

I looked up at the sky, but except for the moon, there was nothing visible, nothing audible. If the Japanese were coming they were still a comfortable time frame away.

At the onset of the war the Chinese had established

an enemy aircraft early-warning system which was remarkable accurate and efficient despite the fact that it was also rather primitive. It consisted of watchers on every hill and mountain top in the country, equipped with field glasses and a telephone. Each watcher reported aircraft movement as he saw it overhead. The knowledge was passed from phone to phone down the line, sweeping with the speed of wildfire across the towns and rivers and rice paddies into our military command centers. This warning network was so swift and so accurate that we never did figure out exactly how they did it.

Suffice to say they did. I could eat my eggs and drink my coffee, secure in the knowledge that the Japanese, if they were coming, would not be here yet.

The mess hall was steamy, warm as a womb, with the ambience of a high school cafeteria. I sat listening to the noise swirling around me, the pilots joshing one another and grumbling about the food, the clank and clatter of the kitchen, the beefy cooks arm-wrestling oatmeal into serving pans, scraping pancakes off the grill, and I felt, as I always did, that I was drinking it all in along with my coffee, the warmth, the noise, the familiarity of my own kind.

Wrapping the feeling around me, I drained the last drop of coffee from the cup and took my dishes and tray to the wash window, where Frank, the K.P. corporal, accepted them with the usual scowl, as much a part of his face as the unlit cigarette forever dangling from his lower lip.

"Thanks, buddy. Great breakfast."

"Huh," was the only response Frank ever gave. Then, amazingly, "See you around."

I added that benediction to my mental insulation and walked out of the mess hall into a darkness barely lightened by the coming dawn.

The base, raw and sturdy as a sod house on the prairie, was springing to life. Men on foot and in jeeps and trucks hurried across the bare landscape, headlights dimmed, voices low. Neither trees nor shrubbery softened the square lines of the single-story mud-brick buildings, each one built of the same specifications regardless of purpose and set on the Kweilin plain in no apparent order, some in geometrical rows, others offset at angles across a wide stretch of dirt.

There was method to the Army Air Force's madness, even if it wasn't obvious. The barracks buildings, for instance, were kept apart so that if one was hit by enemy bombs and its pilots killed, those in a further location, at a different angle, might be spared. The mess halls were separated for the same reason.

"Besides," I thought, resolutely dodging a speeding jeep, "walking from one to the other is good exercise." Little did I know how *much* good exercise was in store for me.

The jeep sputtered away into the dark and turned in to another coal-heated mess hall which would serve as our briefing room for the day.

A thick haze of cigarette smoke and loud chatter assailed me as I opened the door. My fellow pilots, keyed up by the tensions waiting overhead and buoyed up by caffeine and nicotine, generated an almost electric charge in the close room.

A couple of guys from the barracks made room for me on a scarred wooden bench and I squeezed in beside them.

"Hey, you Damn Yankee," I said, punching Bill Law in the arm. He was the only one of us born north of the Mason-Dixon line.

"Hey, there, Roland," he replied, affecting a deep drawl and goo-goo eyes.

Bill Harbor, whom I grew up with in Texas, pulled

my cap down over my eyes in greeting, and took a long draw on his smoke.

We knew we were acting silly, not to mention immature, but the briefings had that effect on you. The dual emotions of nervous anxiety and desire to get in on the action produced a sort of reckless high which, while it lasted, was exhilarating.

We joked around until the schoolroom clock on the wall hit the dot of 5:00 A.M. The burlap-hung door swung open and Colonel Powell, the briefing officer, entered the room, khaki uniform precisely pressed, shoulders square, angular chin jutting forward. The atmosphere changed immediately from locker room antics to dead serious silence. It was as if someone had flicked a switch.

The Colonel stepped up to the front of the room and leaned forward on the podium, in an attempt to bore every word directly into our brains.

"Good morning, men."

A couple of cigarette coughs. The Colonel waited.

"This morning you will be participating in one of the largest bombing raids ever mounted in the China-Burma-India Theater."

A couple more coughs, nervous ones.

"Our target is the Kowloon docks of Hong Kong. There will be three squadrons from our base."

Three squadrons, forty pilots. Forty faces taut with concentration in the smoky room. Forty chances to become an ace or a statistic.

I stole a glance at the guys from my barracks, my buddies, each one emanating a presence or magnetism that was himself and yet contributed to the whole. I have encountered this feeling before and since, but only in situations where each man is responsible both to himself and his fellows for the success or failure of a crucial mission.

We lost men every day, and each time it hurt, but there was always the comfort of knowing that they had given it their all, not just a halfway job.

As I sat listening to Colonel Powell I didn't think about any of this in a concrete way; you couldn't do that on a daily basis and still maintain your sanity. It was always in the back of your mind, of course, but if you dwelled on it you'd be a goner before you ever reached the sky. If I had known as I sat on that hard wooden bench that I would soon be shot down myself, would I have been able to go up that morning? Fortunately, perhaps, I'll never know.

So I sat in blissful, if tense, ignorance and took notes on rendezvous points, target headings and weather. I received my code name for the mission, "Daybreak Charlie," got up with the guys when the colonel had finished talking, and caught a weapons carrier out to my plane.

Her name was Texas Belle and she behaved like a Southern lady, smooth running and silky, her P-51 Mustang engine free from hitches or glitches or nervewracking idiosyncrasies, the shapely blonde painted on her side always smiling saucily.

The sun was just rising as we pulled abreast of the revetment where Belle stood waiting. The light glinted off her glass canopy and highlighted the fearsome tiger shark grimace painted below her nose.

I always got a tremendous lift out of that sight, and I swung my tall frame out of the carrier with a spring. I was a fighter pilot, a Flying Tiger; there were guys who'd give their eye teeth for my job, with good reason. Flight was a thrill you never got over.

My ground crew had already checked over every inch of the plane but I went through the familiar routine of the pilot's walk-around, looking for loose cowling or Dzus fasteners, giving Belle a reassuring good luck pat before takeoff. She was, as usual, A-OK.

I pulled on my brown silk gloves, then the brown leather ones over those, strapped the parachute onto my back and the Mae West onto my front, adjusted my cap and goggles, and climbed into the cockpit.

At once the familiar smell of the plane rose up to greet me, a mixture of cold metal and warm gasoline overlaid with the tang of excitement and the dry, dusty scent of fatigue, which worked their way into an aircraft on its first flight and never left it again.

The sun was well above the horizon by now, streaming down on the wide white runway, built entirely by hand with coolie labor. The crew chief gave the thumbs-up, and we were off. I was the leader of my squadron and we were the first squadron off the ground.

I taxied down the runway, picking up enough speed for lift-off, and eased back on the stick. Belle's nose, then her tail left the ground in a smooth motion, and Kweilin fell away below me in a complex embroidery of lanes and alleys and narrow streets. Houses roofed in red tile hugged the congested byways, jostling their neighbors shoulder to shoulder, and spilled out into the countryside, a quilt of greens, each square more vibrantly verdant than the next. Through them flowed the Li River, a silver serpent carrying sampans and needle-thin fishing boats, diving cormorants and leaping carp along in its shining wake. Jagged-edged limestone mountains, like so many tiger's teeth, cast sharp shadows over the rice paddies and lotus ponds, which grew less and less distinct as I climbed toward the heavens.

I loved this part of flying, sailing aloft between green and gold, free of the earth yet intoxicated by its beauty.

Belle and I soared up to 21,000 feet, and when we leveled off I checked on my two wingmen to the right and left behind me. We were flying a split-diamond formation in groups of three, each leader in front with his wingmen 75 to 100 feet to the rear. Our forty planes fanned out around me in these triangles, propellers a blur, pilots unidentifiable beyond the helmets and goggles.

A wellspring of camaraderie, of shared excitement, bubbled up from deep beneath my flight suit and caught in my throat. We were on strict radio silence, but I threw my nearest buddy a high sign I wasn't sure he could see and smiled into the sun.

One hour thirty minutes to Hong Kong, traveling at 275 miles per hour. Our planes had a capability of more than 400 miles per hour, but with the smaller auxiliary fuel tanks we carried we had a range of only five hours. Fuel was precious and speed ate it up. We would need every drop of gas for the inevitable dog-fights and prayed-for safe return home.

An hour and a half scanning the skies for stray "bandits"—Japanese Zeros emblazoned with the big red "meatball" that was their flag. An hour and a half zealously monitoring the airspeed indicator and altimeter, for just outside Hong Kong we were to rendezvous with the B-24 group we would escort. If we flew too high or too fast on the way in we'd overshoot them. An hour and a half flying a speed-reducing zigzag pattern to keep us in line with the slower 308th Bomb Group.

We droned on. Belle purred like a kitten, though considerably louder, and her perfume of hot oil smoke and crackly, heated radio tubes drifted through the cockpit. Sunlight poured down into the canopy. The world seemed, for a moment, a peaceful place.

And then, there they were up ahead, a whole squadron of B-24s cloaked in olive drab, snub noses sprouting guns like three-day stubble. They rode heavy in the clear air with their deadly cargo, and I felt the smile drop from my face as if it had never been there.

We climbed into position above the B-24s but below the mammoth B-29 Superfortresses, which had their own fighter escort. Sandwiched somewhere in the middle were the sturdy B-25 Billy Mitchell bombers, adding their twin-engine throb to the muted roar. And above us all, at 28,000 feet, cruised the P-38 Lightnings, used for photo reconnaissance.

This was the largest raid I had ever been involved in, with close to 300 American aircraft. The sheer volume took my breath away. A shiver ran down my spine. My hand tightened on the stick and I consciously willed it loose.

The multi-colored necklace of Hong Kong appeared below, and jutting into its harbor was our target, the Kowloon docks.

The battle was on. Wave after wave of planes poured across the sky, bombs raining from their bellies in a torrential silver storm, and where they landed boiling thunderheads of smoke churned back into the air. Flak from enemy ground guns burst up from every angle, and the bomber crews' gun turrets swiveled left and right, spewing shells like hailstones.

A giant red cross blazed from the top of one large building, caving in as we hit it, for we had been told it was a decoy. Tiny toy men raced out of sinking ships and swarmed up the gangplanks. Flames licked at their feet as they ran.

A Zero was on my tail. I dove down through puffs of orange smoke, and came up behind him, leaning on my guns. White tracer bullets arced across the sky like fireworks, and the ruddy glow of bursting shrapnel gave the whole scene an eerie aura of hellfire and brimstone.

The Zero peeled off to the left and another one came in on my right. I banked sharp to the right just under him and came up on his blind side. I had him square in my gun sight. I pressed hard on the trigger, holding my position for a split second until he wheeled around and I saw the bullets from his guns popping at me.

Thick black smoke poured from a B-29 going down just ahead. The air rumbled with the concussion of thudding bombs and vibrated with the roar of overworked engines.

Two more Zeros came head on at me, swerved around and aimed for the B-24 under my wings. My auxiliary fuel was gone. I jettisoned the tank and climbed toward the now hazy sun, then dove down, straight at them. They turned tail and ran.

I climbed again, scanning the sky for bandits, peering through smoke clouds, dazzled by lightning bursts of flak. I thought I could see one coming through a flurry of ground fire. I pulled back on the throttle, and suddenly Texas Belle rocked violently under me like a frightened filly.

We started into a dizzying, diving spin and I fought for control of her. I grabbed for the stick with my right hand, and noticed with surprise that it was covered with blood. The leather overglove had been ripped away, revealing a bright red gash in the silk underglove.

I yanked up on the stick and Belle steadied, but through a gaping hole in the floor I could see a thick stream of orange smoke gushing from her belly. She'd taken a direct hit in the oil system and the engine had seized in seconds. There was no way to maintain control of the plane. We weren't going to make it.

I looked back through the hail of ground fire and

smoke and saw my father standing on our Dallas porch and heard one of his favorite phrases, "Study long, study wrong."

He was right. Now was not the time to *think* about what to do; it was a time for quick action and snap decisions. I considered my parachute, carefully packed and ready for use. I looked out again at the bursting flak and knew I would ride the plane down. Any metal around me would be more protection than a leather jacket and a piece of silk. Belle and I would go down together, but as far from the Kowloon docks as possible. Landing in the waters of Hong Kong Harbor would only make me an easy candidate for a Japanese prison camp.

I turned Belle's nose inland and put her into a glide, coaxing every last mile out of her, searching for a spot open enough to land in but hidden from enemy eyes. We bumped along on air turbulent with concussion above the slums and mansions of the town until they petered out into dry brush, but it was too heavy to come down in. We were running out of glide and keeping Belle's nose up became an effort.

And then, there it was, a dry riverbed set between thick banks of shrubbery. Kuan Yin had been watching out for us.

We dropped into the yellowish sand with a muffled thud and skidded about a hundred yards, until Belle finally stopped with a shudder.

I sat motionless in the cockpit. I had been terrified from the second we'd been hit, but only in a distant, removed sort of way, as if I were watching someone else on a movie screen. I had been too busy to really think about what was happening. But now that I was on the ground and safe for the moment, the heavy build-up of adrenaline flowed out of me in waves, leaving me drained and shaken.

Well. I was young; I was healthy. Lots of guys had gone down and made it back. If they could do it, so could I. I wouldn't think about the ones who didn't come back. I was from Texas and I was a fighter pilot, and who cared if I was cocky? That's what I needed to be, for right now I was my one and only friend.

CHAPTER TWO

Missing in Action

I took stock of the situation. Belle wasn't going to go any further and in fact would only be a giant finger pointing out my position to an enemy spotter. I had to get away from her.

I slid back the canopy, noticing afresh the jagged tear in my right hand. I pulled off the glove and a small river of blood cascaded down my arm.

And now I realized that my left cheek hurt like hell. Cautiously, I put my good hand up and pulled it away covered with sticky warm blood.

"Oh, my God," I thought. I peered with dread into the little cockpit mirror and gasped. Between goggle and chin was a gaping hole.

Well, it probably looked worse than it was. There were numerous small lacerations on my face and scalp, and everyone knew that these things bled far more than they were worth. But if it was nothing, how come I could feel a piece of shrapnel sticking through the inside of my cheek? I decided to stop looking in the mirror.

I pulled off the Mae West, unhooked my parachute,

climbed out of the plane and slid shakily down the wing onto the sand.

More blood. My left leg was full of shrapnel, while the right had sustained what was in comparison only a few mosquito bites.

I had a first-aid kit in my backpack. The thing to do was to find suitable cover and then patch myself up.

I stumbled across the sand into the underbrush, dragging my left leg a little and trying not to drip a trail of blood behind me. I had to get further away from Belle. I fought my way through about a quarter mile of brush, worrying each step that the noise would attract unwelcome attention, and then stopped, exhausted. This was far enough until nightfall.

We had been told numerous times in training not to travel by daylight, when the enemy could spot you as easily as you could him. If you were shot down, you were to hide by day and move only at night. The other thing was not to panic. Someone would surely see you go down, but whether that entity would be friend or foe was a question you might be lucky not to have answered. Therefore you were to lay low until you felt the situation was safe enough, and you were calm enough, to travel.

I looked around. I was in a thicket of reedy saplings—wild plum and scrubby oak and something else which gave off the sharp tang of sage. The screen of brush was so thick that I couldn't see the riverbed at all, but then if I couldn't see it, no one walking up it could see me either. The brush was even thicker at my back and the ground rose in a slight mound, so I felt fairly protected on that side, too.

Of course if someone came along and spotted Belle, he'd have to reason that I would be somewhere nearby, but there was nothing I could do about that. She was too big to hide and I was too exhausted to attempt the massive and probably unsuccessful task of camouflaging her. The sand was dry and shallow, so it hadn't taken an impression of my footprints other than a blurry scuffing. It would be difficult to track me from them. I'd take my chances here.

I sank down in a small depression between shrubs and hefted my backpack onto my lap. From it I took the precious first-aid kit, containing iodine, bandages, salt tablets to be taken in areas of extreme heat and humidity, halizone tablets for purifying water, ampules of morphine, and syringes to inject it with.

These last I set aside; the pain was not that bad, and I didn't want to dim my faculties for the sake of a little relief. I was deep in enemy territory, 300 miles from friendly lines, and convinced that it was only a matter of time until I was taken captive by the Japanese. I was determined, however, to give them a run for their money.

I wrapped my bad hand in several layers of gauze, dabbed iodine on all the nicks and cuts within reach, and taped a thick, clumsy pad over the hole in my cheek.

Placing the bloodied bits of cotton back in the pack so there would be no evidence of my stay after I'd moved on, I sat back to wait for nightfall, or shock, whichever set in first.

It had been just after ten A.M. when I was shot down and it was now past noon. Five hours until sunset, and then one more until full dark.

I tried to get comfortable and relax, but my ears pricked up at every rustle of the breeze in the leaves, and when a bird swooped down close to my head, my heart gave a lunge that sent it rocketing almost out of my rib cage.

The shrapnel in my legs set up a dull throb in counterpoint to the sharp fiery feel of my face and hand, and I began to worry about gangrene. We had been told that the metal shell fragments would cause that dread condition if not treated promptly.

"Relax, Dusty," I ordered myself, and the nickname bestowed by my pilot buddies seemed to work like a talisman. It was a reminder that I was *not* alone, for I knew they would all be pulling for me, and I could draw strength from that beamed concentration of warmth and concern.

I shrugged deeper into my fleece-lined jacket and took mental inventory. Besides the jacket I was wearing a gabardine flight suit bristling with zippered pockets, thick wool socks and heavy combat boots. This clothing would keep me warm enough, for the daytime temperatures hovered in the fifties and at night it probably wouldn't dip below the mid-forties.

In addition to the first-aid kit, my backpack also contained two cans of K-rations, a canteen, a "boy scout" compass, a square of silk half the size of a sheet of paper that would reveal a map of China when dipped in water, and a pointee-talkee, which was a little booklet of pictures of houses, food, airplanes and the like to aid you in communicating with non-English-speaking Chinese.

Strapped to my waist was a cleaned and loaded pistol and a money belt containing currencies of the various provinces we had flown over that morning.

Sewn to the inside front flap of my jacket was a cloth imprinted with what we called the "blood chit," a Chinese flag and some Chinese characters which informed the reader that I was an American pilot and a sizable reward would be paid to the person who escorted me safely back to my base. A square of khaki cloth was tacked over the chit to hide it until the time it might be needed.

I thought about the thick chocolate bar waiting

inside the box of K-rations, but I didn't dare drag it out. I didn't dare move at all, now that I'd got my wounds dressed. I was only twenty miles from Hong Kong and the Japanese were close. Too close.

The hours dragged by. Dry brown leaves dropped from a mulberry tree and whispered around my feet, a sparrow chattered above my head, and once a lizard slithered across a rock. Off in the distance I could see the puffs of multi-colored smoke that meant the battle was still raging, and now and then a parachute came drifting down like a dandelion seed in a storm.

I tried thinking about those guys and wishing them luck, but somehow I seemed to be the only American in all of China, and my situation more horrific than anyone else's. Standard feelings, I hoped.

After an eternity that by my watch was an hour, the vibrating drone of multiple engines drew closer and suddenly the sky overhead was filled with American aircraft. My buddies, going home. I watched them silently, out of sight, trying to fight off an overwhelming desolation and only partially succeeding.

Finally, the sun dropped below the horizon, leaving an afterglow of pale shadows against cold inky splotches. I shivered. Should I start walking now? I peered through the screen of shrubs. The riverbed still reflected the last vestiges of waning light. Best to wait until total darkness descended.

Another hour oozed by, then two. Eight o'clock as I peered at my watch. I was so stiff I wondered whether I'd even be able to creak to my knees. And now the moon had risen, cloaking the thicket in a mottled maze of light and shadow. I could picture myself walking out of the trees, directly into an enemy bayonet. I had heard blood-chilling stories about Japanese cruelty to prisoners of war. I decided to wait

until moonset. The hours crawled by; midnight, one
A.M., two A.M.

Suddenly I heard the scuff of boots on sand. My
heart gave a tremendous leap and then froze solid.
Cautiously, quickly, I sank back down into the shrubbery.

The footsteps continued along the riverbed, closer,
louder. And now there were voices, two of them,
conversing in the high-pitched, rising and falling ca-
dence of Chinese.

I knew as soon as I heard them that they weren't
Japanese, for Japanese voices were more guttural and
their speech chopped and harsh as though each word
ended with the downstroke of a butcher knife. My
heart started up again with a ragged thud and my brain
started whirring.

These fellows could be my ticket to safety. The
Chinese were noted for their willingness to get American airmen back to friendly territory, hence the state-
ment inside my jacket. On the other hand, we had
been warned frequently that *anyone* could be a spy,
and many Chinese had become Japanese sympathizers
in the interests of self-preservation.

The footsteps and voices drew abreast of my hiding
place. I had to make a decision now. I rose painfully
and parted the brush.

Two shadows stood in the sand, listening in rigid
silence for my next move. I must have appeared out of
the thicket like a tall dark scarecrow, either man or
ghost, friend or deadly enemy.

"*Ni-hao,*" I said, which was the greater part of my
Chinese vocabulary and means "hello."

The shadows edged closer, and now I could see that
my potential rescuers were only children, boys of
about fourteen or fifteen. They had short, sturdy peasant frames and squarish faces topped with thatches of

bristle-straight hair. Their clothing, dark colored in the dim light, was too short in the arms and legs and too wide at the waist. They each carried a small cloth pack the size of a grocery bag, and nothing else, not even a walking stick for protection. I towered over them, but they stood tough.

I pointed at my chest. "American."

"We see flag," the older one demanded.

I pulled open my jacket and ripped the khaki cloth from the blood chit. They read it carefully, peering close in the moonlight, speaking excitedly in Chinese.

"Gun," the older one ordered, with a gesture toward my holstered .45.

I took out the clip, put it in my pocket, and threw the pistol to the boys. This was another lesson we had been taught in briefings; if you wanted help from the Chinese civilian, you had to be willing to relinquish your firearm superiority.

The older boy picked up the pistol and stuffed it into his trousers with an authoritative air.

"Bullets," he demanded.

I handed over the ammo clip. He placed it carefully in his pack.

"We take you to Americans."

I assured them that they would be paid handsomely on my return and the younger one smiled in delight.

From this point on the boys and I were a team. They were brothers, Weng and Chien Lee. Weng was the older by a year. Their parents had been killed in an earlier raid on Hong Kong and they were escaping to friendly territory, traveling at night as I planned to do. We agreed to make the trip together.

At Weng's suggestion we stayed put for the short remainder of that long night. I broke out one can of K-rations, which the boys wolfed down in a way that spoke volumes about the size and frequency of their meals in the past weeks. I could choke down only a few bites because of the hole in my cheek, but even so the cold, fatty stew and flat, dry crackers tasted like the finest Texas barbeque, and the chocolate bar was pure heaven.

I gave them my canteen. They disappeared into the brush and came back ten minutes later with water. Only then did I realize how terribly thirsty I was. I reached for the canteen, then stopped short.

There was no such thing as potable water in China. Due to a nonexistent sanitation system and the Chinese farming technique of using "nightsoil"—human waste—as fertilizer, disease ran wild in every city, town and village. Potent, deadly germs flowed down every street, through every field and into every source of drinking water in the country.

The boys, as native Chinese, had a certain immunity, but my water would have to be purified. I dropped my halizone tablets into the clear liquid and waited in an agony of thirst the prescribed thirty minutes before guzzling it down. The cold liquid went immediately to my torn cheek like a knife and I choked, tasting blood.

"Slow," Chien said, grabbing the canteen from my hands.

"I'm okay." I grabbed it back and sucked down the water greedily, but as slowly as I could force myself to take it.

After we ate, we conducted our own version of a briefing session. I had originally planned to go back toward the sea, then work my way west along the coast, but the boys wanted to head inland, almost straight north toward Kweilin. Theirs was a much better plan, shaving off almost half the distance and avoiding the worst of the Japanese territory around Hong Kong. We would leave the next night.

As soon as that decision was made, I put my head back on my pack and fell into an exhausted sleep. Kuan Yin had indeed been merciful in sending me Weng and Chien, and the cricket serenading us from the riverbed promised us luck.

I spent most of the next day sleeping, trying to recoup the energy drained from my body by shrapnel and shock. While the boys kept watch, I drifted in and out of a fog of vaguely sinister dreams, coming to now and then with a jolt as I remembered where I was.

At dusk I awoke to find Chien peering into my face with concern.

"*Ding hao*," I said, smiling to show that I was, really, just fine.

Chien sat back on his haunches and laughed. "*Ding hao*. We go when stars come."

We shared another meal of cold canned stew—the last of the K-rations—and also shared information about ourselves. It seemed as though we had known one another much longer than just a day and a night, as though the threads that connected our lives had been strung long ago. Already the pattern of our relationship was comfortable and well-worn. But within that relationship the boys and I knew nothing of each other's lives and histories and habits.

I told them something about my wife, my parents and family, my friends back in the States, and felt as though I was describing people from a dream, vivid but unreal nonetheless.

The boys spoke English with a curious, clipped British accent which I found disconcerting, until I realized that they had learned the language, like most Chinese residents of Hong Kong, under British rule of the area. Their English was adequate but not fluent, strained to the limits as they described their lives to me.

Their parents had been merchants of some kind, though what they sold I never understood, and the boys had attended school like any middle-class American kids. They were clean, courteous, educated, moving in an entirely more modern world than the peasant farmers outside Kweilin. Their lives had been normal and relatively uneventful—until three days before we met when bombs from an air attack killed their parents and ended the world they had known.

The boys haltingly described the attack. "Planes," they kept saying. "Many planes in sky."

A hole opened up in my stomach, black, fearsome and miles deeper than the one in my cheek. Whose planes had turned Weng and Chicn into orphans, American or Japanese?

I tried to think back, before Belle and I crashed. I had not been involved in a Hong Kong raid in the past week, but bombers could have gone out from any number of other American bases. We didn't do strafing runs on the peninsula for fear of killing civilians, but shells often went miles astray of the intended target. And the planes which dropped them could just as easily have been Japanese.

I could never determine whether the boys had lived in Kowloon or Hong Kong, only that it was somewhere close to the water. Since they could not geographically pinpoint where they had lived, it was impossible to tell what target the bombers might have been aiming for. The answer was always cloaked in darkness.

It was also impossible to understand where the boys had been when the air raid occurred—at school or at home, on an errand or out playing. All I could pin down was that they had been away from their parents at the time, perhaps on the other side of the city. I didn't understand whether they had returned home, laughing and happy, to find their parents dead and their house or storefront gone, or whether someone had brought the tragic news to them. All I did understand was that they had decided, like so many other Chinese, to flee the city, go inland to an unknown place where they might find the peace that had so recently been shattered.

Perhaps it was our lack of common language that prevented them from describing the incident clearly, or perhaps it was a defense mechanism in their minds, a dark curtain drawn tight over an event too horrible to remember.

I thought it likely that Weng and Chien would never know what had happened. Perhaps it was best that I didn't know either, but the question of responsibility lay in wait, gnawing at me in odd, unguarded moments as I observed the boys.

The sky turned from pearl gray flannel to black velvet decked out in diamonds.

It was time to go. The boys picked up their cloth bundles and I grabbed my pack. I pulled out the compass and pointed us northwest, away from the riverbed.

The moon had risen again, distorting shapes and lengthening shadows so that we stumbled over roots and walked into half-seen branches in the thick brush, each one a Japanese soldier waiting to practice his terrible tortures on our little group. My left leg throbbed at every step, and now and then I could feel a warm trickle of blood coursing down toward my ankle. The damp air crept under my leather jacket, and I felt sorry for the boys in their thin cotton ones.

But they marched on, never complaining, and after a while I began to marvel at the resiliency of the human spirit. Here were two young kids who had just lost both parents, who owned nothing in the world but the clothes on their backs and in two pitiably small packs, walking into a future that was at best uncertain; and still they were determined, proud and ingenious. I decided to forget my own small hardships.

Weng and I took turns in the lead. Chien, as the youngest, stayed, in true Chinese fashion, a respectful distance behind, although I could tell he occasionally had difficulty restraining himself from running ahead in sudden bursts of enthusiasm. I wished I felt the same way.

Weng appeared as wary as I was. He took each step cautiously, peering into every inky shadow before moving through it. A few times I swore I saw him testing the air, sniffing it as a hunted animal does before venturing into the wind.

I took the fore more as a formality, to show that as an American and the eldest I was capable of leadership, than out of any conviction for my own decision-making. The truth was that even after an entire day of rest, I still felt weak-kneed and lightheaded, but I was egotistical enough to think the boys needed my show of strength.

I turned out to be wrong—almost *dead* wrong. In my jelly-limbed state I missed an important clue which would have serious repercussions the next day, but of course I didn't realize what I had missed until much later.

We had been trudging through the brush for hours, beyond conversation, almost beyond thought, when my eyes caught the glint of metal reflected in moonlight off to the side of the path. I bent down to take a closer look.

It was a tin spoon, the kind that comes with mess kits, and the bits of rice which clung to it were still soft and fresh. That was the part that didn't register.

Weng came up behind me.

"What you doing?"

"Nothing. Come on."

I rose with difficulty, feeling afresh the blood pounding into my cheek, and led us on toward that eater of rice.

CHAPTER THREE

Walking with Ghosts

Sometime after three A.M. we reached a grassy plateau devoid of trees, shrubs or any decent cover. It was impossible to tell how far the plateau stretched or what was on the other side. We were still in the New Territories of the Hong Kong peninsula, a sparsely populated region rife with Japanese activity. Daybreak would come only too soon on that open plain. We would have to stop here, in the woods, until the next nightfall.

Three low pines clustered along the edge of the plateau, their branches dipping to the ground to form a natural tent. We crawled in among the scraggly limbs and curled up as best we could on a bed of pine needles. My pack kept poking me in the small of the back, but there was no room to take it off and I didn't want to step back out into the open to remove it.

The boys, smaller than I and therefore more comfortable in the cramped space, put their heads on their bags and appeared at once to be asleep.

I listened to their even breathing, in counterpoint to the throbbing of my leg and hand, and tried hard to ignore the fiery ache in my face. Every time the wind rustled in the trees I jumped and my heartbeat swelled to a crescendo, slowing to normal tempo with painful thuds.

The black night lightened to gray and then pearl as I lay awake beneath the trees. The sun rose, bathing the sky with gold and drawing the sharp, clean scent of the pines into the air. I began to feel drowsy. My head nodded onto my chest. I was floating over China.

And then, close to my ear, a twig snapped. My eyes flew open. Cautiously, I turned my head. A straw sandal was poised inches from my face. Its mate came down beside it, followed by a rifle butt and a flurry of guttural speech. The Japanese!

I mentally kicked myself in my bad leg, finally realizing the significance of that tin spoon. I should have seen that the fresh rice meant the owner of the spoon—and it could only have been the enemy—was only a short distance ahead. I should have held us back a day.

Out of the corner of my eye I could see Weng with his hand clamped over his brother's mouth. Chien's eyes were wide with fear.

Only a thin screen of branches separated us from the enemy. I sat motionless, not even breathing, and waited for the end.

The sandals moved an inch to the right, and were joined by another pair. A volley of harsh voices ricocheted around the little clearing. It sounded like five or six different men, which meant there were probably more because not everyone in a group talks at once. Certainly there were too many to be overpowered by one blood-caked pilot and two young boys.

My heart thudded in my chest like a misfiring engine. It echoed in my ears and throughout the clearing, I was sure.

Why didn't those guys go away, back to their brutal bamboo-cage camp, their warm *sake* and warmer geisha girls? Why didn't they leave?

It wasn't possible that they wouldn't find us, not when my own senses were working overtime. I could hear the inhale and exhale of every breath those soldiers took, see each fiber in their worn sandals. I could even smell them, a curious musty scent of rice and fish.

Surely they could smell me. I was more foreign to this clime than they were, a stranger composed of wide open ranges, cow ponies and leather, good Texas beef, corn and milk and coffee.

The aroma of that coffee drifted in from the past, strong and black and pungent. Coffee brewed in a gallon bucket, drunk from tin cups under a sky teeming with stars. Skin still tingling from a midnight dip in the Colorado River and burnt bronze from shirtless days stacking hay bales and herding cattle.

Galloping across the grassland like a wild Indian, treading softly through fields of bluebonnets, munching on windfalls of pecans from the hundred-foot trees that grew along the river banks.

At that moment I would have given anything to have been back on Granddad's ranch, riding with my brothers, fishing with my uncles, shearing sheep, mending fences—doing anything but sitting here waiting for the inevitable. Now I knew how a jackrabbit felt, caught in our old pickup's headlights on the road at night, frozen with fear.

The rifle butt in front of me swung up and out of my line of sight. Its muzzle pierced our pine-needle screen. A khaki sleeve brushed against a branch. I willed myself invisible. A pinecone dropped onto a fallen log with a tiny crash. Someone laughed, harshly, and the straw sandals turned and walked away.

I twisted my head a mere fraction of an inch and looked at the boys. Chien flashed me a victor's grin, rising from the ground with the fluid grace of a cat. I felt I could breathe again, and opened my mouth to say so when a shot rang out in the clearing.

My mouth closed with a snap. Chien fell back to the ground as if he had instantly melted there, and Weng grabbed at his arm convulsively.

Although part of my mind had already given us up for dead, a small, still-reasoning portion told me they weren't shooting at us. Not yet. They hadn't seen us behind the low branches.

With an infinitesimal motion, I put my face up to the pine needle screen and peered out. A single Japanese was standing about fifty yards away, aiming his rifle at a large pinecone set on a stump, evidently using it for target practice.

He shot again, obliterating the pinecone, and half a dozen of his compatriots came running across the plateau, yelling at him harshly. I couldn't understand a word, but it was pretty obvious that they were angry with him for wasting ammunition.

The men's uniforms were tattered and patched, their leather boots long given out and replaced with worn straw sandals. They could ill afford to lose a single bullet.

The shooter, gesturing wildly, suddenly turned and fired at eye level, directly at our shelter. The boys and I ducked into balls, our hearts going like trip hammers.

For a moment there was complete silence. Then, a scuffle of feet, and I saw small hands plucking at something on the ground just beyond our branches. A black wing swept past. The shooter had taken a crow from our trees.

Conversation started up again loud and fast, moving away into the clearing. There were shouts and, by their footsteps, perhaps three or four more fellows joined the band.

Next came a brushing sound I couldn't identify, then clearly, the strike of a match on metal, and the smell of smoke. They were cooking the bird on the spot. They must have been as hungry as we were, ten men sharing a single skinny crow.

They were still less than a hundred yards away. We didn't dare move, and although they probably cooked and ate that bird in fifteen minutes flat, not bothering to dress it, the time seemed like hours.

Finally, they sucked clean every bone, put out the fire and ambled away, their voices dying into the distance. But it was a good half hour before we unwound ourselves, and nightfall before we left the shelter of the trees.

At full dark we set off across the plateau. I felt a little lightheaded, but whether from lack of food, loss of blood, or adrenaline depletion I didn't know. At any rate, it suffused the evening with a surreal quality, a blurring at the edges which made it difficult to tell how long we'd walked or how far. Each time I took a step I felt as if I were setting my foot down in cotton wool instead of on hard ground. My breath echoed raggedly in my ears. The meadow seemed blanketed in mist, but when I shook my head and looked again it was clear.

Finally we came upon a farm at the bottom of a hill. Its rice paddies, laid out in neat squares, gleamed silver in the moonlight. But even in utter darkness we would have been able to identify them by the overpowering stench of nightsoil. I felt myself becoming queasy, shaking all over.

Chien, who had been staring at the farm as if at a palace, grabbed my sleeve. "You sick," he informed me.

"I'm fine," I said, staggering down the shallow slope.

"Sick," he insisted, holding me back and, probably, keeping me upright.

Weng took over. "Stay here," he said, and pushed me down near a convenient boulder. "We get food."

They melted away into the moonlight.

I sat back and closed my eyes. The tiny farm, the moonlight, the rice paddies all swam in and out of a mist which threatened to engulf me. I swallowed to keep from gagging.

And then the boys were back. They had with them half a cooked chicken—in China the size of a pigeon—two pieces of fruit, and a vegetable which resembled a purple potato.

Chien begged me to eat a sliver of chicken, and although the idea made my stomach revolt, I didn't have the strength to resist. It tasted surprisingly good and made me crave a section of the orange the boys were devouring.

I eyed it like the forbidden fruit it was. Because of the sanitation problem, nothing that grew in Chinese soil could be eaten by Americans unless it was cooked. But I figured I couldn't feel any worse than I already did, and it would be a long time before I reached clean mess hall grub again, so I ate it, feeling like a self-testing guinea pig.

The citric acid burned my torn cheek and made tears stand in my eyes, but after I had finished I felt much better. The shakiness and nausea had gone, leaving an oddly calming fatigue.

"You better?" Chien asked and when I firmly answered, "Yes," he drew out a small bundle from under his shirt.

"Lookee we get for you," he said proudly and handed me the package, which consisted of a Chinese peasant's daily wear. The tunic-like shirt and draw-string trousers were of faded blue cotton, worn and patched but clean. I didn't have the heart to ask how he got them, for they probably represented half of some poor farmer's entire wardrobe.

Chien grinned. "You like? Put on."

"This too," Weng ordered, producing out of no-where a wide-brimmed straw coolie's hat. "Now we go people, you look Chinese."

That was in the eye of the beholder. After I had fastened the shirt over my A-2 jacket and rolled up the legs of my flight suit to the knee, which was where the peasant pants hit me, I was a mighty awkward looking Chinaman. Not to mention the fact that at six feet tall, under the coolie hat I stuck out like a sore thumb with a toadstool cap. But in a crowd or at a distance, my new outfit would hopefully provide some camouflage.

We set off again into the night, skirting the mud-and-thatch farmhouse, treading as lightly as possible on the dirt path. There were no lights in the house and I wondered whether the boys had asked for or had "liberated" our midnight snack. I didn't question them because, again, I really didn't want to know. That small meal, like the clothes, represented a feast to its original owners. However it was gained, I was grateful.

After a couple miles the rice paddies gave way to barren, rocky fields, and beyond them a cemetery crested a hill. The stone grave markers shone eerily in the waning moonlight.

I was about 300 yards up the hill before I noticed that the boys weren't with me. I turned and looked down. They were standing at the base as if rooted there.

I did a quick reconnaissance of the area. Had I stumbled into a nest of Japanese? I saw no one. Still, it wasn't safe to yell, so I motioned for the boys to come ahead. They didn't move. I looked around again. Still nothing and no one. I motioned to them again, but they wouldn't budge. I was beginning to get a little spooked.

I hurried down the hill, peering over my shoulder as I went. "What's the matter, fellows?"

Chien pointed at the cemetery, his eyes like saucers.

"What?" I whispered anxiously.

Chien pointed again, his arm floating up zombie-like, but with precision. I could feel the hair raising on the back of my good hand, but I still didn't see anything.

"Weng," I asked, more unnerved every second, "what's wrong?"

"Ghosts," he said solemnly.

I almost laughed with relief. "There's no such thing as ghosts," I explained, but it didn't do any good. An undercurrent of superstition ran strong in China, sending the ghosts of dead ancestors to lurk in every home, every plot of family ground, and especially in every cemetery.

As well they might. Looking about me at the frightened faces of Weng and Chien, at the glittering, frosty ground and the backlit tombs on the hill, I could almost see the faint outlines of an army of starved and beaten Chinese peasants rising from their graves, marching down upon us.

In the last hundred years, the Chinese had suffered every plague in the Old Testament, and many even Moses never heard of. Disease, drought, flood and famine coursed through the land in a tidal wave of misery. The people were oppressed by foreign powers on their borders and by warlords from within. Intolerable overtaxation was the norm. Men were not drafted into the army but dragged away in bonds, for conscription was a death ticket.

In parts of China, the trees had been stripped of leaves and bark as peasants tried to fill their empty bellies. I myself had seen parents, babies strapped to their backs, struggling to reach a deep pit at the top of a mountain so they could throw their children into it. Their poverty was so enormous that they simply could not feed another mouth. I had seen people, bundles of bones, lying half-dead in the streets with no one to help because to offer aid was to take on the responsibility for another life, another insupportable burden.

No wonder there were ghosts in China.

And if we didn't keep moving, we'd soon join them. Somehow I coaxed the boys past the ridge, but it was like walking with two stiff and unyielding mannequins. When we finally got past the graveyard into open terrain, we were all weak with strain.

We pressed on, trudging through patchworks of rice paddies and lotus ponds terraced into the hillsides, past pitiful mud-and-thatch cottages. No dogs barked in warning, for in food-scarce China, any animal was a source of protein. We were too tired to talk. The only sound was the muffled tread of my boots on the dirt path and an occasional scuffling as the boys' sandals dragged across a rock.

Toward dawn we began searching for a hideout for the day. I figured we had covered about six miles during the night, which, added to the five we had done the night before, meant we were still on the Hong Kong peninsula. The Japanese were still right at our backs. Our camouflage would have to be good.

By accident we found the perfect place, a stand of brush backed by a rocky outcropping with enough room to stretch out between the two.

The ground was uneven and pebbly, but I didn't

care. My face was on fire again, my leg ached terribly, and I was exhausted.

I sank down on that damp earth, my head on my backpack, and closed my eyes. The dark, warm cloak of sleep pressed down on me like a shroud. I could hear Chien calling my name, but I was powerless to answer. I was gone, drifting, drifting away over China.

I was so high that the whole country looked like a map on a page with mountain ranges of inverted Vs and rivers of blue ink squiggles. I could even see the yellowed edges of the page and a freckling of mildew spots, and on the wind I caught the musty scent peculiar to old books.

The map began to spin. *I* was spinning, out of control, hurtling through the sky—Belle and I were going to crash—the land was rushing up faster and faster, brown and thick and . . . it wasn't China soil but the carpet in my parents' living room. I was lying on the floor, half-listening to dance music on the radio, engrossed in a library book about the mysterious East.

I was twelve years old, half a lifetime younger, never dreaming that someday I would see that strange land for myself.

In 1932, few Americans had ever been to the Orient. Those who had were adventurers like Richard Halliburton and Frank Buck, men of daring and excitement. They brought back to the rest of us dark tales of opium dens and thieves' markets, sailors being shanghaied and girls sold into white slavery, fierce warlords and mandarins with fingernails like daggers; visions of pearls and jade, rich silks and golden idols, oils and perfumes and mist-enshrouded mountain peaks. It was all fascinating, and as far off as a fairy tale. Far off . . .

Far, far away, I could hear Chien calling me. I tried

to answer, struggling against that warm, dark cloak, but it was too thick and too heavy.

My head was heavy, my eyelids like lead. I fell asleep with my cheek pressed hard against the book. That was why it hurt so much.

I wanted to wake up but I couldn't. My head was spinning, spinning . . . what was I, a delivery boy for a Dallas daily paper, doing in China? What strange forces had transported me to the other side of the world? I knew the answer. It was Ming the Merciless, arch enemy of Flash Gordon and all mankind. I had shuddered at his evil deeds just last week at the neighborhood movie palace.

The floor beneath me began to shake, and then I realized that *I* was being shaken. Someone was calling me, urgently, insistently, but I couldn't wake up.

I was in Belle again and we were going to crash—I awoke abruptly, sweat streaming down my face and burning where it hit the hole in my cheek.

A nightmare feeling of dread enveloped me, draining slowly as I realized I was *not* going to crash again. Through the screen of brush I could see the night sky, teeming with stars.

Chien had me by the shoulders; he was shaking me back and forth like the milkshake machine at the soda fountain. He looked scared, although he seemed to relax a little when he saw that my eyes were open. He turned and spoke rapidly to his brother in Chinese.

Weng moved into my line of sight. "You okay?" he asked gruffly.

"Yeah, I think so." I sat up and wiped the sweat off my brow with my sleeve.

Chien still looked concerned. "I call you and call you, but you don't answer."

"He okay now," Weng said. He picked up their packs and handed one to Chien. "Come, we go."

"Wait a minute, fellows, it's going to be daybreak any minute. We can't leave yet." Besides, I felt as though I'd just ridden a rollercoaster upside down at triple speed. I needed a rest.

Weng swung my backpack up over one narrow shoulder. "Daybreak many hours ago. Now night again. We go."

"You mean I've slept through an entire day? What time is it?"

"Night. Time to go, before Japanese come close."

That got me to my feet.

"We try to wake you," Chien said apologetically.

"I know, I heard you. But Weng's right, we better get going." I took my pack from the boy and shifted it onto my own back.

I couldn't believe I had been asleep that long. That unnerved me as much as anything else that had happened. In my family we had always been up with the sun, and I had carried that tradition into the Army Air Force, rising before anyone else in my barracks. And now here I had been completely unconscious for what I figured was at least sixteen hours.

The boys didn't own a watch. Mine, a cheap Bulova courtesy of the military, wasn't running, probably because I hadn't wound it. That I could tell by holding it up to my ear—the night was entirely too dark to read it anyway.

I asked Weng when darkness had fallen, trying to estimate how many hours of walking we had available.

"Two, maybe three," he said with a shrug. "Now night. We go."

We went, striking off into a thicket of bamboo which whispered our presence at every step. There wasn't any obvious way around it, however, and we had decided when we first laid our plans, back at the riverbed, to head in as direct a line as possible.

And in China at that time, there were very few roads. Peasants traveled from home to market on dirt cart tracks and from village to village on dusty footpaths. The superhighway was unknown, and even minor thoroughfares were rare.

So we pushed through the bamboo, hoping no one other than ourselves heard our rustling passage, going slowly to avoid tripping over exposed roots. Somewhere in the distance a chorus of frogs praised the heavens and a cricket orchestra rehearsed the same section endlessly.

After a while the bamboo gave way to more compact foliage, honeysuckle and jasmine, unscented now because of the season, mixed with scrubby oak. The effect was one of having come out from behind a dark curtain onto a moonlit stage full of overstuffed furniture.

Chien began to dart ahead, enjoying the alternating patches of light and dark. Weng called him back in a sharp undertone and they exchanged a few high-pitched Chinese phrases.

"Japanese," Weng explained to me.

"Where?" I could feel my neck muscles tense, my shoulders bunch.

"Maybe close." He shifted his pack so that he had one hand on his brother's arm and the other on the .45 I had given them. I understood that the Japanese had done far more damage to these boys than to me. I admired afresh Weng's courage, but wondered if he realized the gun was empty.

He must have sensed something in my attitude because he asked if I disagreed that the enemy was probably nearby.

I said I thought he was a better judge than I, and that was the truth. The cotton wool feeling had returned, and I was having a hard enough time staying upright, never mind outthinking the enemy.

In addition, I was as terrified of gangrene as I was of Japanese torture. I was convinced that the dreaded condition would set in at any moment and unsure by what symptoms it would first manifest itself. I had been something of a track star in college and was used to my body doing what I wanted it to do. Its refusal to immediately shake off its injuries and bounce back was frightening me more than I cared to admit, even to myself, so I was more than happy to let Weng take the lead.

I really don't remember much of the rest of that night—it was all a muddle of light shadows and dark, clawing branches and ankle-grabbing roots, throbbing leg and hand and face. I vaguely recall crossing a stream, the icy water cascading over my boot tops, and I think we stopped at a tiny shrine to Buddha because I remember the boys kneeling by the side of the path. Other than that, it was all a blur of silver and black and blood-red mist.

Then we came to the village.

CHAPTER FOUR

In the Hands
of the Kitchen God

We came upon the village abruptly, rounding a bend in the footpath we had been following for the past mile. It popped up so suddenly that it seemed like a fairy tale town, invisible one minute and there the next. From where we stood the ground canted down steeply, so that the village lay in a narrow valley or bowl, all of it laid out at our feet.

It was a tiny place, not more than two dozen mud-and-thatch houses clustered together around a central well. There were no stores, no stables, no signs of commerce or public authority—nothing but crude cottages and around them the rice paddies reflecting a gray-green radiance back at the moon. From where we stood it looked peaceful, dormant, as though it had been asleep for a hundred years. Undoubtedly, life in the village hadn't changed in ten times that long.

Weng and Chien sized it up with a professional eye, carrying on a rapid dialogue in Chinese. The only word I caught was *cha*, which means tea, but I was so unsteady by this time that the only thing that crossed my mind was to wonder why they would want to have a tea party in this time-forgotten place in the middle of the night. After several minutes of discussion they switched to English.

"We get help in village," Weng told me.

"Food," Chien added with a bounce.

"I don't know," I said dubiously. "They may be Japanese sympathizers."

"They good Chinese," Weng said.

"You don't understand. People in the village may be spies, they may work for the Japanese."

"This good village," he insisted.

"You don't know that." After all, none of us had ever been in this area before. We were all traveling blind, with no knowledge of the terrain or the people, and it was commonly understood that there were enemy sympathizers among the peasantry—certainly they had little in the way of material goods or sustenance to bind them to their own nation. Most Chinese were intensely loyal in spite of insurmountable odds, but you never knew when you'd encounter a turncoat.

"Good people," Chien chimed in. "And food!"

"They'll see me," I countered weakly, meaning that there was no mistaking me for anything but an American. I could be turned in for badly needed cash. "I'm staying here."

"We get help in village," Weng repeated, starting down the angle of the hill.

"You too," Chien begged, and when I didn't move, turned and followed his brother reluctantly. Weng was the father figure in his life now, and he would go where the older boy led.

I watched as they dwindled into the muted landscape, wondering whether I should have gone along after all. Maybe the Lees were right about the village. I was definitely not at my sharpest tonight; I might have missed whatever clue told them it was okay. We had scarcely eaten in two days, nor had even had water for almost 24 hours. Food and drink would be wonderful, and it would be a great relief to be safe within four walls for a while.

Then again, maybe they were planning to hand me over to the enemy once inside those mud huts. I dismissed that thought immediately—I knew instinctively that the boys were on my side; I had since the moment I met them.

So I stood there, wavering mentally and physically, staring down at the dark shapes of Weng and Chien until it seemed that they reversed course and strode back up toward me. I sank down on a hillock of grass, my head in my hands.

A darkness fell between me and the moonlight, and I felt small hands under my arms.

"Come," Weng said, "we get you help in village."

"Make you better," Chien added.

Thus, supported by one brother under each arm, I walked down into the village.

As we approached the nearest house, nothing stirred but the leaves in a single tree standing in the bare yard. No chickens clucked, no dog barked, not a cat prowled around the perimeter. The single unglazed window was blank and dark as a blind eye.

Weng rapped on the bamboo door, calling something in Chinese. Nothing happened. He knocked again, calling louder. We waited what seemed like an eternity, and still the house remained silent.

I was beginning to think it was deserted when a shuffling sound started up inside and came closer, stopping just on the other side of the door. A cracked, querulous Chinese voice demanded an answer, obviously asking who we were and what we wanted.

Weng gave a two- or three-word reply and we waited again. After a lengthy pause the voice demanded another answer. Weng said what sounded like the same thing, and added, "American."

Another pause, and then the door opened, revealing a miniature, stooped old man, not even five feet tall, in tattered clothes. He beckoned us inside with an arthritic hand, then motioned for us to sit down.

In contrast with the moonlit yard, the interior of the house was pitch black, and I stumbled over what later turned out to be a rock protruding from the dirt floor. The old man plucked at my sleeve and guided me to a rough bench along one wall. My eyes were adjusting to the dimness and I could see that the bench, a square mud oven, and a bed in the corner heaped with quilts were the only furniture in the single room.

The old man pushed me onto the bench, babbling away in his cracked voice. Now that he had let us in, the dam had burst in his speech and he went on almost without pausing for breath. He seated Weng and Chien on the floor near the oven, hobbled over to the bed and tussled with the quilts until an old woman, as tiny and gnarled as he, emerged from the heap and ran outside.

In a minute she was back in the hut, bearing an armful of rice stalks for the stove. She shoved them into a small aperture in the face of the oven and lit them with a piece of struck flint. Then she hurried back out with an iron kettle, returned with it full of water, and placed it on top of the oven.

All the while the old man had kept up his breakneck conversational pace, though the woman never said a word. Now he turned to her in a manner indicative of years of unquestioned authority and gave her a detailed command. Still without a word, she turned and ran out of the hut yet again.

The old fellow finally wound down. Standing in front of me, he nodded three times, stared at me hard with quick, bright eyes and spoke a few slow words. I could tell he was waiting for me to reply, but I had no idea what he had said.

I shrugged my shoulders in the universally understood gesture and said very distinctly, "No speak Chinese."

Apparently this was not as universal as I thought because he said the same thing again.

"He say his name Wang," Weng said from the floor. "He want to know your name."

I looked him in the eye. "How do you do, sir. My name is Roland." No response. "Roland."

"Ah, Lo-lan." The old man seemed delighted by this bit of information, nodding so low he almost bowled himself over.

It was very dark in the room, lit only by the reddish glow from the oven door. With Weng and Chien almost invisible in the stove's shadow and the hunched little figure before me flickering in the firelight, I felt as if I were in the domain of the dwarf king in some old storybook.

I half expected him to shower me with gold coins or turn me into a toad, but all that happened was that the pot on the stove began to bubble. Wang glanced into it, went to his door and looked out anxiously, muttering something to the boys.

"He says his wife come soon, make tea," Weng translated.

So they *are* having a tea party, I thought to myself murkily, but that's only for little girls, or Alice in Wonderland. I was muddling my fairy tales.

While I was trying to sort this out, the door opened and Mrs. Wang came in. Behind her was what seemed to be the entire population of the village, all crowding into the hut, hesitant at first and then in a rush. There were about a dozen old people, as wizened as the

Wangs, fifteen or twenty children, each wider-eyed and more doll-like than the last, and about thirty younger adults, although it was hard to estimate their ages in the dim light. All had the prominent bone structure of the undernourished beneath the translucent skin of South China. All were dressed in rags and all were carrying tiny parcels wrapped in leaves.

In a room measuring roughly twenty by thirty feet there was barely enough space for everyone, even standing shoulder to shoulder as they were. Mr. Wang went into his machine-gun speech, pushing some people out the door and pulling others to the fore, inches from my face.

I was beginning to feel distinctly odd, like Alice through the looking glass. Everything was out of focus, either too close or too far away.

"Weng?" I called weakly. "Chien?"

Chien materialized on the bench next to me. "Everything okay. You big news. People want to see you."

"Why?"

"You American hero, save China from Japanese."

"I'm not a hero."

"You American. Same thing."

I couldn't think of any reply to that, so I said nothing.

The noise level in the room was rising, a babble of high-pitched voices determined to be heard. Outside, through the open door, things were just as loud, and someone had lit a few bamboo torches. It was like a neighborhood block party.

"Chien," I said rather testily, "the noise. What if someone—the Japanese hear?" I couldn't imagine that the village was normally this festive in the middle of the night.

"Everything okay. They think someone's pig have

babies." Naturally there would be no cause for such glee if a human child was born.

I was too exhausted to care, and anyway the party seemed to be breaking up. I slumped back and watched as each villager handed Mr. Wang his leaf-wrapped parcel, took one last long glance at me and departed.

I must have dozed off because the next thing I knew, Mrs. Wang was pressing a tiny cup of hot tea into my good hand.

"*Cha*," she said reverently. "*Cha*."

"*Cha*," I repeated, dredging up the word *thank you* from my subconscious with immense effort. "*Sheh-sheh*."

Her whole face beamed with delight, and she made firm "drink up" gestures.

The tea was scalding, and served in a delicate porcelain cup the size of a robin's egg, so much finer than anything else in the cottage that it was obviously a rare and prized possession. I was afraid I'd drop it, but Mrs. Wang looked so eager that I clasped it carefully by its base—Chinese cups have no handles—and drank. I was awkward, using only one side of my mouth because the hot liquid was too painful for my torn cheek, but it tasted calm and comforting and revitalizing.

As soon as I was finished, the old woman poured me another cup and after it another, refilling from an old teapot kept on the back of the stove.

I saw that the boys and Mr. Wang had tea also, theirs served in rough clay cups, but when I offered mine to Mrs. Wang she shook her head vehemently, saying, "*Pu-shih*," and poured me another cup.

After this she brought out a bamboo tray piled high with the leaf-wrapped parcels and urged me to take one. Unbound, it proved to be a handful of rice mixed with slivers of vegetable. Only after I had sampled it, picking up the rice grains with my fingers, did she allow the others to take a package. Each small parcel contained the same thing, a few spoons of rice mixed with bits of vegetable or fish, or just more rice.

It was difficult for me to eat, because of my cheek, but even more difficult because I realized the sacrifice the villagers had made in this gift of food. Someone in each family was going to go hungry tomorrow because of it.

I tried not to accept the leaf parcels, but Mrs. Wang wouldn't hear of it. Each time I refused one, she pushed it into my hand, murmuring *"Hao, hao."* When I went so far as to get up and put one back on the tray, her husband said *"Pu-shih"* in tones of consternation and insisted on guiding me back to my bench with *two* parcels.

At that point I happened to glance out the still open door, and saw the whole village standing there, smiling and peering in with great interest. These people had made a great sacrifice on my behalf, and it appeared to be a source of pride, as well as entertainment, to them. It would be rude of me not to accept their gifts, but I still felt guilty. Aware now of my audience, I put as much gusto as possible into eating, smiling widely with the functional side of my face.

In a corner near the stove, the boys were eating lustily, untroubled by any compunction. Their eyes gleamed in the dim firelight and their faces shone with pleasure. Guilt is a luxury of the well-fed, stemming from knowledge of a lifetime of plenty; Weng and Chien did not have that problem.

When the rice packets were empty, Mrs. Wang gathered up the leaves and threw them into the fire where they immediately began to smoke, sending out fans of gray fog. Visibility in the room was reduced to zero, but no one seemed to notice. The old woman passed around the last of the tea, now lukewarm, and we polished it off.

The tea and the smoke were having a soporific effect—I could barely keep my eyes open. The tendrils of dread which kept wisping through my mind had been stilled; I felt as relaxed as in my grandmother's kitchen. My eyes closed, my head slid onto my shoulder . . . a gnarled hand gently touched my arm.

Mrs. Wang gave me a broken-toothed smile and said something beyond the limits of my marginal Chinese.

"Weng?" I waited for him to translate.

The tiny woman put a hand to her lips. The smoke had faded away, the fire had died, and Weng and Chien were curled up to the retained heat of the stove, fast asleep.

I rested my face on my outstretched hand and pointed at the boys, indicating that I would sleep on the floor with them.

This garnered a horrified *"Pu-shih"* from Mrs. Wang. Her husband popped out of a dark corner and he too was shocked. With much gesturing, they made it clear that nothing would do but for me to sleep in their bed.

Again, refusal was impossible, yet I could not bring myself to turn these old people out onto the cold floor. My upbringing would not allow it. Texas is part of the South, and this was something a Southern gentleman simply would not do.

As the Wangs gently pushed me onto the bed, my muddled brain came up with a solution. I lay down full-length on the thin mattress, demonstrating that my legs hung out a full six inches over the end, the bed having been designed for much smaller people. It would be obvious, I thought, that I would have to sleep on the floor.

And that was the last thought I had until sunlight slanted across my face. I could have sworn that I had gotten off that cot and curled up next to the oven, but when I awoke I was lying under the rough cotton quilts of the bed.

No one else was in sight.

The cottage looked even poorer by day than it had last night. The floor was swept dirt, the walls a dun-colored mud. A few straw baskets were set against one wall, and another wall supported a shelf on which were the tea cup I had used, a small wooden figure of Confucius and a paper scroll.

The square oven, built of the same dun mud and set in the center of the hut, held the clay teapot, a gallon-size iron pot and another one half that size.

These, together with the bench and bed, a primitive cot formed of rope strung between bamboo legs, constituted the total furnishings.

I rose stiffly and limped to the door. It was blindingly bright outside, a beautiful morning. I judged it to be about ten o'clock. I had overslept again.

The village was as silent as it had been before we entered last night. I looked up at the path we had taken down, but no watchers stood there. Nor was there anyone in the yard. It should be safe for me to venture as far as the well.

What I wanted more than anything was a wash—even my eyelids felt sticky with grime. I looked for a bar of soap, but that was just one more possession the cottage did not boast. Instead I took the big pot from the stove, then put it back. It would not be fair to squander their undoubtedly meager supply of fuel on the luxury of hot water. I would wash at the source. Setting my coolie hat on my head, I stepped out into the brilliant day.

A breeze stirred the dusty yard and brought close

the smell of the fields—dank earth, wet vegetation, and, of course, nightsoil. To the right of the door was the "honey bucket," the waterproofed basket used for the collection of that noxious fertilizer. It was not empty.

The Wang's house was slightly behind the rest, each house in the village circle being slightly offset, like a mouthful of crooked teeth. I walked cautiously between the blank mud walls, listening for human sounds which would tell me to retreat.

At the center of the circle was the well, thatch-roofed and dun-colored like the rest of the village. Against the wall of one house was a spill of flame-orange bougainvillea, the only bright note in the place.

I sent the bucket splashing down into the well, then drew it up again dripping dark, weedy-smelling water. I must have been weaker than I realized, for the bucket seemed to weigh a ton, and the act of drawing it up with one hand was almost beyond my strength. But the sun felt good on my arms when I rolled up my sleeves, and the water had a bracing tingle as I rubbed it into my skin.

Washing my face made me weak-kneed, even though I tried to avoid touching the damaged side. I had to sit down on the edge of the well. As I did so a disquieting feeling came over me, as though there were unseen eyes boring into my back. I had been about to strip off my shirt. I shrugged it back on, sure I had seen a flash of movement out of the corner of my eye. Probably a bird, although there was no birdsong. A rat would be more likely.

I adjusted my hat and rose slowly, dizzy yet again. When my brain cleared and I could see clearly, there was a child standing in the door of the house with the bougainvillea. Behind her was an old woman, both staring out at me from the dark interior. I smiled at them, but they remained in frozen fascination of this giant from another world.

Now I saw children and old people in the doorways of other houses facing the well. No child was more than a toddler and each adult was crabbed with age. All but the very young and the very old were working in the rice paddies.

I smiled again and called out *"Ni-hao"* for "good morning," but there was no answer.

I didn't doubt I looked pretty frightening. I lowered the bucket down the well and turned back toward the Wang house. Maybe the fact that I wavered a little unsteadily as I walked away was responsible for what happened next.

Behind me I heard footsteps. A hesitant voice called, "Lo-lan." I turned around. It was the old woman from the house with the bougainvillea. I could see her gathering all her courage, for in China women did not take the initiative in such matters. Then she motioned for me to accompany her inside her tiny home.

I had to stoop to get through the door frame. Inside, the furnishings were much the same as the Wangs', except that instead of the bench against the wall there was a low table surrounded by reed mats for use as seats. The stove was a little larger than the Wangs' and was built into the corner. Fastened to one wall was a paper drawing of a squarish fellow in flowing robes, either beaming or grimacing, it was hard to tell which.

The old woman bade me to a seat at the table. With difficulty, I folded my legs under it. Next the woman put a pot of tea on the table and a clay cup. She motioned for me to drink. Her little granddaughter transferred herself from the doorpost to the table, never taking her gaze from me.

I drank the tea, nodding and smiling and murmuring "*sheh-sheh*," but there was nothing I could say to the woman and nothing she could say to me. The silence stretched on. I began to wonder where the boys could have gone and when, if ever, they would be back.

After a long time, the woman touched me on the sleeve and said again, "Lo-lan?"

I pointed to myself, repeating "Lo-lan," then pointed at her. She placed a hand on her chest and said, "*Jiu-mou*."

"*Jiu-mou*," I repeated.

The child giggled, but I must have said it properly because the woman smiled for the first time since I had entered and patted me on the hand.

A fly buzzed around inside the house, recreating somehow the sound of summer. The grandmother brought out a tattered jacket and began mending it, humming tonelessly to herself. The child finally grew tired of watching me and sat down on the dirt floor, drawing designs in it with a stick.

Time stretched out again, with the suspended feel of enforced idleness. I grew drowsy, but roused myself sharply. All I seemed to do now was fall asleep, when what I needed was to remain alert. I had to stay awake . . .

This time when I woke up the house was in deep shadow. Outside, the last rays of sun were draining from the sky. The child was nowhere to be seen. The old woman was lighting the oven. When she saw me looking at her, she came over and patted my hand again. Her skin was as dry and wrinkled as old paper, but her eyes shone in the dying light.

Although she was beginning to seem very dear to me, I was growing distinctly uneasy about where the boys were. I had assumed they were out foraging for food somewhere, but now it was night already, time to move on, and still they hadn't returned. I didn't think they'd go on without me, but the only alternatives were that, or that something had happened to them.

Just as I was becoming really concerned, there was a commotion at the door and in came the old woman's family, two young men and a girl of about seventeen, smelling of soil and hard work. Behind them were the boys. They were all laughing and joking.

I stood up as fast as my stiff knees would allow. "Weng, Chien, where have you fellows been?"

"We work in fields, help Wangs," Weng said.

"Wangs have no children, so we work for them today," Chien added.

"Why didn't anybody tell me? I could have helped." And paid them back for the dinner, I thought.

"You sleep. Good for hurts."

This was kind of Weng, but there was that flash of guilt again.

The child came in, clutching a handful of leaves. She gave them to her grandmother, who put them into a pot already simmering on the stove.

I cannot, I thought, take these people's food again. "Weng, I think we should be on our way."

"Eat first."

"I'm not hungry. I'll just go wait outside."

"We have big feast."

"No, really, I'm not hungry." I started toward the door.

The old woman put a hand on my arm. "Lo-lan." She seemed to be pleading with me not to go.

"You eat fish," Chien said, and from within his shirt he pulled out a good-sized carp, weighing about two pounds. "We catch in river. Very lucky."

Lucky indeed. Chien handed the fish to me, I

handed it to the woman, and she put it in the pot like the great delicacy it was.

Our supper of boiled fish and rice, flavored with the pungent leaves, was served in a single bowl placed in the center of the table. We all ate from the bowl, taking small portions with our fingers and transporting them directly to our mouths.

I tried not to think about germs, although God knew I was hosting enough of my own already. I hoped the sharp pain in my cheek every time I bit down was not a sign of gangrene; surely if I did have that dread disease, everything would have gone numb by now.

No one talked during the meal; food was too rare not to be savored to the last crumb. When we were finished, I turned to the woman and thanked her, using the name she had given me.

"She say to call her that? You know what you say?" Weng asked.

"What?" I replied, fearing I had called her a pig or some other odious term. Chinese is a tonal language, and the same word can mean several entirely different things, depending on which of four tones is used. Westerners, having no familiarity with such a concept, are as apt as not to say completely the wrong thing.

"You call her 'grandmother,' " Weng said.

I was touched, and to my horror, felt my eyes begin to fill. I was in worse shape than I thought.

"We—we need to go now," I said unsteadily. "It's dark enough."

We got up from the table, the boys jabbering away in Chinese, apparently explaining that we were leaving. As we turned toward the door, the old woman took my hand and guided me back to the stove.

She pointed at the picture on the wall, speaking slowly and earnestly as if her words carried great importance.

Chien translated. "That Kitchen God. He watch over everyone in house, then at New Year report to God of Heaven if they good or bad. She tell Kitchen God to watch out for you now, make special trip to heaven. Tell other gods to watch out for you, too; make you lucky."

My voice seemed to have gotten stuck in my throat. With great effort I loosened it. "Thank you, Grandmother, thank you," I said in Chinese, then hurried out the door before my emotions got the better of me.

Outside, the night was very dark, with a pale moon rising. Over near the well, a cricket chirped lustily. Maybe that was the Kitchen God's work, for crickets are lucky.

I took a deep breath, trying to steady my ragged respiration. I wondered what the name of this tiny village was, where the people had such big hearts.

Weng and Chien ran up behind me carrying their bags, which made me remember my own.

"We've got to go back to the Wangs' so I can get my backpack."

"Already have," Weng said, shrugging it off his shoulders and handing it to me.

"We've got to go back anyway, to tell them thank you."

"Already said."

"But I didn't."

"Wangs know."

"But—"

"They sleep now. Rice farmers sleep early."

This seemed to be true. What else was there to do with no food, no light and no entertainment? All around us the tiny cottages were dark and silent, although it couldn't have been later than six-thirty or seven o'clock. We had instinctively lowered our voices as we walked.

Now, passing the Wangs' door on our way back to the footpath we had trod last night, I felt the house was indeed wrapped in slumber. I directed a thought wave of fervent thanks through the bamboo door as we passed by it and out of the village.

This was our third night on the road, my fourth since being shot down. I was getting used to walking to the point of exhaustion, tripping over rocks and roots, always listening for the sound of the enemy, but I hoped the numbing, dazing cotton-wool fog did not become a part of the routine. By this time I was beginning to fear it as much as the impending gangrene.

I scanned my internal systems for signs of breakdown. Everything seemed to be okay—jury-rigged maybe, but okay. The boys seemed jaunty, more carefree than at any time since we'd joined company.

We picked up the path where it intersected the village, following it for about a mile to an intricate embroidery of rice paddies, each laced with mud dikes and decorated with feathery rows of grain. Here the trail petered out. Beyond the roughly five acres of rice was a field of lotus, then another few acres of rice. We would have to thread our way through these fields, for steep hills rose on either side.

The mud dikes, perhaps two feet high and hand-formed, were slippery and it was a constant struggle not to collapse into the shallow ponds.

Rice can be grown on dry land, but it is one of the few crops that is just as happy immersed in water. The Chinese flood their rice fields so that weeds, not possessed of the same amphibian qualities, will be drowned out while the food crop remains strong—an intelligent program for people whose primitive agricultural tools afford barely enough time in a day without the extra effort of weeding.

Mixed in with the water from the irrigation canals was, of course, the ever penetrating aroma of nightsoil. All the more reason not to fall in. I wondered if I'd ever get to the point where I ceased to smell it. I doubted it.

There were frogs in the rice paddies, and every so often one plopped into the water with a loud splash. Otherwise there was no sound. No drone of planes to miraculously see me in the dark and dip to my rescue, no hum of telephone wires to be used in a call for help. Except for the boys, I was completely alone in an alien landscape.

I kept one eye on my feet and the other on the vista ahead. No fog—yet.

I tried to cheer myself up, wondering what the guys back at the base were doing. I didn't think they would have given me up for dead—there had been a number of men who were shot down and took weeks to get back—but I knew my buddies would be waiting for me and worrying about me.

Especially my ground crew. Belle was their baby and therefore I, as her pilot, was their responsibility. They fretted over every inch of her—every seam, bolt, battery, piece of wiring and length of hose. They spent countless hours checking her over, adjusting, readjusting, and checking again. Then, when Belle and I took to the air, they sat up on the revetment, cigarettes dribbling ash between their fingers, and sweated out our return.

Many's the time I'd seen some poor guy's ground crew watching helplessly as a squadron returned from a mission, plane after plane dropping to the runway, every one safely home but theirs. Hours after everybody else had gone in to debriefing and hot coffee, the ground crew of a missing plane would be found, still sitting atop the revetment, eyes skyward, waiting.

The thought of my guys waiting like that increased my sense of desolation. I shivered, and hurried to catch up with the boys. My leg was beginning to drag again, and they had gotten ahead of me by a couple hundred yards.

Suddenly the moon was blotted out by a huge winged form, too large for a bird. Irrationally, I thought it might be a dragon, come to carry me back into nightmares. The tendrils of dread, held at bay during our stay in the village, brushed against my clammy skin and I found that I was sweating in the cool night air. I realized then that I was only feverish, and laughed at myself. The "winged form" was only a low cloud moving across the face of the moon.

But the cloud cover was dropping lower and lower, until it blotted out the rice paddies, the silver water, and the thick lotus leaves beyond. I passed a hand over my eyes, willing the fog away.

When I opened my eyes the fog was gone. The rice paddies gleamed like pewter, the three-quarter moon like ivory silk, but something was wrong. The lotus field had disappeared.

CHAPTER FIVE

Into the Wild Blue

Where a moment before a carpet of deep green leaves lay over the landscape now there was an empty hole, a black field filled with stars, as though a piece of night sky had suddenly been grafted onto the earth.

The ground seemed to sway beneath my feet. I felt dizzy. A glance at the boys told me they had noticed nothing wrong. They walked steadily on, chatting softly to each other in tones too low for me to hear. I must just be tired, I told myself, nothing to worry about. *Don't panic.*

But when I looked again, the rice paddies too had been swallowed by sky. We were walking into a void.

It was like passing through a door. On one side were pain and fear, dirt and stench and fatigue. On the other side were red plush seats, warm, dry air, the smells of steak and potatoes drifting from the dining car, the comforting clack of the wheels on the rails, and the gentle, rhythmic rocking as the train sped through the night.

En route to Ogden, Utah, across the salt flats of

Nevada, glowing faintly under a thin wash of moonlight. Clumps of sagebrush standing out in dark patches on the land. Rocks glittering with fool's gold in veins of quartz.

I knew I was hallucinating, but I didn't care. The motion of the train was soothing, lulling me into a safe place. I let myself slide back through time.

The train was climbing now, into the mountains, through deep tracts of pine, impenetrable in the dark. My reflection skated across their surface on the windowpane like a spirit from a different world.

I *was* from a different world. Union Station, Los Angeles, a Spanish hacienda masquerading as a railway station, full of sunlight and deep shadows and girls in high heels kissing their guys good-bye.

My wife, Ovella, and I had spent the two weeks since the bombing of Pearl Harbor struggling with our hearts, our consciences, and our fears, finally deciding that I should join the Army Air Force. I had been working as a flight instructor at a tiny airport in Hawthorne, near L.A., and it was only right that I use my skills to help the war effort. I was a 600-hour pilot—a hot pilot, I thought, and ready for action.

I drove downtown to the induction center on a Wednesday, December 17th, and five days later found myself at Union Station, hugging Ovella in a fierce grip I hoped would last us for the months or years until I saw her again.

All around us other couples echoed our efforts to grab hold of a feeling with such force that it could never get away. Some embraced secretly in the shadows of the arches, some kissed passionately beneath the great wrought-iron chandelier in the middle of the waiting room, and around us all two small children raced, giggling and screaming, their clattering foot-steps reverberating on the Spanish tiled floors.

That was early afternoon, as a civilian. Now it was early morning, three A.M., and I was only an hour away from Ogden and Hill Field, the Army Air Force training base where I would become a U.S. fighter pilot.

I was excited, my head filled with visions of sleek, snub-nosed P-40s, myself at the throttle, knocking off Japs with a dashing flair. I gazed out the window, beyond the fleeing night forests, to the cocky airplanes awaiting my arrival.

A biting pre-dawn chill, breath coming out in white cloud puffs against the lamplit sky. Stamping my feet and swinging my arms to keep warm. California cloth-ing was not enough. It was cold in Utah, with little drifts of snow piled along the roadways like spun sugar.

We had been bussed from the train station in Ogden to Hill Field, a drafty, jouncing ride during which no one spoke much, except a very young corporal who tried to convince us that we were entering a proving ground no one could hope to pass. His bravado was that of the schoolyard tough who dares you to contra-dict him while secretly praying you won't. I hoped this kid was as mistaken as those bullies. His version of military life was not very attractive.

I would soon find out, for here we stood, one hun-dred inductees, hopeful fighter pilots, in front of the orientation hall, about to be introduced to the Air Force.

We were divided into four groups, or squadrons, and assigned drill instructors. Ours was a tall, muscu-lar, raven-haired staff sergeant who looked like Hia-watha and had the personality of Geronimo. He couldn't have been more than twenty-five, but he had honed the art of intimidation to a keen edge.

"I just got out of Leavenworth," he told us with a blood-chilling scowl, staring into our faces as though searching for particularly tender scalps to add to his collection. "Don't get on my wrong side or I ain't gonna be responsible."

His charges shivered in the cold air. No one dared look him in the eye.

He hustled us into formation, bawling out simultaneous orders to straighten up, turn around, slow down, move it faster, look sharp and keep your eyes to yourself, and quick-marched us across the quadrangle to the mess hall, glowing warm and yellow through steam-glazed windows.

He rammed us through the double doors with a warning to be finished eating and back out on the pavement in twenty minutes, "or I ain't gonna be responsible."

Apparently time was of the essence, and fast wasn't fast enough. The Air Force would feed you, but they weren't going to waste any time on niceties like digestion.

Amazingly, the food was good, hot, wholesome and fragrant, although I noticed that ketchup and Tabasco sauce were the most popular items on every table.

We went through the chow line feeling embarrassed and out of place in our civvies among the combat-tough fatigues and smart, knife-creased khakis, as though we had walked into the War Department in our pajamas. My spiffy pleated pants and two-tone wing-tips looked juvenile in comparison. I couldn't wait to get into real fighter pilot gear.

That morning was my first lesson in the military tactic of "hurry up and wait." By the time I had got my food, found an empty table and sat down at it with three other guys from my group, ten precious minutes had fled by. Cramming the toast and eggs into my mouth and carrying my tray to the dish stand in the corner used up another nine minutes. *I* was not going to be the one to be late; when the wild Indian said twenty minutes, I believed he *meant* twenty minutes.

I hurried through the mess hall, my breakfast thudding in my stomach as I went. The doorway was narrow and jammed with officers, and I couldn't decide, in my semi-civilian status, how much deference to show. I kept waiting for them to clear out but more kept arriving, so finally I just closed my eyes and shoved through. No one paid me any notice at all.

Feeling like I'd run the gauntlet, I raced out into the charcoal-colored dawn. Twenty minutes exactly. The important mission we were being rushed through breakfast for would not fail on my account.

At twenty-five minutes the Indian showed up, bawled out the guys who were just arriving, and lined us up again in perfect formation. Then we waited. A half-hour went by, forty-five minutes, an hour. Our sergeant offered no explanation of what had gone wrong, why we were waiting, but merely scowled out into the lightening day as if wishing himself anywhere else on earth.

Finally, an asthmatic old bus wheezed up, coughed open its doors and admitted us for another bumpy ride. The big rush was over; the major campaign was divulged as a trip to the clothing stores.

I decided I might as well enjoy it and leaned back on the cracked leather seat to admire the scenery.

Hill Field hugged the foothills which gave it its name, contouring itself to stands of fir and pine dusted with sparkling snow. After the static winter sun of Los Angeles, the whole place looked like a Christmas card.

The base was old, built in a manner suggestive of

impermanence, peppered with foundationless frame buildings coated in a dull gray paint that looked like it was peeling when it wasn't. The major landscape efforts consisted of gray gravel and white rocks, with occasional handkerchief plots of grass. There was a movie theater, a library, a softball field, all with the same temporary look.

Still, the big trees and the snow-cloaked mountains visible beyond them formed a majestic backdrop for the base, framing it like a rough stone in a richly worked setting.

The bus wheezed along, pumping carbon monoxide into the pure air, and at last pulled up in front of the supply depot. My heart took an extra, excited beat despite the Indian's dire warnings to keep track of every item we were to be given, or he "wasn't gonna be responsible." I was about to receive my official fighter pilot gear.

Inside the cavernous building, which smelled of dust and canvas and old wood, we were led past long dull-green counters; behind them were cubbyholes and shelves stacked ceiling high with military attire. In the dim, dust mote filtered light it was easy to imagine that most of that stuff had been stored here, unused, awaiting the light of day, since the Great War, or even the Spanish-American War. The amount of gear we were given didn't make the slightest dent in those stacks.

And we were given a lot. Our arms were piled high with olive drab fatigue pants and shirts, blankets, khaki pants and shirts, caps, visors, socks, army boots, dress shoes, dress hat, ties, raincoat, greatcoat, zippered lining, brass and cloth insignia, backpack, canteen, mess kit, sleeping bag, pup tent . . . my arms sagged under the weight and I could barely see over the top of the load until they gave me a duffel bag to shove it all into. Then past a final counter manned by a final surly airman, and I was handed my pilot's jumpsuit and the coveted leather combat jacket.

I was in heaven. Now I was a confirmed fighter pilot, itching to get at the controls of a honey-voiced P-40. I could hear her engines singing already.

The Air Force, however, had a different opinion on the matter.

The next two days were taken up entirely with lectures on rules and regulations, how to care for your gear, how to care for your body (which now belonged to Uncle Sam), with running from classroom to barracks to mess hall and back and with so many shots that I dreamed about that insidious silver needle, aiming at me like a mosquito from hell, and my arms got so sore I could barely lift them.

On the third day, we were addressed by Hill Field's commanding officer. An imposing, craggy-faced fellow with ramrod posture and a steely eye, he stood before his new recruits, one hundred young hotshots, eager, cocky, confident.

"How many of you are pilots?" he barked. "Raise those arms in the air."

A hundred hands shot up with pride. The C.O.'s face took on a deep frown of displeasure. His eyes narrowed. We knew we were in trouble.

"Not in the Air Force, you're not," he growled. "Just forget you've ever seen an airplane. Now you're here, you're going to fly our way or you're not going to fly at all."

That took the wind out of my sails. I was insulted. How dare the Air Force insinuate that I didn't know my job? I wouldn't have joined up if I didn't think I had something to offer.

I was already an experienced pilot with more than 600 hours in the air when I arrived at Hill Field. I had received my license at age seventeen, and had already been flying for four years. I knew all about gravity and lift, thrust and drag, how to dive into a roll and how to pull out of a stall. So did the other fellows in my group. But according to the Air Force we were novices still wet behind the ears.

Out of the corner of my eye I could see the other guys' mouths set into hard lines. Obviously they felt the same way I did. A hundred arms covered in brand-new khaki sleeves came down in a hurry.

But we couldn't back out now, nor did we want to. We had pledged ourselves to Uncle Sam and we'd just have to bite the bullet.

And it turned out that Uncle Sam didn't want you to fly all that differently; he just wanted you to maintain discipline while you were up there.

So we learned to salute everything and everybody, to end every question or answer with "yes, sir" or "no, sir"; to stand at attention, chin in, chest out; to march in single file and fall in in neat, orderly rows. We learned to be officers and gentlemen, and that along with the privileges of rank went respect and responsibility.

We ran everywhere; double time became a way of life and sleep was a distant memory. We stayed up until three o'clock in the morning polishing brass and spit-shining shoes, then were rudely awakened two hours later by the sergeant, who would slam into our barracks bellowing that we had five minutes to get up, dressed and outdoors for morning inspection.

On the rare Saturdays when sleeping in was allowed, half the guys complained that they couldn't sleep because they were too mad at the sergeant.

I ignored them. Mornings were not their best time, and when they weren't complaining about the sergeant they were belly-aching about me.

I had been appointed squadron leader, not by popular vote, but by the Indian, a move I never understood, since he never gave any indication of why he chose me, and instead acted as though he had never come across anyone with less brains (although he treated us all that way).

One of my responsibilities, as leader, was to get everyone up in time. This involved a lot of cajoling, cussing, and, on occasion, buckets of water in the face, which prompted one of the guys to tell me, "My only hope is that when you get home to your wife after the war, you'll let her sleep past six o'clock in the morning."

I figured I'd worry about that when the time came. In the meantime, I was more concerned about demerits. Twenty-five and you were washed out of the program, and one of the easiest ways to get gigged was not being out on the inspection line on time. I wasn't going to let that happen to anyone in my squadron.

Actually, once I got over the shock of not being considered a bona fide pilot, I was happy with the routine. I hated being bullied, of course, and the endless round of inspections was wearing, but I realized that discipline was important to the mechanics of the military, and that adherence to the rules was an important part of the game. I was very competitive and I wanted to get ahead, so I played along with it. There wasn't any point in fighting it . . .

Why fight when you could drift along through the star fields in the lotus ponds?

Or was I running . . . running through the wooded tracts of Hill Field, breathing in sharp lungfuls of crystalline air, my pack wedged comfortably in the small of my back, trotting with the rest of my squadron toward the spot on the map where we would bivouac for the night . . .

Or running around the track beyond the softball field, determined to beat the sergeant to the finish line? I could see him up ahead, his crow's-wing hair glistening in the sun, legs pumping up more speed as he bent into the curve, face already chiseled into a victor's grin.

I knew I could beat him. Let him think he could win; he didn't know I had been a track star in college and my legs still remembered all the moves. I leaned into the straightaway, feet pushing off the dirt surfaces like pistons, and pounded into the curve a hair's-breadth behind him.

He felt me behind him and lengthened his stride, but I was prepared and in the instant he wasted slowing to look behind at me, I surged ahead and pounded on past. My blood rang in my ears and the trees clouded before my eyes, but I laid on a final burst of speed and lunged across the finish line a hundred yards ahead of him. I felt wonderful.

The sergeant charged across the line and then stopped abruptly, his coal-black eyes snapping sparks. He turned, glowered at me, and then walked up and clapped me on the back. "Good race, Sperry."

That was it. He strode off the field alone, glaring into the distance. Neither of us ever mentioned the race again, but I remembered it every time he bawled us out, and smiled a secret, interior smile. I knew we were equals.

And I knew that when we were finally allowed to fly, I'd be miles above him.

But I was at Hill Field for six weeks before I even saw a plane at close range. Until then we spent long hours in the classroom learning navigation, figuring wind drift, cruise, and range. We had courses in instrument flying, radio, and morse code. My head was filled with staccato dots and dashes, with the swinging Aquadrants and N-quadrants of the navigational circuit, when all I longed for was the feel of the stick in my hand, lifting me and my fighter plane high into the blue beyond.

At last the day came when we piled into the burly trucks called weapons carriers and rode over the ridge to the airfield. There below us was the runway, running out like a licorice whip into a stubby field of winter grasses. At one end was a cluster of hangars, dark mouths gaping like cave entrances, hiding all the treasures of Ali Baba in the guise of fuel barrels, oil rags, axle grease and airplanes. I was sure my P-40 was waiting for me within.

But the Air Force had another surprise in store. There weren't enough fighter planes to go around, so we recruits were relegated to a collection of old biplanes, mostly open-cockpit Stearmans and chunky open-cockpit Waco 10s and UPF-7s.

The first plane we trained on was a Republic P-43. Because it was only a one-seater, the student had to sit on the wing, observing, while the instructor slowly taxied down the runway.

Then we were allowed to sit in the cockpit ourselves, going through the pre-flight procedures, checking dials and gauges, talking through takeoff and landing techniques with the instructor standing by.

I might have been bored, but I was so thrilled to be in a plane again that I didn't care. All planes fly basically the same; going from one to another is like going from, say, a Toyota to a Cadillac to a Ford pickup. Each has different power settings and stall characteristics, and these you can learn only in the air. But sitting there on the runway, I gave the old plane every ounce of my attention.

Finally, after two or three hours of ground training

in another old open-cockpit model, my instructor glanced out at the winter-gray horizon and said, "Okay, it's yours, Sperry. Go fly."

I took off, buzzing down the runway like a kid escaping from school at summer's start. A sweet push on the throttle and the front wheels parted from the tarmac like molasses from a spoon, smooth and slow. Then the tail wheel slowly left the ground and we were airborne. I was free again.

I climbed to ten thousand feet, getting the feel of the plane, making her acquaintance gradually. I leveled out and banked into the sun, coaxing her along slowly until I felt I knew her style. Then I took her upstairs, trying out some lazy turns, a couple rolls, nothing crazy until I got used to her and she to me.

I had first learned to fly in a Waco UPF-7, back in Texas, and I had almost forgotten the thrill of it, the wind blowing in my face, pushing to get under the leather helmet and goggles, my scarf flying out behind me. The old gal wasn't a sleek and sassy fighter, but she was exhilarating. I felt like I was a part of the sky, or it was a part of me, coursing through my blood like warm blue ice. The world fell away beneath my feet, and my heart soared up on canvas wings. Even in a rickety biplane I felt like an ace.

In those old crates we practiced strafing runs, coming in at an angle on a target and letting go with a burst of bullets.

From high altitude, I dove down at a big red bull's-eye draped over a railroad car, trying to come in from the sun so the enemy couldn't see me through the glare. My finger poised on the machine gun's button, I homed in on that freight car like an eagle after a rabbit, slotting the target into the gunsight, coming in closer and lower, then leveling, firing off a flurry of tracers and zooming up, up again and away.

Then came ground training again, this time in a P-40. The Air Force was ready to admit I was a real pilot. I climbed into the cockpit, hoping the goofy grin of delight I felt wasn't going to rip out of the back of my throat and spread clear across my face. I tried to settle into the metal seat as though I'd always sat there, and immediately gave up trying to be nonchalant. I was finally where I had longed to be; I might as well enjoy it.

I examined the controls carefully, running a hand across the glass covers of the altimeter, tachometer, rate-of-climb indicator, turn and bank indicator. I intended to learn these faces intimately.

And not just by sight. I soon found myself, a black bandana tied over my eyes, memorizing the position of every control—landing gear, switches, fuel flexor valve—so I could operate them by touch if I were ever blinded in flight.

We were prepared for every eventually. We learned to soar into the air, and we also learned to fall, strapped into parachute harnesses so tight we could hardly breathe.

Climbing the narrow outside staircase to the top of the eighty-foot parachute training silo was almost more terrifying than jumping. The steps seemed to get more insubstantial the higher I went, and the instructors' warnings not to look down grew more difficult to heed. Halfway up, I simply could not resist the urge to peek below my feet; an instantly dizzying sensation left me clinging to the handrail, afraid to move. I never minded heights in an airplane, but this was different. I had no wings.

Forcing myself to look only at the steps directly in

front of me, I carried on to the top and through the little door leading to the parachute platform.

The wooden platform was four feet square, suspended over a ten-foot-wide water tank far, far below. It reminded me of the circus trapeze high-divers who jumped into a bucket of water.

Of course I had more safeguards than the circus performers. I was strapped into the leather harness over my flight gear, and the harness was attached to a "trout line," a strong cable that connected me to the platform at the top. Even if I forgot to pull the rip cord to open my parachute, I couldn't fall all the way to the bottom. At most I'd get a dunking in about five feet of water. "Easy," the instructor said.

Right. I swallowed hard, nodded to him that I was ready. He pulled a lever at his side, and a trap door in the platform yawned open. I was falling, plummeting as fast as my heart had leaped into my throat; falling—I grabbed the rip cord and yanked hard. The parachute billowed open, setting me down gently like a dandelion seed in an April breeze. Easy.

After that first time, I had no fear at all. Except once. For some reason, I dropped into the silo at an angle, swinging into the metal sides like a pendulum, with great painful thwacks. I bruised my ribs so badly I was sure they'd wash me out of training. Fortunately, they didn't.

Falling through fields of stars, or lotus fields . . . Belle and I were crashing, falling into the earth. Sweat poured into my eyes, blinding me, and I saw no more.

CHAPTER SIX

Discovery by Daylight

I came to with a start, the kind of horrified snap that jerks your body alert some nights just as you're falling asleep. Belle, the parachute silo, the star fields all slid away into the darkness beyond the rice paddies as smoothly as a nightmare which leaves you awake and shaky but unable to grasp its content.

The boys were still walking ahead of me, chattering away, apparently having noticed nothing out of the ordinary.

'Come on, Roland,'' I urged myself. "Just keep going.'' I put one foot carefully in front of the other, as deliberately as a drunk on his way home from a toot.

I wasn't sure how long I'd been out; it felt like months but couldn't have been more than a few minutes—the rice paddies and lotus fields were in basically the same position and at the same distance as when I'd seen them disappear.

Thank God the world had jolted back to normal.

"You okay?" Chien turned to me with a frown creasing his usually sunny face.

"Sure, great. *Ding hao*."

One foot in front of the other. Somehow I had the idea that if I didn't tell the boys how I felt, the dizziness, the disorientation, the clammy grip of fear would all go away, leaving me as strong and sure as I had been before the crash. Already the gulf of experience between now and then stretched so wide that last week appeared as distant and diaphanous as a previous lifetime.

The rice paddies were still ahead, still no closer. As far as we walked they remained fixed in place, like a painted backdrop in an old movie. A silent movie. The moonlit land had the same silvered look as old film.

But it wasn't silent. Crickets poured out their hearts to the night, frogs splashed and croaked in the ponds; somewhere a night bird sang a single note over and over. Weng and Chien chattered on like a couple of parakeets. I had no idea what they were discussing.

We walked on.

I began to think about the Wangs, envying them their one-room cottage. At least they could stop for the night. They were sleeping peacefully now, secure in the accomplishment of a day's work well done, knowing where they'd be tomorrow and how they would fare.

I realized this was ridiculous. The Wangs had problems I would never want to share; I was darn lucky I *wasn't* a Chinese peasant—most dogs in America lived better than they did. And yet I went on feeling sorry for myself, thinking that at least the Wangs were at home, they had each other, they were in their own country, while I was a stranger, all alone in a hostile land.

"You sure you okay, Roland?" Chien turned back to me again, as if reading my mind.

"Fine," I muttered, not wanting to be distracted from my misery.

The boy gave me a puzzled look, hesitating a moment before resuming the conversation with his brother. This time they seemed to chatter on at double speed. Chien gestured back toward me once or twice and Weng stared up at the moon with concern, then halted suddenly.

"We stop here for night."

"Why? What time is it?" I asked dumbly. I knew he didn't have a watch.

"Time enough. You tired."

I looked up at the moon myself, trying to calculate its position in the sky. It was still at a midpoint between heaven and the horizon.

"It's early, Weng, only midnight. We've got hours till dawn."

"We stop here."

"Weng, we need to keep going. Don't worry about me."

"You sure? We stay here if you sick." His eyes narrowed suspiciously.

I smiled in spite of myself; then I felt guilty. Who was I to complain about being alone here? I had Weng and Chien, who obviously cared. Enough to hinder their own progress, endanger their own lives just because they thought I was tired.

Well, I could carry on a little longer.

The moon slowly dipped toward dawn, gliding along on its invisible, well-worn track with infinite ease. Finally, it slipped behind a clump of willows, and stuck. Morning was imminent.

"*Now* we stop," I told the boys. They agreed readily.

We had long since passed the terraced rice paddies

and had come out into a sandy valley, cut through with rivulets of river water and thickets of bamboo.

There were no farms, no houses, not even a discernible trail. Apparently no one ever came this way. Except maybe the Japanese. We were still in a direct line of interception with their fragmentation armies. We would have to choose our daylight hideout carefully.

We needed a thicket dense enough to hide us all but high enough so we wouldn't find ourselves sitting in river water by midday.

I looked around. The willow mooring the moon had chosen would have been ideal, but we would have been backlit by lunar light until dawn, so I ruled it out. Everything else was either too sparse or too low.

"Maybe we'd better keep going, at least past that ridge." I pointed to a low hill about a mile farther north.

Weng squinted at it anxiously.

"Must hurry."

Already the moon was dissolving into a silver pool at our feet. The sun would soon appear.

It seemed to take forever to reach the ridge, walking through the colorless chasm between night and day. Twice Chien tripped on half-buried rocks and fell flat— even he was getting tired—and once we came upon a paper food wrapper Japanese. The hairs on the backs of our necks stood straight.

At last we fell within the shadow of the hill, chill and damp but welcoming as a pair of open arms. A cleft yawned just to the left, almost completely hidden by a dense stand of bamboo. Weng literally pushed his brother up the hill and into the protection of the brush, then slipped in beside him like a wraith. They both seemed to disappear before my eyes.

I ducked in after them, dragging my bad leg over a

knot of roots, and sank down gratefully on the dirt floor. It was cramped for the three of us, but safe.

I said I would take the first watch.

"You too tired," Weng said.

"*You* too tired," I said. "You worked all day, and walked all night while I laid around sleeping. I'll wake you up in a couple hours."

"I not hurt. I take first watch."

"Weng, don't argue with me."

It was becoming a matter of pride for both of us.

"I not argue. I help you."

"I know that, Weng. Thank you. I'll just sit back for a minute, then I'll take the first watch."

I fell asleep immediately, sitting straight up against the rock wall with my good leg crossed under the bad one, Chien resting against my shoulder. I think Weng pulled our packs off and shoved them to the rear of our little shell, but I couldn't be sure. I was out cold.

And then suddenly I was awake.

Sunlight was butting against the wall of bamboo, trying to force its way in. Chien was still lying against my shoulder, as heavy as a lead weight. Weng sat with his back against the rock, his dark eyes glittering in the chinks of light.

"Not your turn to watch."

"I know."

I had no idea what had awakened me. It wasn't Weng, who still sat as immobile as a statue. Chien slumbered on with the deep, even breaths of a child. I strained my ears but there was nothing else to hear. Beyond the bamboo I could see nothing.

"You hear anything?" I asked Weng.

"You?"

"No, I guess not."

I eased Chien's head off my shoulder and onto the rock, then crawled awkwardly to the mouth of the

cleft. I put my eyes to the bamboo, garnering a splin-
tered view of an apparently empty hillside. The reeds
were thick and green and rustled like a windstorm in a
wheat field with every touch.

Weng was instantly at my elbow.

"What wrong?"

"Nothing—I hope."

I pulled the reeds apart a fraction and swept the hill
with both eyes. A rocky outcropping here, a clump of
willows there. Nothing that shouldn't be. . . .

I caught a glint from between the shrubby trees.
Metal. My breath caught in my throat.

Then I saw the bulky pack, khaki-colored, sticking
out from the willow fronds, and recognized it for what
it was. Regulation Air Force issue.

"That's an American pilot!" I whispered excitedly
to Weng.

"You sure?" again suspiciously.

"Never been surer." I was already halfway out of
the little shelter, crawling on hands and knees.

Weng put a hand on my sleeve. "Wait!"

I turned to face him.

"Be careful."

"Don't worry about me."

"I think I go with you."

"No, Weng, stay here." I knew it was an American
behind that willow clump; I recognized the equipment,
but more than that was a feeling, a sixth sense that
told me one of my own people was just a few hundred
feet away. Maybe that sixth sense was what had awakened me.

But I wasn't a psychic. A Japanese could have
picked up an abandoned Air Force pack any number
of places; it would have been a war souvenir to him.
My intuition about the person hidden in the brush

could be all wrong, and if it was, I didn't want Weng with me.

But Weng was already poking at his brother's arm. "Chien, wake up. We go, fast."

Chien, sleep-dazed, started to say something in Chinese but Weng cut him off with a hand over his mouth.

"Guys, I want you to stay here."

"We a team. You said so first night."

"But that was different."

"We team, like New York Yankees."

"How do you know about the Yankees?"

"Everybody know Yankees," Chien said disdainfully.

Weng, as usual, was more serious and to the point. "We know *you,* Roland. We go with you."

I gave up. "Okay, but stay behind me, and stay quiet."

They didn't say a word, just looked at me with eyes like saucers.

We crept out of our shelter and across the exposed hillside, trying to tread silently on the frost-tipped short grass. I wanted to call out to the man, but again, if he wasn't American that wouldn't be a smart idea.

As we came within a few feet of the willow clump the wind shifted toward us and I caught the unmistakable scent of fresh blood. Whoever he was, he was banged up pretty bad. But he wasn't unconscious, for now I heard the click of a trigger being cocked.

Weng stopped dead, his arm across his brother's chest, both of them already poised for flight.

"It's okay," I said to them in an undertone, then louder, "It's okay. I'm American. We're friendly."

The nose of a pistol came poking out from the brush, followed cautiously by a pair of cornflower blue eyes.

"It's okay," I repeated. "Come on out."

"Lord, I'm glad to see you!" The voice was pure Midwest.

"We'd be mighty pleased to see you, too."

Sheepishly, "Oh, sorry."

The shrubbery parted to reveal a man about my age, a fellow pilot, judging by his flight suit and leather jacket. Sweat-darkened brownish hair fell over his forehead, shadowing a stubbly chin. He raised himself painfully to his feet with the aid of a stripped tree branch, and I saw that his left leg was a mess.

From the knee down the khaki pant leg was in tatters, stained brown with dried blood. He had done his best to bandage his wounds, but the heavy gauze was soaked with fresh blood.

"How long you been here, buddy? I'm Roland Sperry, with the Twenty-third Fighter Group, and this is Weng, and Chien, my team."

I thought this would please the boys and relieve them a little, but instead they continued to stare at the fellow distrustfully. Then I realized it was the gun that was bothering them. He still had it clutched in one hand.

"Would you mind handing your weapon to Weng here?"

"Why?" he asked incredulously, looking from me to the boys and back.

"Because otherwise they aren't going to lead you back to base with us."

He hesitated, but complied, mercifully thinking to empty the clip into his jacket pocket before turning the gun over to Weng, who somberly stowed it in his knapsack.

"Now you part of team!" Chien said, his good humor restored.

That broke the ice and we all laughed, but our laughter was too loud.

"We shouldn't be standing around in the open like this." I said. "Can you make it across the hill to our shelter?"

"Sure," said our new friend, "lead on. By the way, my name's Dalton, Emory C."

Once we were holed up again, Dalton and I compared notes. He had been shot down in the same battle I had been in, the bombing raid on Hong Kong. Like me, he had chosen to ride the plane down instead of trying to parachute out into a sky full of flak.

"Not that they didn't get me anyway," he groaned, moving his leg gingerly in effort to get comfortable on the hard-packed dirt.

"I came down in a tumble of brush about ten miles inland, said good-bye to my baby—"

"You leave your little child?" Chien was surprised. He knew Americans did not abandon their offspring as the Chinese were often forced to do.

"My airplane," Dalton said, but his voice carried as much pain as if he had left a human companion. I knew how he felt.

"Anyway, I left her there, in the brush, and started walking. I picked up this," indicating his walking stick, "laying on the ground right outside the plane like it was waiting for me. But it's been tough going.

"I'd been walking all last night, trying to make up some time I lost the night before when my leg was really killing me, and the dawn kind of caught me by surprise.

"I heard you guys come in and I thought for sure you were the Japs. Lord, I was scared. I just pulled in, like a turtle into a shell, and prayed you wouldn't find me."

"But we did," Chien piped up.

"Yeah, you sure did," Dalton said.

The addition of Dalton made our tiny shelter twice as cramped as it had been before. He was only an inch or two shorter than me, lean but with the big-boned musculature of the northern Plains. His injured leg, like mine, had to remain outstretched, and together we took up half again our share of the space.

And he didn't bring much in the way of spoils to share. He had half a bar of chocolate, two hardtack crackers, and a quarter canteen of water, purified. The boys and I had nothing but water, unpurified.

But it was breakfast time, and we decided to eat. Miniature chocolate sandwiches, washed down with nature's first beverage. First, though, I had to purify my water. I dropped the halizone tablets in my canteen, and waited, trying to estimate thirty minutes without aid of a watch.

We all sat watching the canteen. The place was filled with the warm smell of seeping blood, the dank odors of damp canvas and soggy leather and sunless rock, and the odd Chinese spiciness that was the boys. It was dark and chilly and dangerous, and yet, waiting for the halizone tablets to dissolve, listening to the champagne-like bubbles fizz against the metal sides of the canteen, I felt as giddy as if I were drinking the real thing.

The four of us were here, for the moment, safe and secure and *alive*. For the moment, we had beaten the odds. Just for the moment, our little gathering felt like a party.

CHAPTER SEVEN

En Route to Adventure

We dragged out the moment, taking tiny bites of chocolate and hardtack to try and make it last. But it was gone all too quickly.

"That was a hell of a good chocolate bar," Dalton said hungrily. "Too bad there wasn't more."

"And mashed potatoes and gravy and corn on the cob."

"What *corn on the cob*?" Chien asked.

"Little baby peas with pearl onions."

"Corn bread with real butter, none of that margarine stuff."

"What *corn bread*?"

"For dessert, lemon meringue pie . . ." I could almost taste it.

"Chocolate icebox cake. . . ." Dalton said dreamily.

"Roland!" Chien tugged on my arm. "What *corn on the cob bread*?"

I laughed, took a slug of water and choked on it. I doubted if I could have eaten much of that imaginary meal if I'd had it; my face still burned like fire and every time I swallowed I tasted blood.

Dalton didn't seem to be doing so hot either. He didn't say anything, but his face contorted with pain every time we bumped his leg, which was frequent in the cramped space, and his bandages were soaked through with blood.

"I think I have some more gauze in my pack," I said. "You really ought to change that dressing."

Dalton hesitated, looking from his leg to me with trepidation. "Nah, it's okay."

"Not look okay to me," Chien said.

"You don't want to get gangrene," I added. "Americans get germs fast."

"I said, it's okay," Dalton said brusquely.

Weng, who had been examining his newly acquired pistol, glanced over at him dismissively. "Maybe he afraid of blood."

"You want me to do it for you?" I volunteered. I hoped he'd say no; I wasn't too crazy about the sight of gaping wounds either.

Dalton flushed. "I—just don't like to look at my own blood. It makes me kind of sick."

"I know what you mean," I said.

But curiously, ever since Dalton had come into our midst, my own injuries had been greatly reduced in my own mind. Maybe being around someone who was in worse shape brought out my leadership abilities and made me more protective, or maybe it was just my old competitive spirit shoving to the fore; I had to prove to myself that I could stick it out better than the next guy.

I don't know that I consciously thought about any of this, but I grabbed my pack, pulled out antiseptic, cotton and gauze and had Dalton's tattered trouser leg ripped off before either of us could blink.

I tried to suppress a strong desire to faint. No wonder Dalton was in pain. Big chunks of shrapnel had gouged into his calf, tearing deep jags through which the bone showed whitely.

Dalton had his eyes closed, his face screwed up in agony. I wished I had a bottle of whiskey to give him as an anesthetic, like they did in old Westerns.

The wound looked clean enough, but what did I know? With shaky hands, I patched the holes with antiseptic-soaked cotton, wound the strips of gauze around the leg as tightly as possible, and tied the whole thing off in a neat square knot.

"There. Done." My whole body was shaking.

Dalton's face was white and little beads of sweat stood out on his forehead. "Do I have to say thanks?" he asked weakly.

"That's a swell job," I countered. "You couldn't get a Red Cross nurse to do better."

"Yeah, but she'd be a darn sight better-looking than you."

I smiled, but I still felt shaky. I picked up the bloodied rags and hid them in a crevice in the rock wall at our backs. Out of sight, out of mind, I hoped. I tried a change of subject.

"Why don't you all get some rest, and I'll take the next watch."

Weng opened his mouth to object, but I didn't give him a chance. "I'm the senior man around here and I say it's my watch. Understood?"

Amazingly, Weng laughed. "Understood."

He and Chien settled back against the rock, apparently as comfortable as in a feather bed.

Dalton shifted his leg a fraction, groaning under his breath.

"Want some morphine? I have an ampule in my pack."

"No, thanks, I've heard what that stuff will do to people. You seen any of those opium dens?"

I personally had not been inside one, but on the streets of Kunming I had sometimes seen wasted, vacant-eyed men moving thickly, as if through heavy water, and had been told they were opium addicts. They were not a sight to encourage drug use.

"How long have you been out here anyway?"

"I told you, just since dawn."

"No, I mean, how long have you been in China?"

"About two years, but it seems like forever."

We were whispering now. The excitement over, the boys were sleeping soundly.

"Remember when you first got to China," Dalton continued, "how strange everything seemed?"

I remembered, all right. Even the flight to China was strange. Strange and exciting, especially for a kid who'd never before been outside the States.

Thirty-Sixth Street Air Base, Miami, Florida, June 1942.

Inside the flight lounge an old electric fan kept up its constant vigil, its dusty blades thumping the air in a valiant attempt to dissipate the early summer heat.

I turned my face into it for one last greedy moment of comfort, grabbed up my B-4 bag and stepped out onto the runway. A thick layer of humidity lay over the tarmac like a hot, wet blanket. My neatly pressed khakis were immediately soaked with sweat and my hair clung to my forehead in a damp wave.

But I didn't care. I was vibrating almost as much as the electric fan, buzzing with excitement. I was on my way to China to become a member of that elite flying corps, the Flying Tigers.

After graduating at the top of my group at Hill Field, I had been shipped to Hamilton Field, San Francisco, where I received my papers, ordering me to report to Kunming, China, to the Flying Tigers. I was thrilled, proud beyond words. To think that I had been selected out of how many far less fortunate thousands was intoxicating. My head filled with visions of myself as a tough, steely air ace, swaggering around old China in my leather jacket with the American flag on the back.

Even if I didn't quite turn into John Wayne or Tyrone Power, I knew I could learn a lot from General Chennault and his savvy pilots. Certainly enough to help win the war, and probably enough to become an ace.

I couldn't wait to get to China.

But first there was the troop train to Miami. Unlike the rail ride to Ogden, when everything had seemed so new, so mysterious, this trip was boring, endless. I wanted to be soaring over foreign skies, not sitting aimlessly in a passenger car with a bunch of guys in khaki, watching the smoke plume billowing back from the locomotive and wishing I was as airborne as the soot cinders drifting in through the open windows.

Then there was the week in Miami, going through the tedious routines, standing in line to be shot in the arm with thick silver needles, standing in line to be issued piles of clothing, standing in line to get on the bus to the hospital and the supply barracks. All this in preparation for China.

But today, at last, I was headed out, on my way to the other side of the world.

I crossed the tarmac to the twin-engine C-47, perched on the runway like an olive drab homing pigeon, eager to be airborne, following its secret inner compass bearings around the globe.

I gave my papers to the chubby, sweat-stained crew chief, who checked them against the list on his clipboard. He squinted at me against the sun.

"Goin' to China, are ya?"

I strove, with difficulty, for nonchalance. "Yup."

"Gonna fly one of them shark-faced P-40s?"

"Yup."

"I hear them Japs are pretty good; shoot ya down before ya even know what hit ya."

"Not me, brother."

"Sure." He handed me back my papers with a cynical glare. "Climb aboard, hot shot."

As I mounted the metal steps of the plane, I heard him mutter under his breath. "Wish I was goin' with ya."

Inside, it was obvious that the plane had been designed for transport rather than comfort. Narrow wooden benches lined the sides of the cargo area, with enough room for ten passengers on each side. There were no magazine racks, no trays for drinks or snacks, no cozy blankets or pillows; there wasn't even padding on the seats.

I stowed my belongings—the B-4 bag, a government-issue, green gabardine and leather wardrobe case, and my parachute—in the aisle with everyone else's and chose a seat. At least they were all by a window.

I knew about half the guys on the flight. We were all going to China, but only four were assigned to Kunming. The rest had been divided up among three other bases.

Bill Griffith was one of those headed for Kunming. He was a down-to-earth, likable fellow from some small town in Arizona, a typical country boy. I was glad he was heading out with me; I had a feeling there'd be a lot of time for chewing the fat on this flight.

The crew chief slammed the cabin door shut, the plane revved her props jauntily, and we were off, taxiing down the runway toward China, adventure and excitement. I grinned widely in spite of myself.

Because the Japanese controlled the entire Pacific beyond Hawaii, our route was to the East, from Miami to Brazil to Ascension Island, adrift in the Atlantic, to Accra on Africa's Gold Coast to Karachi, India, to China. This route was twice as far as if we had flown west, but westward there were no possible stops between us and China, no safe harbors or ports of call where a plane and its passengers could put in for refueling and feeding.

The C-47, which in its civilian incarnation was called a DC-3, carried extra fuel tanks, but these increased her range to only ten hours. Not long enough by half to get from Hawaii to China in one hop, even if we had *wanted* to try it and risk being shot down by the Japanese.

So we took the longer and safe route, the "scenic route," as one of the guys put it.

Leaving Miami and its muggy air behind, we flew southeast across Cuba, the West Indies, and the breathtakingly turquoise Caribbean Sea. Myriad islands shimmered in the clear blue water like emeralds, their sandy shores reflecting platinum against the sun.

Thoroughly bedazzled, we dipped below the Caribbean, skipped across the tip of Venezuela like a stone skimming a lake, and began our descent into Georgetown, British Guiana.

My first experience in a foreign clime. And it certainly looked foreign. The air base had been carved out of raw jungle, a tangle of vines and leaves and trunks that aggressively challenged the perimeter of human territory. The air within was charged with the rich scents of loam and wet **earth and** rotting and renewing vegetation.

The barracks we were assigned to had been built at

the very edge of the forest, high above the ground on thirty-foot stilts, and yet the dense foliage breathed in and around us as if we weren't there.

We were told that the reason for the stilts was to keep the denizens of the jungle away while we slept. There were jaguars, they said, and thirty-foot snakes, and lizards.

I remembered all that when I crawled into bed that night. A faint breeze brushed across the room through the open windows, and on it were carried the night sounds of the jungle, barkings and screechings that sounded sometimes distant and sometimes eerily close. But my dreams were undisturbed by fearsome creatures. Sleeping in the barracks aerie was as restful as sleeping in a treehouse, and I awoke refreshed and ready for another day of travel.

I clambered down the ladder from our perch, had a leisurely breakfast of eggs and coffee, and climbed back into the plane for the next leg of our trip, Georgetown to Natal, on the coast of Brazil.

We gained altitude quickly and leveled out over a vast sea of green, the Amazon jungle, threaded with the red-brown river that gave it its name. We skimmed over that jade-hued carpet for hours and yet it never thinned, never gave way to towns or fields or any sign of civilization that I could see. The flight chief told us this was the most dangerous part of the trip; if we went down over the Amazon, the jungle would close over us in an instant and we'd never be found.

I pressed my nose to the window glass and peered down into that impenetrable mass. I could almost hear the screams of the jungle monkeys, the screeches of the vibrantly colored parrots, and the inexorable advance of the forest, creeping steadily over the rotting hulk of a crashed C-47.

I found myself listening carefully for any change in the rhythm of the engines, any little skip in the heartbeat of the plane. Fortunately, I heard none.

The engine throbbed like thunder, reverberating against the plane's metal skin with a hum that set deep into my own bones. We flew on, banking east, toward Natal, and finally landed, safe from the gaping jaws of the jungle.

The base at Natal was built like the one at Georgetown, on land roughly wrested from the jungle, its barracks set on stilts like a native village.

And again I spent a restful night, lulled to sleep by the wind ruffling my hair and awakened in the morning by the birds singing in the branches just outside the window.

We spent two and half days in Natal, while the plane was refueled and rechecked and while the military carried out whatever mysterious business it did to use up the other excess hours.

Unlike my tenure at Hill and Hamilton fields, however, I was happy to let the Air Force take as long as it liked; we were allowed to wander Natal at will and I was having fun. It was like being on vacation.

We explored the town, and Bill Griffith and I each bought a huge bunch of bananas, the fattest and yellowest we'd ever seen.

I bought a watch, a beautiful gold one that cost only four dollars. The price should have clued me to the fact that two months down the line, in Kunming, the gorgeous gold would flake away to reveal the cheap brass underneath, but it didn't. I never minded, though, because it *was* beautiful while it lasted and it had sentimental value, being one of the first things I purchased overseas.

We spent a day at the beach, swimming in the creamy surf, and watching the Brazilian girls parade past in their exotic tans and two-piece swimsuits.

We were on our way to war and we were having a ball.

When we got back on the plane, every one of us was clutching a big bunch of bananas. And as it turned out, they were the last bananas we were to see for a long, long time.

I took my familiar rock-hard seat, buckled on the green webbing safety belt and watched as our C-47 followed the Brazilian coastline down to Rio de Janeiro.

Our pilot gave us a Cook's tour, circling twice around the hundred-foot mountaintop statue of Christ, dipping low over the famous Copacabana Beach.

I never was quite sure what business brought us 2,000 miles south of the regular route to China, but whatever it was, it was quick. Only a few hours after we landed at the Pan Am terminal of the civilian airport we were airborne again, heading northeast, away from Brazil's foamy shoreline, out over the Atlantic, a deep indigo in comparison to the crystalline waters of the Caribbean.

We flew for hours, chasing our shadow across the South Atlantic over miles and miles of empty blue ocean. Far below, the chop of the waves was almost visible, signaling the presence of whales or sharks or schools of fish, or maybe just a freshening wind teasing at the surface of the sea.

For seven hours there was nothing else to see, nothing to hear but the throb of the engines, nothing to feel but the ever increasing hardness of the wooden benches. We told jokes, played cards and ate bananas, which helped relieve the tedium, but the seats remained as hard as ever.

Finally, as the sun swung over our tail, our trusty C-47 homed in on Ascension Island, a tiny dot of land in the vast sea. It didn't grow much larger as we came in for landing.

Ascension was a fueling base, strategically set midway between Natal and Accra like a permanent, slightly oversized aircraft carrier. Only a few mechanics staffed this lonely, desolate rock; not even trees, except for a stalwart few, grew in its windswept soil.

The Air Force had provided its exiles with a little movie theater and a miniature PX; nature had provided a rocky beach. Outside of that there was nothing to do. The men were issued quantities of ammunition, which I assumed was for target practice as entertainment. There certainly was nothing and no one, besides themselves, drawing breath to shoot at.

We spent a cool night there, with the wind howling unchecked around the barracks, and I thought it must be the most desolate place I'd ever come across.

In the morning, when we reboarded the plane for the next leg of our flight, we could look right out across the runway to the sea. As the C-47 lifted off into the cloudless sky, I felt my spirits lifting too as the melancholy of Ascension sank below our wings.

More miles of featureless blue as we soared above the Atlantic. More jokes and cards and bananas. More hours of trying to get comfortable on comfortless seats. But I didn't mind. I was riding high, excited about seeing Africa with all its primitive natives and exotic wild animals. I couldn't wait.

At last we landed at Accra, on the Gold Coast, and piled out of the plane, ready for more adventure. That's when we found out the party was over.

The U.S. Air Force, in Africa, had apparently tired of playing genial host and had reverted to type. We were given so many shots I felt like a punching bag for sadistic syringes, a sensation I thought I'd left far behind in the States. We were smeared with thick and smelly mosquito-resistant ointments, and required to sleep under claustrophobic mosquito netting instead of high in the scented breeze.

To be fair to the military, the mosquito problem in Africa was horrific; a bite from one of those insect Draculas could easily kill you.

But besides the medical treatment, we were also subjected to the same Hill Field–type lectures, how to behave like an officer and a gentleman; how to represent the Air Force and America; how to behave among the natives. We had rules we were supposed to fly by, drive by, live by and breathe by.

I perked up at the behaving toward the natives part; it meant we were actually to be allowed out among the people. We didn't see much in Accra—during the two days we spent there, we were only off base a few hours, but it *was* exciting.

The men wore long bolts of cloth tied around their waists like skirts, and the women wore little more, exposing me to a cultural frame of reference I had previously found only within the pages of the *National Geographic*. I could see where some of the guys from the base might need the "officer and a gentleman" lecture.

A lot of fellows did violate the rules, but only by giving the natives candy bars and chewing gum.

The Africans were friendly and had learned quickly about the white men encroaching on their land. Most of them spoke English, picked up from the British who had come to Accra before the Americans. They wanted to do for us, and in return expected us to do for them, in the form of tips, candy, gum.

We saw little of the countryside. The base was only a half mile from the sea, and we could walk down to it, but by the time we got there it was time to turn around and come back.

So that was Africa. No lions, tigers or giraffes. No monkeys or elephants. Only giant mosquitos and our plump little C-47 sitting on the runway, waiting to carry us on to Karachi, India, on her final stage of our journey toward China.

The last of the bananas disappeared as we flew over Central Africa, banking northeasterly toward the Arabian deserts and the Arabian Sea, finally fetching up in Karachi like a bird blown in to shore by the trade winds that gust along the Sahara.

It had been a miserable flight. Hot, humid air rose up from the tropical savannas in waves and turned the plane into a flying steam bath. I was already out of my seat as we slowed to a stop on the runway, looking forward to a long, cool Coke and the relief of cooler, fresher air.

I unstuck my damp khaki blouse from my back and stepped down from the plane. Karachi was as hot as Africa, or hotter, but at least less muggy.

Karachi was the aircraft distribution base for the entire CBI Theater. This was where engine overhaul and maintenance took place, where new planes were picked up and tested. It had a busy, bustling attitude that the other bases we had checked in at did not; it knew it was at the forefront of the action.

I felt the wide smile sneak back over my face as Bill Griffith and I strode across the tarmac to the mess hall, past planes with pockmarks and bullet holes, through knots of pilots with leather jackets slung casually over one shoulder. We were in the thick of it now. We were flyboys too.

We laid over in Karachi for three days, waiting for an available flight to Chabua, the last stop before China. Each morning we checked in with Base Operations; then we were released to spend the day as we chose.

We walked around the city, browsing in the tiny shops, marveling at the cacophony of the streets— carts, wagons, bikes, cars, camels, horses, all vying for the same congested space. Brass bells, auto horns, merchants in turbans, and women in veils, all competed for our attention.

It seemed that everything was handcrafted—there were the brass and copperworkers chasing intricate designs in metals; there were leatherworkers, from whom I bought a beautiful pair of officer's dress boots, made for my feet alone in three days; there were the basketweavers and the jewelers and the tailors with their rich silks and finely embroidered cottons.

There were sacred cows wandering freely on the streets and dozing on porches, fruit drink vendors who sold their product by the gallon, souvenir hawkers and snake charmers.

We stopped to watch one woman, arrayed in orange and pink veils and brass bangles, piping a hypnotic melody on a flute. Sure enough, the snake began to rise from the basket at her feet, and then to dance.

I had no intention of stopping to watch this spectacle. I had been taught early, in the rattlesnake country of my granddad's ranch, that snakes are nothing to play around with, and are to be feared and respected. But as the rest of the crowd was drawn by the snake charmer's flute, so was I, mesmerized by her fluid motions and the liquid sway of the cobra.

When the snake had risen to its full height, the

woman laid down her flute and kissed the snake, face to face. I wondered if maybe it had been defanged, and if it was true that cobras are deaf and can't hear the flute at all; but somehow I didn't like to believe either one. The act was too mystical, too much a piece out of *The Arabian Nights* not to be believed.

By the fourth day, when we climbed aboard another C-47 for the flight from Karachi to Chabua, I was ready to leave the snake charmers and jugglers, the bazaars and the beggars behind. The Indians were all very kind to us, but the country was too poor, her white-tunicked, veil-trailing, brass-bangled, sandal-wood-scented people too inured to poverty for me to handle with ease.

I was glad to turn my back on the "scenic route" and my face toward my new career.

The base at Chabua, nestled at the foot of the Himalayas, was much smaller than the one at Karachi, and was the last step between China and the rest of the Allied world.

Here we boarded a huge C-46 transport plane and took on the Hump, which was what all the old hands called the treacherous mountain route between the worlds.

It was cold flying at 21,000 feet over the snow-covered peaks. I gazed down in awe at ice-sheeted valleys, deep granite crevasses, and blinding white snow banks, every bit as terrifying as the Amazon jungle. A plane that went down here would be buried just as surely and even more quickly than in the tropics.

Thick gray clouds, laden with snow, drifted past the windows and we shivered in our leather jackets. No one talked during the three-hour flight, as if in fear of angering the mountain gods.

When the air in the cargo compartment began subtly to warm and I saw dust motes dancing in a shaft of sunlight, I realized that we were over the Hump and starting our descent into China.

An auspicious beginning, I thought, not knowing that I was already thinking in Chinese terms, measuring every event in quantities of luck. Or maybe all pilots count on Lady Luck to carry them through, relying as they do on unseen forces, on the very air to keep them aloft and safe.

I shook myself to throw off the chill, from the Himalayas, of course, not from any contemplation of mortality, and turned to the window. Kunming Lake, big and bluish-green, rumored to be bottomless, shone like a beacon as we banked in over the base and landed on the dirty runway. I was in China at last.

CHAPTER EIGHT

In the Land of
Flying Tigers

Here I was all right. I looked at Weng and Chien and
Dalton and myself, all squeezed into the tiny cleft in
the rock, and wondered whether that sun-sparked
welcome *had* proven to be auspicious.

I had been shot down, lost my beloved plane, been
wounded, none of which could be considered the least
bit lucky. On the other hand, I was still alive, I was on
my way back to Allied territory, and I had help. Kuan
Yin, Lady Luck, whatever you wanted to call her,
seemed to be on the job. I only prayed she wouldn't
desert me now.

Dalton had dozed off with his head tilted over onto
one shoulder. He was going to have some stiff neck
when he woke up. I thought about rearranging him,
lifting his head back onto his pack in a more comfortable position, but I was afraid he'd wake up and catch
me acting like a nursemaid. I needed to sustain my
tough pilot image, if only, here in the dim filtered light,
to the only conscious member of the group, myself.

I thought back again to my arrival in Kunming,
where I had really learned to be a pilot.

* * *

Twelve miles southeast of the lake, Kunming Air Base lay sprawled over a flat plain. From the sky, the main compound was a rectangle of neatly nested squares and rows, with toy airplanes parked all along its length. A lane of trees bordered the north end of the rectangle and led off into the tilled and tended countryside. Beyond it, a curving road led past a long runway to a handful of buildings and revetments scattered through the fields in no apparent order.

We descended quickly, the dirt runway looming larger with each second. Here was the squeal and bump as our wheels touched down, the rapid deceleration as we taxied to a stop.

My heart banged against my ribs with a thud that surprised me; I hadn't realized I was so excited, or nervous. I grabbed my B-4 bag and parachute from the aisle and followed Bill Griffith out of the plane.

A faint breeze wafted across the runway, carrying with it my first whiff of China. Fish and fertilizer and manure mixed with something sweeter, less tangible, floating lighter on the air, that tantalized the sense of smell even as it repelled.

The ground crew sergeant, checking us off on his clipboard, laughed at the look on my face. "Kind of a shock, isn't it?"

I didn't want to be rude. After all, he lived here.

"Well . . ."

"It ain't just Kunming; the whole country smells like this. And you never get used to it."

"Swell," Bill said in my ear. "We'll think we're living in an outhouse."

The sergeant laughed again. "Oh, it's not so bad." He stopped, apparently consulting some inner voice. "Or is it? Anyway, welcome to China. You fellas go on over to Operations," motioning to a mud brick building at the edge of the runway, "and they'll assign you to a hostel; pretty soon you'll feel right at home."

I hoped so. All of a sudden I felt like a kid on the first day of summer camp, lost and homesick and not sure I didn't want to turn right around and go back where everything was familiar, and clean-scented.

This was the end of the line, I thought, trudging across the runway. I was going to be here, on the other side of the world, for a long time. No more dreaming about being a hot shot pilot; here I'd have to prove myself, either make it or break it.

The operations shack smelled comfortingly of coffee, and I cheered up immediately. Of course I would make it. It was only natural to feel strange in strange surroundings, but I'd get used to it soon enough.

The atmosphere inside was jovial. Pilots and mechanics with time on their hands crowded around, anxious to see who had just arrived. They introduced themselves, asking who we were, where we were from, who we might know that they knew, how things were going in the States.

"After all," one of them told me, "we've been out here a long time, and you guys are like a message from home."

They were all dressed in various degrees of uniform, khaki slacks with combat boots and baseball caps, or shirts with the sleeves rolled above the elbow and officers' caps tilted back on their heads, but I could tell at a glance which ones were fighter pilots. They had the easy confidence that comes from skill honed to a fine edge.

Two of them, whose names I remembered as D. V. Hill and Something-or-other Swanson, leaned on the edge of a desk smoking cigarettes.

"So you're Flying Tigers?" I asked casually, I hoped. These guys were my idols.

Swanson reached over and stubbed out his cigarette in a tin ashtray on the next desk. "Have to say yes to that one."

He must have noticed my eager stare and Bill's self-conscious stance behind me because he looked over at Hill and chuckled. "Hell, we've been here since the General thought up this AVG business."

He lit another cigarette. "We're old men compared to you kids."

They were only in their late twenties or early thirties, but they did, indeed, seem infinitely more worldly-wise.

"AVG. Then you're civilians, not Air Force."

"They'd give us commissions if we wanted 'em, but we're gonna teach you boys to fly as hot as we do; then we're goin' home."

"We've had enough of China," Hill added wearily, but I barely heard him. My head was echoing with the line about teaching us to fly like they did. I was determined to learn everything I could.

A skinny corporal with glasses and spit-shined shoes piped up from the back of the room. "Hey, listen up now. You guys that just got in, file on out to the jeep. I'm gonna drive you out to your hostel."

Hostel, it turned out, was another name for barracks, and ours was beyond the main runway, at the far end of the base.

The neat, rectangular part of the base was the top brass's compound, containing their hostels and offices. Security was heavy here, and the roads were constantly patrolled so no one could enter except with a special pass.

Past this section was the main runway and then a series of outer roads and runways, leading off to various hostels, revetments, and supply and maintenance buildings.

Kunming Air Base was every bit as primitive as the bases in the jungle, except instead of being hacked out of the foliage, it had been plunked down on a bare dirt plain. All the buildings were simple one-story rectangles of mud brick, constructed of the same material as the huts of the Chinese peasants, on the outskirts of the base.

And even these were elegant compared to the quarters Bill and I were assigned to. Our new home was really a tent, a 12-by-16-foot wood frame sheathed in canvas. Set into one side was a pair of multi-paned windows which gave the place an odd, stagey look, like a set for a vaudeville routine. The floor was bare earth covered with rush matting. We would soon discover that when it rained our flooring turned to mud.

The corporal dropped us off, with instructions to stow our stuff and be ready in one hour to be picked up for supper at the mess hall.

At dinner we were each given a mess kit. A staff sergeant handed them out grudgingly, as if they were made of gold rather than tin.

"One per customer," he barked. "Don't lose 'em, 'cause there ain't no more."

I could see that supplies were limited—if you didn't even have a floor, how much else could there be—but I hadn't realized I'd be carting my eating utensils around with me forever like I was on a permanent camping trip.

The food was another surprise—it was terrible. We had rice mixed with gluey chunks of tinned beef and, for dessert, canned pineapple shipped over from Australia. The cooks swore it hadn't gone bad, but the sickly sweet odor was not very convincing.

I felt like I had been put on a prison diet, until Swanson passed by my table. "We eat just like the Chinese, kid. Except ours are only war rations."

I had forgotten for the moment that we were in a war zone. I was so excited about having reached my destination, so concentrated on achieving my goal of becoming a great pilot, that I had blocked out the reason I was here.

"Right," I said sheepishly, but I still couldn't eat the pineapple. I scraped it into the garbage can, swished my mess kit clean in a bucket of hot, soupy water, and stepped out into the early evening.

The peculiar smell of the land hovered in the dark air, fetid as a sewer. Off in the distance a plane took off, the roar of its engines growing fainter as it gained altitude. I had always imagined night in China as sweet with the scent of jasmine and the song of the nightingale. Maybe somewhere else, but not here and not now.

For a week we were left to our own devices, free to wander about the base, poking our noses into the operations shack and maintenance bays, exploring the revetments and runways. It was an indefinite, suspended time, without the "on vacation" feel of our days en route to China, yet also lacking the sense of purpose that comes with an assigned job.

It was not unpleasant, however. I got along well with my tent-mates, and we all spent many hours stretched out on our sleeping bags, planning how we would win the war with our combat tactics, or talking about our lives. Besides Bill, there were Frank Nixon, stocky and cheerful, and John Chennault, son of the general, thin and dark and soft-spoken.

When the afternoons got too warm inside the canvas

walls, we'd hitch a ride on a passing jeep and go wherever it was headed.

They were building a new runway on the northeast section of the base—by hand. Fifty Chinese peasants, men and women, dragged a rock crusher across the field. The crusher, a huge stone cylinder, must have literally weighed a ton, and the people strained on two ropes, pulling it along the 10,000-foot length of the runway for hours in the summer sun. Ahead of them, children worked ceaselessly, collecting larger rocks in baskets and dumping them in a growing mountain off to one side.

The people were all painfully thin, their knees and elbows jutting out from baggy shorts and blouses like blades. Some of the men already looked like cadavers. I didn't see how any of them had the strength for this heavy labor.

The skinny corporal, our driver that day, took off his glasses and rubbed his eyes. "Kind of gives you the creeps, doesn't it?"

"What do you mean?" I asked warily. I thought he was going to say something derogatory about their sweat-stained clothes or gap-toothed grimaces.

"Well, we sometimes think we're wonderful gods from the West, bringing our planes and our technology to save these people. But look at them. Look what they're willing to do to save themselves. Would we do that? It's—I don't know, doesn't it kind of give you a chill?"

He was right. It did. The Chinese were a determined people. I would do well to remember that.

On the first day of July we were told to report that evening to the main mess hall for a full briefing—my first one.

I was so excited as we filed in past the serving line, now cleared of food, that I thought I'd burst. I chose a seat up front near the lectern—I didn't want to miss a word. There were about forty pilots and seventy mechanics and ground crew in the big room, but my eyes saw only the five men who were to brief us.

There was the usual fidgeting, coughing and whispering from the audience while the five guys at the front waited for everyone to file in and settle down, their eyes combing us all for possible flaws.

When the room quieted, a tall, lanky fellow detached himself from the group at the front and stepped up to the microphone. "Evening, men," he began in a slow, Texas drawl, "I'm Tex Hill."

Tex Hill, Flying Tiger group commander! I could not have been more thrilled if Superman had walked up to the lectern.

"Welcome to the best fighting air outfit that's ever been assembled."

I could feel that goofy grin creeping across my face. I was in—*I* was a Flying Tiger. I struggled to look nonchalant.

Tex told us something about the history of the Flying Tigers, about his part in the group's formation and how he knew we'd work hard to maintain its sterling record.

I hung on his every word, and on the words of the other three officers who spoke in the same vein.

Then General Chennault was introduced, and as he stepped up to the podium I felt even more awe than with Tex Hill. Claire Chennault had founded, even invented, the Flying Tigers, and it was his fighting tactics, his innovative strategies, that had made the group a success.

Every line of his body said "fight and win," from his square jaw and thin-pressed lips to the narrow, calculating eyes to the set of his shoulders as he addressed the microphone in a deep Louisiana drawl. His men called him "Old Leather Face" and I could see why. This guy was tough.

But he was also fair. I could see that too. We would be given ample opportunity, he said, to prove ourselves here in Kunming, as pilots, or mechanics, or crew chief, whatever our specialty was. We would have every chance to learn to be the best, and to practice at it. But if we failed, through laziness or sloppiness or inability, we'd be busted back to the States before we had time to turn around and see what hit us. The Flying Tigers was for winners only.

He went on to say he knew we were all winners, or else we wouldn't be here. He thanked us for our dedication. Then he fixed us with an eagle's glare, turned without another word, and walked away from the microphone.

I didn't sleep all that night, nor the next one. I lay awake in my sleeping bag, staring up at the canvas ceiling, reviewing the briefing over and over. General Chennault had made an indelible impression on me; I knew he was the boss, without question, and I wanted to grasp and retain every word he said.

The next day we were assigned to a classroom to learn air combat tactics. I had thought we studied hard at Hill Field, but that was nothing compared to this. Twelve hours a day for ten days straight, we studied blackboard techniques.

General Chennault was a born teacher, an excellent communicator, but the only formation procedures he accepted were his own; the only combat tactics were those he had tried, tested and proved worthy. You learned to do things his way, or you went back home. He tolerated no nonsense at any time.

There was a test every day, and the lowest passing score was an 88. On the final test I scored a 96, which put me in the top three percent of the twenty-seven pilots in the program. It also put me on Cloud Nine. I was intensely proud of myself.

Now we were taken out to the airdrome and assigned three to each P-43. As a replay of Hill Field, we had to memorize the cockpit blindfolded, scoring at least a 90 to qualify for flight. We all passed and one by one, over a twelve-day span, took the little fighter up for six two-hour flights.

That was thrilling, soaring alone over China, looking down on the intricate mosaic of fields and towns, so different from the vast sweep of forest and plain that had been Utah. But the real thrill came when we practiced two simulated dog fights, executed just the way the General had taught us.

Now I really felt like a pro. I was awarded full pilot status and pronounced combat-ready. I gave the P-43 a mental pat on the wing; she was a swell little plane and I already felt affectionate toward her. But the Air Force had another of its surprises for me—for once a good one. I had graduated to the P-40, a shark-toothed beauty sitting out on the runway waiting for me. The P-43s were used to build time and combat readiness; *real* fighter pilots flew P-40s.

I spent the next couple days grabbing whatever hours I could in the P-40, getting the feel of her. She was so much fun I felt like I was out joyriding. She was touchy on landing, but otherwise was a real trouper. I had her in dives at 350 miles per hour, and she'd pull right out and back to 250 cruise speed without a whimper. Her gauges were accurate and easy to read; even fully combat-loaded with ammo and extra fuel, she handled like a lady. I fell hopelessly in love with her.

Of course, she wasn't *my* plane. There were never enough P-40s to go around in those early days, and you had to be prepared to share whatever plane was available with whoever's turn came up next. Still, I felt a proprietary pride in the whole squadron of P-40s, like the sultan of a harem, or a proud horseman with a stable full of stallions.

Two days after I became an official Flying Tiger, I was awakened at five A.M. by jeep headlights shining in through the open window. The sound of footsteps, and my friend, the skinny corporal, banged on our door. "Hey, guys, you gotta get up. Briefing in twenty minutes at the operations shack. Get up!" My heart slammed into my throat. This was it—real combat at last. I wasn't scared, but excited, with a brain-jarring buzz that sent the blood pounding through my head.

A cold shower in the outdoor stall, icy water cascading down around me in the dark; tugging my clothes on over still damp skin; shrugging on the leather jacket with a smile the other guys hopefully couldn't see in the lamplight; running the two hundred yards to the briefing shack.

The briefing took about fifteen minutes. Black coffee; no breakfast. Seven of us pilots sitting in the small room, ready to jump up, already keyed up for action.

I watched what the other guys were doing, trying to gauge my movements to theirs. I was still excited and trying to disguise my combat rawness with a gloss of nonchalance. It hadn't occurred to me that my buddies were probably doing the same thing. Only Captain DeFure, who was very young himself, and his two wingmen had any experience. The rest were as green as I was.

Colonel Wingate, a staff officer who would not be going up with us, immaculate in knife-creased khakis at five o'clock in the morning, stood at the lectern. We had two targets that morning, he told us, the Hankow Rail Yards and a Japanese army moving south toward Kunming. Captain DeFure would be our leader. Our call signal for the mission was 74, derived from the fact that this was July 14th, the *seven*th month, *four*teenth day.

"Any questions?" Wingate looked out at us like a coach readying his team for the big game. "All right then, men, get out to your planes. And good luck."

A jeep took us out to the separate revetments where the planes were parked, dropping each of us off at his assigned aircraft.

At my stop, I jumped out of the jeep, strapping on my parachute as I ran up to the plane and clambered into the cockpit. Sergeant Hanks, my crew chief, was already standing on the wing, waiting to strap me in.

"She's all ready for you," he said, buckling the safety harness across my chest. "Take good care of her."

I pulled on my helmet, goggles and gloves. "I will, Hanks, don't worry."

A tiny voice in the back of my brain whispered, "What do you mean, 'don't worry'? You're going into *war*, buddy. You could get *killed*."

I told the voice to shut up, in fact, pretended I hadn't even heard it, gave Hanks a big smile and a thumbs-up, and pushed forward on the throttle.

The engine gave a roar and we rolled out of the revetment toward the runway. While we were taxiing, I checked the magnetos and switched from main to auxiliary tanks and back again, so I'd be ready when I reached the runway.

Dust from the dirt taxiway billowed into our windshields, enveloping the converging planes in an ochre cloud. Now all seven planes were on the oiled-down runway. The dust feathered away into the pearly morning light.

DeFure advanced his throttle and rolled on down the runway, straightening out as he picked up speed. One by one we followed him, gathering speed on the runway, lifting off in about 2,500 feet, trailing single-file behind him. Then with throttles opened all the way and our landing gear retracting, we pulled into two split diamonds, with the Captain still in the lead.

Thirty-five miles north, my radio crackled with DeFure's voice. "Seventy-four, split formations."

He stayed ahead as we peeled off into three-plane formation, guiding us on toward our first combat situation.

The radio crackled again. "Seventy-four, hot lead check." One at a time, we test fired our guns. My finger was steady on the gun button, and my eyes were keen as they followed the white-hot tracers through the sky. I felt good, ready for anything.

"Seventy-four, climb to sixteen thousand and hold."

I pulled back on the stick, and the P-40 rose joyfully into the sky, leveling out smoothly at just the right instant.

Up ahead was the biggest, blackest cloud I had ever seen, and I thought that Texas had shown me them all. We maintained our heading, passing through the thick, swirling mist like piercing the underside of a swamp. When we came out on the other side, the sun was so bright it dazzled my eyes.

Hankow was about 900 miles from Kunming. The first part of our mission called for us to jettison our auxiliary, or belly, tanks into the rail yards. We had about twenty minutes, and twenty gallons, of fuel left when the Captain called for drop release.

I pulled the release lever and watched as fuel tanks rained down on the tracks below, exploding into fireballs as they hit the target. It was tremendously satisfying.

The Japanese must have thought they were being attacked with 500-pound bombs, but we encountered no ground fire and no bandits approached us from the air.

We were still thirty minutes from our second target, an army of about 500 men heading toward Kunming. As we got close to the target zone, I could see small arms fire coming from a wooded area along a river bend.

We dove down at 350 miles per hour in close formation, holding our fire until we were only 200 feet off the deck, or ground, for a blazing strafing run.

"Seventy-four, on your own."

This meant that we were each to call our own shots, but see and be seen. It was as important to frighten the Japanese and throw them off guard as to hit them.

I picked out a weapons carrier and rolled in with all four guns blazing. I got out a couple of great bursts, pulled away, and came roaring back in for another pass from a different angle.

Soldiers were running in every direction, diving into the shrubbery, the water, behind boulders. I saw them not as individuals but as nonspecific targets. I knew I was hot and I wanted to keep blazing away, making pass after pass, but we had a particular area to concentrate on, the thicket where their fire was coming from. We shelled that area for about ten minutes, until there were no more bullets arcing up out of the trees; then we climbed back up to 15,000 feet and leveled out to a low fuel burn for the trip back home.

The return flight was uneventful. I spent it with my eyes peeled for bandits in the distance, and possible problems with my cockpit gauges, as I had been taught. We had learned to be always alert in the pilot's seat, not relaxing until we reached home, or we might never reach home. I kept up my vigil, my mind never straying from my job, but underneath my flight jacket, my blood bubbled with excitement.

I had done it! I had succeeded in my first combat mission, diving out of the skies with my tiger shark's teeth bared, knocking the enemy into next week. I relived everything with the back of my mind, and enjoyed it all over again.

We touched down at Kunming with one sortie completed, two hours and forty-five minutes of combat under our belts.

We pulled our planes into their revetments, and jumped out, adrenaline still pumping away like hot pistons.

Sergeant Hanks and Corporal Simpson, my armament man, were waiting for me at my revetment. They unbuckled me from the plane, clapping me on the back and offering me congratulations. A jeep pulled up and they sent me off to debriefing, but first I had to thank that beautiful P-40. I gave her a loving caress as I walked away, thanking her for a job well done.

Breakfast was waiting for us at the debriefing, and I thought coffee and powdered eggs had never tasted so good. The room was noisy with the excited chatter of the pilots, still keyed up from the mission, everyone eager to tell his story.

It got quiet in a hurry when General Chennault entered the room, accompanied by Col. Robert L. Scott, another top staffer. I had understood that the General never attended briefings or debriefings and I was flattered that he was here.

The debriefing itself took about forty-five minutes. Colonel Wingate, who ran the meeting, asked us a hundred questions about what we had seen, in terms of troop movement, equipment, rail lines, bandits encountered, anything and everything that might help them anticipate the enemy's next move. Occasionally, the senior officers would pitch in a question, always asked as cordially as if they were guests. There were also questions about how our equipment worked, how we had handled ourselves and our mission, if we had any comments.

About halfway through the session I was handed a note, which said that my plane had been examined and I had had only 150 rounds of ammunition left when I landed. Obviously, I had not counted on any action on my way home. It was a valuable lesson. I had forgotten that you had to monitor your ammo and your fuel going and coming; they were your ticket home. I never made that mistake again.

It made an impression on me, but it didn't deflate my ego any, either. I was darn proud of myself.

The General and his staff were proud of us, too. They encouraged us to eat all we wanted; then we went back to our huts for showers and several hours' rest.

I wished I had a shower and a hot breakfast now, cramped up in this dank cave. I wished I had a few hours' rest. I wondered how long it was until my watch was over, until this whole ordeal was over. *If* I would be alive to know it was over.

I gave myself a mental kick. Enough self-pity. No more giving in to fear. I *was* a hot shot pilot, remember? I had done okay before; I'd do okay now.

CHAPTER NINE

Another Encounter

I had planned to break our watches into three-hour stretches each, figuring on one vigil per person in a day in hiding of about twelve hours. It was all calculated very neatly and scientifically; the problem was that without a wrist watch or clock it was extremely difficult to tell how much time had gone by.

I began to realize that time is a subjective element. When you're part of a technological society it's all ticked off in tidy increments of hours, minutes and seconds. There's a sense of security, of control, in being able to measure the flow of time as the hands sweep around the dial. But now that safe world was gone and time took on a different face, one that could be measured only in the less concise, more emotional aspects of shifting shadows and the changing angles of the sun's rays.

So I sat and watched the sunlight creep across the field, melting the dew from the grass blades, steaming the damp from the exposed rocks. The willows bent in a stiffening breeze. The breeze died away. Slowly, imperceptively, the sun rose higher in the sky, until at last I judged that my three hours were up.

But somehow I did not want to relinquish my watch. I didn't feel safe lying back and closing my eyes here in this cramped little space. Of course, I didn't feel safe anywhere in this occupied part of China, but particularly at this moment I did not have a good feeling about this spot.

Maybe because it was an enclosed space and our backs were against the wall. I kept thinking of that food wrapper we'd seen, with its ominous Japanese printing. If *they* found us here, we'd be trapped, with no means of escape.

The more I thought about it, the more concerned I became, until that concern turned into an adrenaline rush of anxiety. Every nerve twitched to get out of this place, to move, to go, to get up. I felt not claustrophobic, but horribly constricted. I *had* to get us out of here *now*.

I knew it wasn't safe to be on the move in the daytime, but I was certain I could find another shelter, one with a better exit and better visibility for us. And we had to go now.

I roused the boys easily. A gentle touch on the shoulder was all it took to render them fully alert.

"What wrong?" Weng said instantly.

"Nothing. I—I just think we should get out of this cave to someplace safer."

"This safe," Weng said.

"No one see us here," his brother added.

"No." I almost yelled it. "We've got to leave now." My nerves were screaming for action. I didn't feel I could waste a moment on explanations. "Get your gear."

The brothers looked at each other, as if wondering what on earth I could be thinking of. I didn't wait for their okay. I was already trying to wake Dalton, who refused to come around.

"Wake up, buddy. Come on, now," I pleaded, shaking him by the shoulders. He groaned and turned his head away. I shook him harder.

"Whaa—" he finally mumbled, pushing my hand away.

"Come on, pal, we're movin' out."

He sat up with such a start I could just about see his heart thud. "The Japs?"

"I don't know. Here." I handed him his walking stick.

Grasping it with both hands, he hauled himself painfully to his feet, suppressing a groan. The bandage on his broken leg was red again with fresh blood.

I felt a twinge of guilt for shoving him out, not allowing him more time to rest, but it wasn't enough to make me stay here. Instead, I offered him my shoulder.

I parted the reeds at the face of the cave and peered out. The willows rustled in a fresh breeze. A bee hovered in front of a stand of bamboo. A pair of thrushes soared over a boulder. Otherwise, empty hillside.

I looked back at Dalton and the boys. "Ready?" I found I was whispering.

Weng and Chien nodded, eyes wide. They still weren't sure what I thought I was doing. Dalton didn't say a word; he was concentrated on moving without crying out. His hand was heavy on my shoulder.

We walked out into the sunlight, blinking like people who'd spent years underground. Everything seemed too bright, too exposed, but the anxiety I'd felt in the cave was dissipating in the open air.

I took out my compass. The needle pointed north, straight over the hill. There were clumps of bamboo all along the ridge, so we'd be fairly protected once we reached the top. It was getting there that would be the problem.

About a fourth of a mile of ground separated us from the ridge, not far except that we could not walk fast with Dalton's leg injury. Speed would not be our strong suit, but there were clumps of willow and bamboo scattered along the hillside, and if we could make short hops from one to the other, we should be okay.

I drew in a couple of deep, cleansing breaths, like I did before a race, and we started up the hill. It was slow going.

Dalton's leg must have stiffened during the hours in the cave; he seemed barely able to drag it. He had let go of my shoulder, I think to give me more freedom if we ran into difficulties, and each step was obviously painful. We would walk about three yards, wait for Dalton to catch up, walk another three yards.

The boys kept about fifty feet ahead of us, like an advance guard, but all they found was another food wrapper, frightening proof that the Japanese had been through here recently.

It took what must have been half an hour to reach the first clump of trees, a safe anchorage in the sea of grass. I looked back at the way we had come. The dew had dried and our feet had left no footprints. No one would ever know we had been here. I hoped.

A plane droned overhead and I instinctively pressed myself against the gray-green branches. It was an American plane, a B-24, traveling north toward Kweilin. Lord, if only *they* knew we were here; if only we could be rescued. But we were hidden in the trees and they were already gone, miles above and miles away.

We achieved our next objective, a small stand of

bamboo, in another half hour, and the next tiny thicket about a half hour after that.

Dalton's breathing was shallow, and his face had a grayish tinge. It wasn't until I happened to glance down at my own leg that I noticed the trickle of blood oozing out of the bandage. Funny, I didn't feel it at all.

We found another cave, actually just another cleft in the rock, behind the third bamboo stand. As we were resting beside them, the reeds began to rustle. Someone was on the other side. My heart stopped. But it was okay. We were in the open. We could still run.

Then I realized the rustling was at ground level only. A man, even creeping, would be making noise higher in the reeds. I parted the bamboo, and saw a huge lizard, three feet from head to tail, scurrying into the rock cleft.

He turned and stared up at me with bulging yellow eyes, then ran to the back of the cave and stopped dead. There was nowhere further for him to go. He was trapped.

I let the reeds close back over his hideaway. That is what would have happened to us had we stayed in our tiny cave. I knew it as surely as I knew my own name.

Now that I felt justified in dragging us out into the daylight, we seemed to move a little faster.

We reached the hilltop and rested for a while in a group of willows whose branches, spreading down to the ground, welcomed us into their sheltering shade.

On the other side, the hill fell away to a long stream-fed valley. Ferns carpeted the gentle slope between thick stands of tea and mulberry and willow. It looked like paradise compared to the open area we had just come through.

We polished off the water in our canteens, which

amounted to two short gulps each, and started down the hillside.

Dalton seemed to be having a little easier time of it—down is always easier than up—and the boys were almost enjoying themselves again. And why not? The sun shone benevolently, the sky was an intense blue dotted with white cloud puffs, a fresh, soft scent rose up from the ferns at our feet; one could almost forget that a Japanese army was just ahead of us and possibly circling around just behind us.

We didn't talk. Our voices would have carried on the breeze and given us away long before our footsteps reached the attention of any unwanted listeners. My mind wasn't taken up with conversation, and I found I wasn't really thinking, either, not in any abstract way.

Instead, I was completely occupied with interpreting sounds carried to us on the wind—a bird pecking at a branch, the rustle of the leaves in the trees, a soft thud that could have been a footfall but turned out to be a seed pod dropping from a dry bush. And every motion caught my eye—the shadow of a passing cloud, a dead leaf swirling into a spider web, a dragonfly dipping down to a fern frond.

I was alert, and anxious—I was beginning to wonder what it had been like not be to anxious—but I wasn't a jumble of screaming nerve ends like I had been in the cave. Out in the open was not nearly as bad, as long as I kept alert.

Then I began to get tired. My face was throbbing again, along with my hand and my leg. Images of gangrenous limbs intruded on my concentration. Dalton, about fifty yards behind me, looked to be in about the same shape. The boys, on either side of me, were dragging a little as well. They weren't injured, but they too were operating on a minimum of food, drink or sleep. Adrenaline gives you a good push when you need to move, but after it drains off it leaves you exhausted.

We were almost to the bottom of the hill. I figured this was a good time to stop, before we got into the valley. From here we had the double advantage of protection and visibility. It would also be wise, I figured, to stop before we got so tired we made a stupid mistake. Our first would be our last.

I motioned for the boys to stop and we all waited for Dalton to catch up.

"I think we ought to stop until night under those trees," I whispered, pointing to a mix of mulberry and willow.

Dalton, breathing raggedly, nodded his assent.

"Look okay to me," Weng agreed. "We eat berries from tree."

"I no silkworm," Chien said in mock protestation. Mulberries are the only thing silkworms will eat. We all laughed for the first time in what seemed like a long time.

The little grove was slightly to the left of our course. Feeling better already with our destination in sight, we veered off toward it.

Fifty feet to the right, in the corner of my eye. I caught a movement, a bird fluttering onto a fern clump. I offered Dalton my shoulder. I caught the same movement again, turned and looked. No bird. It must have flown off. Dalton clamped his sweat-damped hand gratefully down on my shoulder. There was that same motion again. I turned around and looked. A bright glint, like dewdrops in the grass. But it was a warm afternoon; all the dew had long since evaporated.

I motioned for everyone to stop short. Dalton's grip tightened on my shoulder, and he and the boys looked where I pointed. Someone was definitely there.

The best thing to do would be to keep going in the direction we had been heading and hope that whoever it was wouldn't catch on to our presence. But like before, when we had found Dalton, I felt myself compelled to investigate.

I started walking toward the spot.

"No!" Dalton grabbed my arm as well as my shoulder.

"He know what he doing," Chien whispered, but he didn't look as though he believed it.

I wasn't sure I knew what I was doing either, but on some instinctive level I reasoned that the fellow—person, I wasn't even sure it was a "he"—behind the ferns wasn't Japanese. For one thing, he didn't smell Japanese, and the breeze was blowing from him to me. For another, the bank of ferns was too small to shelter more than a single individual and I didn't think a Japanese soldier would be alone out here. If he was, the four of us should be able to overpower him.

Should be. I took another step toward the ferns. What in hell did I think I was doing? Three steps. I should turn around now and run. Get away. Five steps. Leave.

I could see his head now, lying flat below the ferns. Dark hair. My brain fumbled. Dark like Japanese hair? No . . . my heart started beating again . . . dark brown. American hair.

"Don't shoot," he said into the ferns. I could see tremors running through his neck and shoulders.

"We're Americans," I said quietly. I didn't want to spook him further.

"What—what?" He was still lying in the ferns.

"It's okay. You can get up. We're Americans."

I waved to Dalton and the boys, mouthing widely, "It's okay."

I gave the fellow a hand to his feet.

"Horton?" I whispered. I knew this guy. He never flew with the same group I did, but we'd run into each other every couple months, stopping off at each other's bases between missions, and we'd become friends.

D. J. Horton was always good for a laugh; he loved to clown around and I could count on him to enliven any evening. His trademark was the two .45s he always wore crisscrossed over his chest in beautifully tooled leather holsters. His dad owned a leather shop in Atlanta and that's where he got the holsters. I don't know how he got the second .45; he conned the Air Force out of it somehow.

He had the two pistols on him now. I could see them beneath his unzipped leather jacket. His flight suit was mud-spattered, and his back pack had a tear along one side; otherwise he looked in pretty good shape. Actually, he looked remarkably good; he looked like home to me.

"You okay, buddy?" I whispered, clapping him on the back.

"Sure," I could tell he was still shaky from fright, but he allowed himself a smile. "You look like hell though."

"You should see the other guy."

But he wasn't looking at me. He had stiffened, staring past me at the boys, who had followed me down the slope.

"Who are they?"

"Weng and Chien. They're helping us back to Allied lines."

"Japs?" he asked incredulously.

"No. They're Chinese. They're on our side."

"You sure?"

I was very tired and I was getting exasperated. "Of

course I'm sure. If they weren't friendly, I wouldn't be here now."

"Sorry," Horton said. "It's just, well, it's just been real scary bein' out here alone. You know?" He smiled the famous Horton smile, full of mischief.

The boys, as when we had found Dalton, had their eyes fixed on his guns.

"Ya'll are admirin' my weapons," Horton said.

Weng said something to Chien in Chinese, then he turned to me and waited. I seemed, again, to have become the spokesman in these delicate negotiations.

"They want your pistols," I told Horton. "But you can take the clips out."

"They ain't gettin' 'em." He said this not in an unfriendly way, but as someone who could not be parted from a prized possession, which indeed, the pistols were.

I was getting exasperated again, and getting tired of having to conduct this whole conversation in whispers. My face hurt, and I was tired of talking, period.

"Look, if you want them to lead you out, you're going to have to give them your guns."

"I did," Dalton said, finally catching up with us.

"Good, but I ain't goin' to," Horton said stubbornly. Then to the boys, "You kids already got two pistols, and I got two, so this makes us even."

Weng had his chin stuck out and his mouth drawn down. He wasn't buying this.

"And besides," Horton said, "if I keep my pistols, then I can defend you if it comes to a shoot-out. If I give 'em to you, how am I gonna help you?"

"Shoot-out, like cowboys and Indians?" Chien asked hopefully.

"Yeah, there you go."

"We *have* two guns already," Weng said thoughtfully.

"Then he keep them," Chien said.

"Okay."

"Thank you, sir," Horton said. He stuck out his hand, but Weng didn't see it. He was too busy taking inventory of his own weapons.

That taken care of, we walked through the ferns to the shelter we had selected before coming upon Horton.

Unfortunately, there were no berries on the mulberry tree. Horton had eaten all his rations days ago. We had polished off ours. We had no water. There was nothing to do but sleep, and this time I let Weng take the first watch.

CHAPTER TEN

Night Spirits

I slid easily into a sleep composed of alternately running and hiding figures, like a jigsaw puzzle in fern greens and weathered leather browns. I had mixed feelings about teaming up with first Dalton and then my old pal Horton. I was glad to see them, of course, and would never have left them out there alone; yet it had been easier when it was just the boys and me. The larger our group became, the harder it would be for us to move unseen through enemy territory.

That had already proven to be true with Dalton. Today, on that exposed hillside, his inability to move quickly had severely hampered us, fortunately without any ill consequences. But if we had run into trouble, we could never have gotten away in time. And we could not have abandoned him.

Horton wasn't injured, so he could move fast enough; but it's easier for three people to evade capture than four, and easier for four than for five.

But there was no turning back now on people, or events. We'd just have to hope Kuan Yin was still watching out for us.

* * *

When I awoke it was dusk. Venus, the evening star, was shining in through the willow branches. My first waking thought was of overwhelming thirst, my second was that our canteens were empty. I remembered reading somewhere, some adventure story, that sucking on a stone alleviates thirst, but I figured that in China even a stone would have to be boiled before it was free from germs.

Horton had his canteen out and was fiddling with it, putting it to his mouth as if desire could magically fill it with water. "Hey there, you're awake. We can get goin' now, straight downhill to the stream."

"We like to wait until it's completely dark," I said.

"Well, how long's that gonna be?"

We Americans couldn't seem to get off watches and clocks.

"Let's plan our course," I said instead of answering him. "Nobody has any halizone tablets left, so we'll make a fire by the stream and boil some water. Then we might as well keep heading north; it's the straightest path. If the terrain stays flat like it is down there, we should make about five miles tonight."

"Sounds okay to me," Dalton said from the shadows at my elbow. It was already dark enough that I couldn't see him clearly, but his voice sounded strained and full of pain.

"I think we come to village soon," Weng said.

"Get food," Chien added.

"Amen." That was Horton.

We didn't ask Weng why he thought we'd come upon a village tonight. I imagined that in his blood he carried an instinctive knowledge of China, the layout of towns and cities and farms, and the spaces between them.

I wondered if I had within me a map of my home. If

set down anywhere in Texas, could I find my way through the empty stretches of desert, the scrubby hills, the rivers and ranches? I supposed I could. I had lived there long enough that the rhythm of the land, the spacing and phrasing, the flow of the place, was in my bones.

But that was Texas and this was China, and they were a million miles apart. Yet again, I was thankful I had found Weng and Chien.

When Venus rose above the topmost branch of the mulberry, we started down the hill, I in the lead, followed by the boys, then Horton and finally Dalton. The half-mile slope to the stream was a gentle one, and we could easily see our path by the light of a hundred stars.

At the bottom, the boys fell upon the stream, dipping their faces in the clear water and taking long gulps.

"Ding hao!" Chien said. "Good! You like?" He scooped up a handful of water and let it cascade back into the stream. It sparkled in the starlight like silver.

"Let's light that fire before I die of thirst," Horton said, fumbling in his pack for his matches. Chien and I collected an armful of twigs and we laid them between two boulders, so the light from the fire would be fairly well hidden. Then we set three flat-topped rocks from the stream bank within the twigs to serve as a cooktop.

Horton set the match to the twigs and our fire flamed to life. I thought I had never seen anything so beautiful. But it was also terrifying because the light crept out between the boulders, creating a glow that could be seen from the top of the hill and away across the valley.

We would have to cook fast.

As soon as the flames sank below the level of the rocks, we placed our full canteens in the magic circle.

It's true that a watched pot never boils. A cricket chorus started up. A frog couple plopped into the stream a few feet away, startling the breath out of us. A night bird sang. The fire flickered and crackled and spat. But the canteens were barely warm.

We didn't dare build the fire up higher; it would be more attention-grabbing, and it would only scorch the outsides of the canteens without contributing any useful heat.

Now the shadows had eyes. An owl soaring in on white-tipped wings was a Japanese soldier in a white headband, jumping out of the tree onto our little group. A deer mouse, claws clicking on the river rocks, was an enemy army, drawing their bayonets.

We watched the night and it watched us back, malevolently, until the hairs on the backs of our necks stood straight. Then came a new sound, a popping and burbling—the water was boiling at last.

We let it go for ten minutes; then we threw sand on the flames until they died away. Safe again in the night, we pulled our canteens from the rocks by their canvas straps, uncorked them, burning our fingers, and blew on the openings until they were cool enough to drink from.

Warm water is not a thirst quencher. It assuages the dryness at the back of the throat and alleviates dehydration, but it doesn't give you the satisfying sensation of cold liquid pouring through and filling the parched hollows of your body.

Still, water was water and we weren't complaining.

We checked to make sure the sand covered our tracks; then we moved on. The tinny slosh of water in the canteen at my side was comforting. I would refill it in the village; I planned never to let it get empty again.

The valley was marshy, which explained why there were no farms. Chien navigated us through it, finding little patches of high ground and skipping from one to another. Sometimes the higher patches were rocky and slippery with water that had seeped up from the marsh. Water weeds snaked up out of the water and lay in wait for an unsuspecting foot. If you slipped into the marsh, thick, dank mud rushed up over your boottops and let go only after a considerable struggle.

Poor Dalton had such a difficult time trying to balance himself and his stick that Horton and I ended up carrying him. This wasn't easy, either, because you had to compensate for the extra weight before hopping from one dry patch to the next. And I was very worried that if we fell, the mud would get into our wounds and cause more damage than was already there.

We seemed to slog on forever. At one point, we came across a pond of clear water with a couple of large birds asleep at its edge.

"Ducks," Weng said. "Village close."

Shortly after that the marsh drained away into farm land, rice paddies and lotus ponds and trails between them. The moon had risen, and by its light we could see, off in the distance, a small town. It was no more than a village, really, but twice the size of the Wangs' pitiful hamlet.

I let Dalton down and massaged my aching shoulders with my good hand. "Do we go in?"

Once again I felt the conflicting emotions caused by the presence of a town. On the one hand, a town meant help—food, water, possibly even medical attention; on the other, it meant exposure to the unknown—

any person or combination of people who could be Japanese infiltrators or Japanese sympathizers.

Dalton leaned wearily on his stick; his eyes were glazed with fatigue. "I guess so . . ."

Horton readjusted his shoulder holsters. "Why should we? We're all right out here, aren't we?"

"Weng?" I asked.

He looked out at the village, a huddle of dark shapes in the moonlight. "Village safe. We go there."

"Lead the way," I said.

The village was walled, protected by the same mud and daub building material that our hostels were made of back at the base.

Just outside the wall, Weng motioned for us to stop. Another motion indicated that we should crouch in the shadow of the wall. Then, with a finger to his lips, he turned, slid over the wall as easily as spilled ink, and disappeared from our view. Chien, following at his heels, also slipped over the wall and disappeared.

We three Americans waited in the dark. From the village side of the wall came a soft clucking, as from a dreaming chicken, and a creak of wood, maybe a door opening. A quick intake of breath and a gasp from someone. Then all was silent.

I felt, rather than saw, Horton fingering his pistols again. Then I heard his breath in my ear. "How do you know what they're doin' in there?"

I put my finger to my lips, hoping he could see the gesture in the dark.

Apparently not, because next he whispered, "Maybe they're turnin' us in for dough."

I put my hand over his mouth. That worked. He sat back against the wall, but I could feel the tenseness radiating out from him like a shield.

Now we heard the wooden creak again, the door

opening back up. "Good, they're coming back," I thought, but they didn't materialize. The chicken clucked again, sharply. She was awake. Now a flurry of Chinese, spoken in undertones, but still shrill with its falling and rising cadences. Now a deep, dragging sound and a wave of dust flowing along the wall. The town gate, twenty feet further along the wall, was being pulled open.

Weng and Chien darted out and ran back to where we sat.

"Come. They wait for you inside." Chien pulled me to my feet, then did the same for Dalton. "Come on," he said to Horton, who lingered in the shadow. "No shoot-out."

"Okay, kid, I'm comin'." Horton lumbered to his feet and followed us through the gate.

As soon as we had got through, the gate was pushed shut by a small boy, about eight years old, who stared at us with enormous eyes. A man of about thirty-five or forty, short and stocky, waved the boy away with another flurry of Chinese. The child ran off, stumbling as he went because he could not take his eyes off us long enough to watch where he was going.

The man motioned us along a path leading toward the center of the village, peering nervously from side to side and hurrying us in front of him like a gaggle of geese on the way to market.

As we were rushed along, I tried to take stock of the place. The first thing I noticed, again, was the smell. It had faded into the background this past day and night, probably because we were in open country away from the cultivated fields. But here it was back again, attaching itself to my nose like a leech. It was even stronger here, and this walk through the streets showed me why.

The village, which was composed of several intersecting streets and alleys, was built of mud and daub. The streets were tamped earth, and raw sewage ran through the gutters, trenches that were dug along the face of each house. The effect was worse than honey buckets, which at least were self-contained.

But there was a perfectly proportioned bridge across a stream in the center of town, a miniature pagoda with three tiers, curving eaves and red roof tiles, and a tiny pond with three golden carp swimming in it. If you were selective in your vision, the place looked like a picture book.

The man steered us around a corner and hustled us over the doorstep of a rectangular building with sloping eaves, turning to look furtively over his shoulder before closing the door. Where most of the houses in the village jostled shoulder to shoulder in the narrow streets, this one stood alone. A small terrace off to one side, defined by red-painted posts, held a few bamboo tables and chairs.

Inside, the building was pitch black and we stood hesitantly in the doorway. The man pushed past us. We could hear him fumbling with something, and then the room sprang into being as he carried a clay lamp to a bamboo table.

"*Cha*," he said, which I remembered as the word for tea, and then I realized where we were: a restaurant or tea house.

The place was small, about 20 by 30 feet, or approximately the size of my favorite diner back in Hawthorne, California. But there were no stainless-steel malt machines, no red leather booths or swivel seats, no flapjack grills or toasters or electric coffee pots.

Instead there were seven or eight bamboo tables with matching chairs on a dirt floor, a long wooden table bearing a variety of clay teapots and cups, metal canisters of tea, and two kettles for boiling water on a raised fire pit similar to the Wangs'. On a shelf underneath the table were a few platters, knives and ladles, a glass jar of rice and another of beans, an empty, beautifully decorated flower vase, a collection of wooden chopsticks in a clay jar.

Our host showed us to a table, seating us with care like any good restaurateur, and bustled around getting tea ready. He had a shock of coarse hair hanging over his forehead which he constantly pushed back in what seemed to be a characteristically nervous gesture, although he seemed much calmer now that we were indoors.

"He make jasmine tea," Chien said. "You like, very good."

"Who is he?" I asked, as our host filled a teapot with boiling water.

"His name Lin," Chien said.

"No, I mean, is he the mayor? The police chief?"

"Not understand."

"What does he do in the town? Is he—" I fumbled for an analogy—"the boss?"

Chien still looked puzzled.

"Is he an elder, an old man of the village?"

Chien said something to Lin in Chinese and he laughed, looking at us and shaking his head.

"He not old. He young man."

Lin arrived at the table with tea on a tray. "*Cha*," he said. "*Cha*." He laughed again and poured the tea.

The tea was fragrant with the milky, feminine scent of jasmine, the only thing in the village that smelled good. I figured if I kept my nose in its steamy fragrance I might make it through our stay without the continual urge to retch.

It burned where it hit the hole in my cheek, but I drank it down anyway, grateful for the warm caffeine rush.

"Hey, this is good," Horton said, surprised.

Dalton, looking exhausted, murmured assent without looking up from his cup.

"*Sheh-sheh,*" I said to Lin. "Thank you."

The little boy from the gate rushed in as if blown by a gale, carrying a pile of rugs he could barely see over. Once over the threshold, however, he was rendered motionless by the sight of white people. He stood and stared at us over his burden until Lin snapped at him in Chinese. He dropped the rugs and went to stand shyly by the fire, still staring.

"That Lin's son, Li," Chien advised.

"Hello, Li," I said, smiling my kindliest. The child's eyes grew even wider and he shrank into the shadows beyond the stove.

His father came forward with another tray, piled high with square, sticky slabs.

"Rice cakes, bean cakes," Chien said. "Very good, you like."

Weng hadn't said a word since we walked into the restaurant. I was beginning to wonder why and it was beginning to make me nervous.

"Weng," I said. "Is something wrong?"

"What?" He hadn't really heard me.

"What's the matter?" I dropped my voice to a whisper. "Why did Lin rush us through the village like that? Are you sure this place is safe?"

The more I thought about it, the more convinced I became that Lin's behavior had been suspicious. I didn't doubt him, but he certainly acted as though he were trying to hide us, quite unlike the Wangs had done. Maybe the man had taken on more than he could handle; maybe he was trying to sneak us past deadly enemies.

Weng was still staring off distractedly, as though he

knew he had made a terrible mistake and was trying to decide what to do about it.

"Weng? *What is it?*"

"What? Oh . . . nothing."

I didn't believe him, and turned to Chien questioningly.

"Lin have very beautiful daughter."

Weng cuffed his brother on the arm.

"She lovely, like moonlight on water," Chien continued.

Weng kicked him under the table.

Relief flooded through me, like moonlight through water.

"That's nice," I said, my voice cracking with joy. "Where is she?"

"In house. Father not let her out at night. Spirits might take her."

So *that* was it. Lin was afraid of evil spirits, lurking in the night to capture us all. Thank God he had decided to brave them on our behalf.

"You'll see her in the morning, Weng," I said. Thank God there would be a morning.

"Long time," Weng said broodingly. Then, changing expression, he fell upon the rice cakes and devoured three in one bite.

I ate three myself. They were gluey, without any flavoring, but they were filling. I could feel them sticking to each rib. The bean cakes, surprisingly, were tasty, sweet and grainy and thick.

While we ate, Lin hovered at our shoulders, smiling and nodding and urging more tea on us. I motioned to him to sit down and join us, but he wouldn't. After we had polished off the tray of cakes, however, he pulled up a chair and pulled out from his jacket a clay bottle with a ceramic cork. He unstoppered the bottle and poured a generous dollop of clear liquid into each of our cups, including one for himself.

He said something in Chinese, holding the cup aloft in an obvious toast, and we raised ours too. We drank it down. I don't know what it was, but it burned like moonshine fresh out of the still. This would surely keep the spirits at bay. My eyes watered and the room tilted. My entire body was filled with a wonderfully warm and soothing glow, and I felt better than I had in days, months even. I was asleep before my head hit the spread-out rugs.

CHAPTER ELEVEN

Unexpected Visitors

By the time we went to sleep it must have been three A.M., the deepest, darkest hour of the night. Beyond the shuttered windows of the tea house, the wind rose, howling around the corners of the building and screeching as it searched for a way out from under the curving eaves. Dry leaves scuttered along the streets like whispering feet, and a tree branch scraped across the roof with a sound like long-nailed, long-dead mandarins scrabbling on the tiles, clawing at the ceiling to grab us up and away. The spirits of the night had risen.

I had been listening for some time before I realized I was awake. Lin's powerful liquor had worn off, leaving me still exhausted but wide awake.

The fire had burned down to embers in the stove and the tea house was in darkness. Again I felt, rather than saw, Horton's eyes on me as I tossed and turned. I heard him making his way over to me between the other sleepers, then felt his breath in my ear.

"So you're finally awake."

I nodded. He could see that.

"Don' you think we ought to get out of here?"

"Not yet. I believe these people can help us some."

"*Help* us? What makes you think they're gonna help us when that Lin fella goes slippin' us a mickey like that?"

"It was only alcohol, Horton. A hundred proof, probably, but purely drink, a goodwill gesture."

"It's goodwill to knock somebody out cold and then sell 'em to the Japs?"

"He didn't do that, Horton."

"Only because you and I got constitutions like horses. We're Southern gentlemen—we know how to hold our liquor."

This was said with some pride. I would have laughed if it hadn't occurred to me that there was some truth to the matter. I had been lying there only half asleep not because of any night spirits, but because I was listening for the stealthy sound of human footsteps in the dark. We really had no idea who was in the village and what their motives might be. But I didn't want to tell Horton that; it would only get him more upset.

"We're safe here tonight, buddy," I said, soothingly, I hoped. "Go back to sleep."

"No chance."

"Then sit down and be quiet so I can sleep."

But although I closed my eyes, propped my injured hand carefully on my chest and my bad leg on a heaped-up section of rug, sleep would not return.

"You still awake?" Horton whispered.

"No."

"The hell you're not."

There was a silence, then: "You see where he put that firewater?"

"No, why?"

"That's one surefire way to put yourself right out."

Horton always made me laugh.

*   *   *

When the morning sun filtered through the shutters, I was still awake. Sometime during what had remained of the night, Horton had drifted back to his own pallet, to sleep, I assumed, and Dalton and the boys were still deep in slumber.

I lay there watching a dust mote spiraling lazily down, and thought about Ovella. About waking in the early morning entwined in her sweet scent and soft hair. Watching her arise sleepily and drift toward the kitchen. Listening to her hum along with the radio as I dressed and shaved. Then the heady aroma of fresh coffee perking and bacon frying. Hurrying clean and fresh into the kitchen to catch her up and dance a step or two to Harry James's velvet horn.

That world was long ago and far away. Now all I heard was the cluck and bustle of the town's single chicken. All I smelled was the pungent odor of the streets and my own sweat-stained clothes.

I clambered to my feet—Lord, was I stiff—and peered through the shutters. A woman was herding a flock of ducks along the street, guiding them with a long stick that reached over their heads to dangle in front of them. A group of children were playing some kind of game with a handful of sticks. Men and women, coolie hats firmly in place, headed for the village gate and the rice paddies beyond.

And here came Lin, rushing up the street, pushing the hair off his face. He opened the door of the tea house, exclaiming something in Chinese.

At whatever he said, Weng and Chien suddenly awoke, jumped up and rolled up their rugs.

"Morning," Chien said, smiling at me sweetly, but Weng, always more serious, anxiously said, "Must get up quickly. Wake captain and major."

He tapped Horton on the forehead. Horton sprang

bolt upright with a muzzy yell that died away as soon as he saw it was Weng.

Dalton was harder to rouse. Again, he seemed reluctant to come back to the conscious world, waking only after prolonged shaking, and with a painful groan.

"Time to hit the road again?" he asked weakly.

"We have company," I said.

"Swell." I handed him the walking stick and as he reached for it, I noticed his hand was raw and blistered from gripping its rough tip. I gave him my shoulder instead, and we stood, blinking in the light from the open door.

Lin bustled around us, folding up our rugs almost before we got up from them, lighting the fire, putting water on to boil, setting out cups and teapots, straightening tables.

His son flew in, arms full of kindling, and deposited it next to the stove. Then he grabbed up the folded rugs and rushed away with them, even though they were piled so high he could barely see over them. Now here he was back again, pouring rice from a jar into a pot on the stove.

Father and son whirled around in a rapid blur. Watching them made me dizzy, and I fumbled for a convenient chair. In an instant Lin was beside me, brushing the hair nervously off his face and talking at me a mile a minute in earnest Chinese. I looked to the boys for translation.

"He say, please you sit over here," Chien said, leading me to a table in a shadowy corner of the room. "You, also," and he guided Dalton and Horton to chairs beside mine. It was becoming obvious that Lin wanted us out of the way, and it couldn't be for any pleasant reason.

"Chien," I said, "why does Lin want to keep us over here, in the shadows?"

"Sun not come this far in restaurant."

"No, Chien. I'm asking if he's trying to hide us."

"He not want to hide from you, he right there, cooking."

So this is what was meant by a Chinese puzzle.

I tried attracting Weng's attention. He was standing beside the stove, staring out the open door, and didn't even see my subtle gestures.

"Weng!" I tried a stage whisper. No response.

"Weng, Captain want you," Chien yelled across the room. So much for subtlety.

The older boy reluctantly detached himself from view of the door and came over to me. "You need?"

"Lin seems awfully nervous about us being here. Are you sure it's okay?"

Weng straightened his shoulders defensively. "Yes, okay. He making plans for you." He unbent a little, and said in a softer tone, "You safe."

His whole body unbent and his face took on a different cast. I recognized that look from my own not-too-distant youth. Sure enough, coming in the door was a girl who had to be Lin's daughter.

She *was* beautiful. A cloud of dark hair framed wide almond eyes, a button nose and perfectly proportioned pink lips. Translucent skin glowed like pearl. Out of this face shone an expression of serenity to make the angels weep. Dressed in the same loose, colorless tunic and trousers as her father and brother, she still managed to convey an aura of overwhelming femininity. This was not a girl but a vision.

Weng stood, transfixed, as she glided across the dirt floor as if it were polished marble and halted obediently at her father's side.

"Go over and talk to her," I prompted.

"Cannot. Must wait for father to give permission."

Lin was unlikely to do that. He had other things on

143

his mind. He gave the girl a tray heaped with rice bowls and sent her to distribute them at the various tables.

A sound from the street caused him to rush to the door, brushing the hair from his eyes, wiping his hands on his trousers.

And suddenly the restaurant was filled with men, all conversing in Chinese, striding about with gruff expressions and demanding voices. Their tunics and trousers were stiff and rough; many wore baseball-type caps that gave them a distinctly military air. I was glad now that we were back here in the shadows. These guys did not seem friendly.

Lin scurried about, bowing, seating people, pushing his daughter forward with fresh tea, calling for his son to put, I assumed, more kindling on the fire. When everyone was seated and set up with rice and tea, Lin made some kind of announcement in Chinese, and motioned for us to come forward.

I was alarmed to see beads of sweat on his forehead. The man was growing more nervous by the minute.

"He want to introduce you," Chien said in my ear. "These important men in village."

A picture leaped into my mind of what was going on here. I hadn't figured out before exactly how the boys insinuated us into the village; I didn't ask and they didn't volunteer. But now I saw it all.

Here are the boys slithering over the gate last night, creeping through the moonlit streets, seeking out and identifying somehow—by some mental radar—the house of the one man in the village who would be immediately sympathetic to our plight.

Here they are, rapping on his door like spirits in the night, their eyes gleaming like cat's eyes as Lin peers out into the dark. In low voices they tell him they need food and shelter for three American flyers. Lin hesitates in his doorway, his own eyes hidden beneath a lock of hair. He shakes his head no, closes the door, then opens it again, slowly, brushing the hair from his eyes. He has no love for the Japanese; he will do what he can to help the Americans and will get his neighbors to do the same. He and the boys hurry toward the town gate.

Why Lin was our prime sympathizer in the village I didn't know. Generally, the Chinese peasants—farmers and rural townspeople—didn't have a firm grasp of the politics of the war. It was too far removed from their hand-to-mouth, day-to-day existence. They knew the Japanese were brutal, but so was their own government. They were more interested in staying alive than in becoming partisans.

Perhaps Lin, however, had had family killed by the Japanese. Perhaps they had seized his farmland. Or perhaps he was simply a good man with a conscience that would not allow him to turn away strangers needing help.

He certainly didn't have the demeanor of a decision-maker in the village hierarchy. Perhaps owning the tea house gave him a certain cachet, or gave him the fuel with which to sway his fellows.

At any rate, now it was up to Lin to convince the rest to help us. He had chosen to endanger them all by taking us in, and now he was not only revealing his actions but asking them to participate. That was the cause of his nervousness. And it was well founded. Theirs was an occupied land, and they would be assisting the enemies of their oppressors. Dangerous dealings.

I faced the village men with anxiety in even greater measure. They were an unknown quantity, and if their own compatriot, Lin, was concerned about their reaction I was even more so.

I knew what happened to Americans who were turned over to the Japanese. They were paraded through the streets in chains, unwashed, unshaven, beaten and bloodied, an example to the people of Japanese might. I shuddered at the thought.

"Captain," Chien gave me a nudge, "you show your jacket." He meant the flag on the inside.

"They worried to keep you here," Weng said, managing somehow to tear his eyes away from Lin's daughter. "Maybe flag will help."

I stood, conscious of the fact that I was already, like that horrible mental image, unwashed, unshaven and bloody. I pulled the jacket off. The friction of the cuff against my injured hand was enough to make me dizzy with unexpected pain. I swayed, and would have fallen if Horton hadn't caught me by the other arm.

Weng and Chien proprietarily guided me back to a chair, talking over their shoulders to the men in Chinese.

"We say you too sick to show off. They must let you sit."

"No," I said, shrugging them off. "I'll show them the jacket."

"Let 'em see mine, too," Dalton said. He dropped his walking stick and awkwardly, off balance on his one good leg, worked off his jacket.

Chien took the jackets from us and started to hand them around. But now no one would touch them. Shaking their heads and putting out their hands as if to ward them off, the men all refused to look at the flags.

"Now what's wrong?" Horton asked.

Chien spoke at them in Chinese, then turned to us. "They say they not need to see flag, they see you

146

brave men. You stay here today; tomorrow they have plan for you to escape.''

Now all the men were talking again, smiling and pushing us into chairs. The daughter gave us each a cup, and Lin brought out his famous firewater. We all gave a toast and drank it down.

CHAPTER TWELVE

Bridge Busting

This time I was prepared for the heady effects of the liquor. I sat back in the chair and let its warmth wash over me like a golden haze. The same haze that had colored the air on my second mission.

Was it sun haze that gave everything that glow, or was it the pride I felt in being a full-fledged Flying Tiger with a successful mission already under my belt?

At four-thirty in the morning, the sky was dark with no promise of the coming light, but the golden glow permeated my dreams. I smiled in my sleep, and when Bill Griffith and I were called to report for a mission I rose happily, eager to face the day.

I set a match to the kerosene lamp and it flared to life. Frank groaned at the sudden light and put his pillow over his head; he hated to wake up any earlier than was absolutely necessary.

The lamplight flickered over the canvas walls of the hostel, mottling the olive drab of my flight suit and darkening the deep brown of the leather jacket. I passed a washcloth damp from the night before over my face, ran a comb through my hair and clapped my suntan officer's cap on my head. I was ready.

A quick breakfast in the mess hall, which seemed too quiet at this early hour. Two cooks banging pots back in the kitchen, a couple of maintenance guys, hands permanently blackened with engine oil, drinking coffee, one other pilot I knew by sight but not by name wolfing down stale powdered eggs like they were fresh off the farm.

Bill and I conversed in library-soft undertones until one of the cooks, a sweaty sergeant with ham hocks for arms, started pounding out "Beat Me Daddy Eight to the Bar" on his pots, and the other one sang along. The performance only lasted a minute, but it was so incongruous in that early morning stillness that everyone else in the mess hall was rendered mute; and when it was over we all laughed uproariously and it wasn't quiet at all any more.

At five A.M. exactly we reported to a small briefing room on the other side of the mess hall. There were fifteen pilots in the call, mostly old pros. Why did they look more tense than Bill and me? Maybe their golden glow had worn thin.

Colonel Wingate, again immaculately pressed, faced us across the podium. "Morning, men."

There were a few grunts in reply, a few drags on cigarettes.

The colonel cleared his throat, adjusted his tie. "We have been informed that a squadron of Jap bombers is heading out of Burma toward Kunming."

Shuffling of feet, deep drags on cigarettes.

"We're going to intercept that squadron, gentlemen, and deflect it from course. You will form up at two thousand feet and maintain altitude until you reach

Burma Airfield, their takeoff point. ETA is three hours, so fuel management is the word of the day.''

He rattled off a list of who was flying split diamond with whom, and I was amazed to hear my name called as leader of one formation with two experienced pilots flying as my wingmen. Someone must think I was pretty good to give me this opportunity on only my second mission. Bill caught my eye and gave me a tiny high sign.

The colonel wound up his list and stepped away from the podium. "Chaplain?"

I hadn't noticed the chaplain before. A small, balding man sitting off to one side, he had the patient, professional air of doctors and ministers, people who are used to giving and receiving bad news.

It was understood that if you didn't want to go up on a mission, you had only to tell the chaplain and you would be replaced; the Air Force believed that an insecure pilot was a threat not only to himself but to the others in his squadron and to the mission as a whole. You would be excused with no questions asked. I had the feeling, however, that the chaplain was sitting there like a psychiatrist, watching everyone for signs of strain, just waiting for the opportunity to put God between you and your plane and separate you from the action.

More feet shuffling. The cigarettes were put down, left smouldering in their ashtrays. The chaplain stepped up to the podium. The gold crosses on his lapels glittered. God was winking at us, smiling after all.

"God is with you, men, here on the ground and up there in the sky. Remember that he is watching over you. Godspeed." He bowed slightly and left the podium to be replaced by Colonel Wingate again.

"Any questions, men?" There were none. "Then good luck and good flying."

We all trooped out into the rising light.

I caught a jeep out to the revetment. The driver didn't ask me any questions about the mission and I didn't volunteer anything. We all knew that there were spies everywhere, and even at this advanced point in the mission, you could let something slip that might critically influence the outcome.

Chinese soldiers, stiff in khaki shorts and puttees, stood guard over our planes in the night, but since so many of them had been revealed as enemy infiltrators we had to post our own men to guard the Chinese. Protocol made it impossible to eliminate the Chinese—after all, we were in their country—but in time the guards guarding the guards became something of a joke.

As my jeep pulled up at the revetment, there were no Chinese soldiers in sight. They had probably been dismissed when the crew chief and mechanic came on duty, two or three hours ago.

This time I had a different P-40, a grande dame who had seen plenty of combat—I could tell by the patches on her fuselage—but her shark's teeth gleamed white with new paint and her eyes were sharp as a hawk's.

The crew chief was a sallow, brittle-boned little guy named Slavsky, who even as I climbed out of the jeep was still swarming over her with his mechanic in tow, triple-checking every nut and bolt. He jumped down from the wing and looked me up and down critically, apparently unaware of the six-inch height difference between us.

"You know anything about flying this baby?"

"Of course I do." I would have been insulted if the golden glow hadn't been insulating me.

"What's this, your second mission?"

"Sure is," I said proudly.

"Your *second*." He sighed. "Just be careful, will you?"

He wasn't nearly as concerned about me as he was about what my inexperience might do to his precious plane. But he buckled me in securely and fastened the canopy with a tender touch.

I didn't have time to think about him after that. I checked the mags, the main and auxiliary fuel tanks, gave the compass a fingernail tap, and keyed my mike, testing to see that everyone in the formation could hear me.

Then came the go ahead signal from the tower. A gentle pressure on the throttle and we rolled into position, sixth in a single file of fifteen beauties rolling into the morning sun. It was like being on parade.

The P-40 was designed for fast action, not idling. She would overheat in only minutes. To compensate, the first five planes taxied into position on the runway, while the rest rolled into a holding area fifty yards off the runway. The five planes held their position for three minutes, then took to the air just as the next five received the signal to start their engines; then the next five rose to the sky. It was as choreographed as a ballet and every bit as beautiful.

I felt confident and in control as I started my engine, rolled onto the runway and held my brakes until my two wingmen rolled in behind me, but it occurred to me suddenly that I was only a rookie and lucky to have two pros on my tail to show me the ropes. I looked over my left shoulder as I turned off the main runway with full throttle forward, and saw Hank flash me the victory sign. The show was on.

The squadron formed up at 2,000 feet and headed southwest to the Burma Airfield. This would be a three-hour flight, and remembering our fuel management watchword, we throttled back to a comfortable sixty-gallon-an-hour burn.

Two hundred miles later the squadron leader alerted us that we should intercept bandits within the next thirty minutes. Now we were flying along with one eye on the sky and one eye on our watches, and the pilot's invisible third eye keeping guard over the cockpit instruments.

Within minutes of the alert we spotted a squadron of aircraft at eleven o'clock low. They were obviously fighters; they were moving too fast to be anything else. A call came over the radio, "Bandits at one o'clock low." And suddenly there they were, three more Zeros rising up from nowhere, right underneath us, soaring up into our midst, guns blazing into the heart of our group.

Our first flight moved onto the one o'clock group, diving below them, then soaring back up, guns popping, throwing their own medicine back at them. The rest of us flew cover, keeping far enough back to stay out of the way, scanning the skies for surprises that could render us all immobile.

Six minutes of sky filled with red and black bursts, circling the action with the adrenaline pounding in my veins; then it was over as quickly as it had begun. The Zeros simply disappeared from the sky.

"High-tailed it back to Burma," Hank keyed into his mike.

"Decoys," the squadron leader said. The Japanese had hoped that we would be distracted by their little show long enough for their bombers to slip through and hit Kunming before we had a chance to turn around and catch them. It was a false hope.

There, just below us, was the bomber formation. We circled for more blue sky, soaring higher so we could come in from the sun where they would be blinded, and dive straight down at them.

Five bombers and eight fighters. They were sitting ducks. I went in with the second attack, screaming down on them like lightning, spewing out a storm of bullets.

We shot down five bandits and sent the other three scurrying back to Burma, their tails between their legs, herding their bomber squadron in front of them like sheepdogs anxious to get their charges to safe pasture.

We too turned and headed for home, but with our heads held high. We had successfully saved our base from destruction, and even though the battle had been waged three hundred miles distant and half a mile up, the thrill of victory bubbled in our veins as strongly as if we had been biblical warriors defending our hilltop with spears and bows.

A deep sigh of sheer joy escaped my lips. The sky shimmered like liquid gold. My P-40 hummed all around me, instrument dials speaking softly of fuel supply, compass heading and altitude. Her throttle and stick fit my hand as neatly as a glove. The metal seat held me as snugly as if made for me, jouncing me ever so slightly as we sailed aloft so that I could feel each breath of life in the plane.

Suddenly I recognized the golden glow for what it was. I was in love. I had fallen for that plane as deep and hard as I had for any girl, even my wife. I loved Ovella, of course, but now I had a mistress as well. And the P-40 was not about to let me go.

We all made it back safely to Kunming, and another debriefing. We had lost no planes during the mission and had come away with only a few bullet holes.

I sat in the briefing room, writing down my flight time on the Form 5. Two hours twenty minutes more.

Strange to think all that excitement took place in such a short time.

Form 5 was a piece of paper the Air Force had designed to extract as much written information as possible from each pilot after every mission. Some of the older guys grumbled about it, but I liked filling in all the lines, checking off each square. It meant I was official. I planned to complete at least a hundred Form 5s before I went back to the States.

"A hundred . . ." I chuckled to myself as I set down the empty cup on the tea house table. Little did I know way back then, after only my second mission, that I would complete 235 Form 5s, 235 combat sorties, before I ended my career.

But my career wasn't over. I *must* stop thinking like that. I was on my way back to home base once again, back to more successful missions. This time it was just taking a little longer to get there, that's all. I was capable of doing anything I set my mind to, and I had firmly set it, like an instrument gauge on the P-40, to "Return Safely."

General Chennault always said his Flying Tigers could do anything. He coined the phrase "triple threat" to describe us, because we acted as pilot, navigator and bombardier all rolled into one. A triple threat to the enemy in one compact package.

He had taught us that we *would* survive if we learned three things and learned them well:

1. *Be a good pilot and follow orders to the letter.* I was doing that. I had been a good enough pilot to get Belle and myself out of the battle zone, even without an engine. I was following orders, rules about how to survive in enemy territory, and so far I was still safe.

2. *Be a good navigator as China is the toughest*

country in the world in which to navigate. I was on course, heading as straight as I dared for home.

3. *Take good aim and drop your bomb on the target.* That was much harder than it sounded. You had to be able to calculate your speed and the bomb's descent rate so you'd know exactly when to pull the release lever; otherwise you'd be way beyond the target by the time the bomb hit the ground. Here and now, I had no bomb to drop. *I* was the potential target, lying low on the ground. But I remembered my first bombing mission, remembered it well . . .

I had been assigned to bust a bridge on a small river. The Japs were using the concrete and steel bridge to move light supplies into the center of China, a mobile supply depot which kept their troops ready to move as needed.

Two of my buddies were assigned to destroy two other bridges, all within the same short range. Although we would each be hitting a different target, we would fly as far as possible together, on what was called a straggle mission, before separating to our separate tasks.

This was only my third mission, and my first time up alone in actual combat. I was excited about this sortie. I had practiced bombing raids every chance I got, taking aloft P-40s begged or borrowed from their crew chiefs and dropping make-shift bombs on a target area just outside Chenkung Lake. I had an eighty-five-percent target-area hit rate, and I knew I was good.

We lifted off the main runway in a smooth takeoff, banked sharply over Kunming and headed east to our assigned targets. We would not be flying over hostile territory, so it was safe to straggle. Visibility was clear at 12,000 feet. Winds were in our favor. It was a perfect summer day, the kind just made for picnics in the park or a country drive with your girl. I patted the P-40's stick. My girl and I were going for a different kind of ride.

We each carried a 500-pound bomb set to explode on impact. The bomb left us no room for auxiliary fuel tanks; we would have to manage our regular tanks perfectly or risk a calculated return to an alternative base.

Below us now was the Tanez River, one hour thirty minutes outside Kunming. I took a bearing, peeled off from my buddies, and headed for my bridge.

There it was up ahead, visible with the all-seeing eyes of the fighter pilot or the falcon at great height. I would have to come in low, much lower. I had been briefed to hit it at 200 feet or less. It was up to me.

I started a descent with power cut back. Gun sight on and trigger safety off. Bomb release set. Down to 1,000 feet. Setting fuel selector. Down to 400 feet. Setting up for a straight-in run. All I had to do now was hop over a small ridge about 300 feet high and a green river bottom. Then a hair's-breadth seventy-five yards to the bridge.

I cleared the ridge. Passed the river. Down to 300 feet. There was the bridge, dead on target, and amazingly, a ten-truck convoy right on center, smack in the middle of the bridge. Down to 200 feet. I released the bomb right into the center bridge support. Perfect contact.

The bridge and ten heavy trucks raised up as if jerked on a string and then pitched into the murky river like lead. The river surged over its banks as though swollen by torrential rains.

I pulled up to about 500 feet to get my bearings. Coming in over the ridge, I had seen a group of trucks and other equipment in a staging area about a mile from the bridge. I lined up on that target and went in with all guns blazing. Then back for another strafing run, slicing through trucks and jeeps and tents with a knife-sharp hail of bullets.

Now I went for altitude, in case I had misjudged the opposition. It wouldn't do to be caught wallowing in my success by a hidden machine-gun nest and be knocked out of the picture myself.

Back up at about 1,000 feet, I keyed in my mike and alerted my buddies that I had spent half my ammo and felt we should place a fix on Kunming and head home. I got two "Rogers" in reply, and throttled back to allow them to catch up to me. They had busted their targets, too, and were ready to go. We maintained radio silence all the way back to Kunming—now that the Japs knew we were around there was no point in guiding them straight to us—and the three of us flew home reveling in the shared glory of a job well done.

When we reached Kunming, we dragged the field at fifty feet, coming in so low we could almost touch the runway, and performed a victory roll to top it off before landing in a showy haze of dust.

The usual crowd of restless pilots and chain-smoking mechanics was hanging around the field when we jumped down from our wings. They ran forward, clapping us on the back and congratulating us on a great show. They didn't know what we had done, but our acrobatics demonstrated we had a great story to tell.

The debriefing went like a dream. I was recommended for the DFC, the Distinguished Flying Cross, for having knocked out a complete Japanese battle group. I had destroyed nineteen trucks, a mess area, their most important bridge and a large ammo storage area that I knew nothing about until a reconnaissance plane flew over the target and brought back photos. Our intelligence estimated that 200 to 250 troops went into that swollen river. I was justifiably proud of myself.

My two buddies had had equal success at their assigned targets and were each awarded the Air Medal for their efforts.

I walked out of the briefing room on a cloud. I was doing good and valuable work, and I was being rewarded for it; I had been promised a promotion soon. I knew I had found my place in the world. But most of all, I had found a new love.

I was crazy about that airplane. She was beautiful and sexy and strong. I gave her loving care and in return she gave me everything I asked for at a touch. I hated to be parted from her. I wished I could sleep in her.

I could feel her loving arms around me now, smell the jasmine in her hair . . .

I was getting confused. "Ovella?"

Of course it wasn't Ovella. It was Lin's daughter, bending over my face with a damp cloth, patting ever so gently at the accumulated grime. I tried to pull away as she got to the right side of my face and my torn cheek but she murmured something soft and held my arm down.

Chien loomed in front of me. "She not hurt you. She put good medicine on you."

"What kind of medicine?" I asked warily.

"Don't know."

The girl had a tiny cup of greenish-black salve in one hand. She dipped some up with a dainty finger.

"Weng?" I didn't want something that looked like gangrene applied to an already infected wound.

"She not hurt you," Weng said sullenly, appearing over my other shoulder.

"I know, but what *is* it she's got in there?"

"At least she look at you."

The girl had her finger an inch from my face.

"Weng," I begged, "tell her not to put that stuff on me."

"She not talk to *me*."

"I'm sure she'll talk to you. Please?"

Gingerly, he placed a hand on her arm as if she were glass and might break at a touch. She turned and looked at him with those huge almond eyes. He stammered out something in Chinese and she put down the salve, but now her eyes looked hurt.

"Tell her I'm sorry," I said. "Tell her thank you anyway." I caught her eye and added, *"Sheh-sheh,"* but she wouldn't look at me, casting her eyes to the ground with that hurt air. Now I knew how Weng felt.

He said something else to her, motioning toward me, and she gave an infinitesimal shake of the head. He talked some more, and finally she replied, in a voice so soft I could barely hear her even though she was standing right beside me.

"She say she don't know what in medicine, but very good for you. Handed down from great-grandmother," Weng said.

"Much honor to share with you," Chien said.

The girl still stared at the ground.

"All right," I sighed, "let her put it on." I couldn't bear to see that look in her eyes. I'd rather get gangrene.

I braced myself. She picked up the salve, gently peeled off my rough bandage, and applied the awful-looking stuff with a feathery touch I barely felt. The salve stung for a moment, then turned ice-cool and I felt my cheek go numb. Whatever the folk remedy was, great-grandmother had obviously known the secret to some sort of natural anesthetic.

I relaxed under the girl's ministrations as she applied the stuff to my hand and leg wounds. I knew it would be all right: this angel could never even touch something dangerous.

"You like?" Chien asked.

"Mmmhmm." My eyes were closing.

"Wake up, Captain!" It was Horton. "We have to stay on the alert with these people."

"Where'd you come from?"

"I've been sittin' right over there," he motioned to another table, "watchin' this girl smear God knows what all over y'all."

"Calm down, Captain," Dalton called from the same table. "It's just an old home remedy, and it feels great. First time my leg hasn't just about knocked me out with pain since it happened."

"I think it's that white lightnin' that's makin' you boys think you feel better."

"Who cares what it is? We're stuck here until tomorrow when they put this escape plan into action, we might as well enjoy it."

"Enjoy," Chien piped up. "You like."

The girl, who had been kneeling at my feet while she tended to my leg, rose in a fluid motion, bowed to her father, took the salve and hurried out of the tea house.

Weng watched her go like one seeing the sun set for the last time.

"Go talk to her father," I said.

"Cannot."

"Yes, you can."

"You not understand. In China, girls given to marry the men when they babies."

"You mean they're *betrothed*."

"Yes."

"So she's probably already betrothed to someone else."

Weng nodded in sheer misery.

"Probably she not even know him, if he from next village."

"Maybe it could be canceled, stopped."

"Never," Chien said. "Soon she marry, all dressed in red silk. Husband come for her, carry her away to new home. She live there, obedient to husband's mother, keep house for husband's family. Never see her family again."

"Weng could try talking to her father."

"No." Both brothers were firm. That was the tradition of China and it was not to be challenged.

"I know just how you feel, son." Horton put his arm around Weng and guided him away from the open door. "I remember a girl back in Atlanta, had the meanest daddy . . ."

His voice faded away into the increasing boisterousness of the village men. Apparently they had not stopped at one of Lin's powerful drinks. Someone brought out some kind of stringed instrument and they all began to sing, louder and louder. Never mind the work day, it was a party. Everyone was joyous.

And then Lin's son ran in the door, seemingly pursued by the four winds, as always. His small face was red with exertion and streaming with sweat. He rushed up to Lin, pouring forth a torrent of speech. Lin stopped short, as if stricken, and every other voice stopped as well.

CHAPTER THIRTEEN

Lake over Thunder

I felt the breath freeze in my lungs. Dalton dropped his stick. Horton stopped in mid-sentence. The Japs must be right outside the town gate. We'd have to hide. There must be a cellar—did Chinese houses have cellars? A hayloft—but there were no animals to be fed hay so there couldn't be a loft. An attic maybe. My mind raced wildly. I fancied I could hear Jap boots in the streets already. My eyes combed the tea house for man-sized cubbyholes.

Then I noticed that no one else looked panicky. In fact, they all had a hopeful gleam in their eyes. It passed from face to face around the murky tea house like a bright spark, stopping finally in the furthest corner of the room where three old gentlemen, whom I took to be the village elders, had their gray-bearded heads together in a heated discussion. This went on for three minutes or so, although it seemed like three hours, then the eldest motioned Weng close and gave him some kind of order or direction.

Weng bowed respectfully, then turned to me. "Lin's son go to next town," he began.

And what? The Japanese were there?

"Third son of village elder live in next town. Son have fish market in town."

"Yes?" My nerves were shredding as he made his way through the story. This must be what people meant when they described Chinese water torture.

"Very prosperous town."

"And?" Dalton retrieved his stick, holding it close like a club.

Weng finally delivered the punchline. "Town have telephone!"

The villagers leaned forward eagerly for our response.

"You call Americans, they come get you," Chien explained.

That would be wonderful, to be able to ring up Kweilin and tell them exactly where we were. Put the responsibility for getting us out in someone else's hands. Just sit back and wait to be rescued. But I was afraid it wouldn't work that way at all. If we used a telephone we risked interception by the Japanese or their sympathizers. We could lead them directly to us. However tempting, a phone call was out of the question.

"Fellows?" I addressed Horton and Dalton. "What do you think?"

"Y'all don't think we could get a message through? Code it somehow?"

"Not on an unsecured line," Dalton said.

"I guess it wouldn't be real smart."

"Then we're agreed," I said. "Weng, please explain to the villagers that their offer is very generous, but it's too dangerous. We can't use the telephone."

"You sure?"

"Yes," I said.

Weng delivered a spate of Chinese to the village

men, who were visibly disappointed by our rejection of their offer.

"They're still going to help us escape, aren't they?" Dalton asked.

"Sure," Chien replied. "They just think telephone make it easy."

If only that were true.

Lin passed around pots of fresh tea and another round of liquor and the tea house soon resumed its air of festivity.

"Don't these guys have to work?" I asked Chien.

"Women in rice paddies," he said, as though it were the most obvious answer in the world. "Men work, too, but today special. Not work today."

"It's some kind of religious holiday?"

"No. Want to see you. You much exciting."

We must be quite a novelty in this place where nothing ever changed except the seasons. Perhaps a handful of strangers came through in a year. And none of them looked anything like we did.

I wondered if we appeared to the villagers as some sort of coarse giants. Besides the fact that we towered over them in height, even our bones were thicker and sturdier. Our leather boots and jackets were heavy and cumbersome compared to the straw sandals and light cotton garments of the villagers. I wondered if we looked like we were walking around encased in armor.

After a while Lin prepared another meal—breakfast? lunch? I found I was losing track of time again—and we ate boiled rice flavored with bits of dark meat, duck I think. It must have been lunch for the sun was at about midpoint in the sky when I peered out the door.

Sunlight barely penetrated the deep overhang of the tea house roof. Inside it was cool and dim and quiet, now that the meal was over and everyone was dozing it off.

Everyone but me. I had had enough of lying around and I was anxious to get started again, be on our way. But I dared not set foot on the village streets during daylight; there were too many people about in this place, even though they all seemed to know about us anyway.

Lin bustled about, collecting the used cups and bowls on a tray, then rinsing them in a wooden bucket of water. He fended off my efforts to help him, brushing his hair back from his forehead, and nodding at me and smiling. I peered out through the shutters but there was nothing to see other than a dust whorl in the street and a silent thrush on a rooftop. I leaned back against the cool clay wall, and I too dozed off.

This time what woke me was the sound of wood brushing against bamboo. A very old man, gnarled and brown as an oak burl, sat in a far corner of the tea house separating a handful of dried plant stalks into piles, laying them out on the tabletop, observing them carefully and then gathering them up and separating them again.

The stalks passed, from two stacks on the table, through his knobby, arthritic fingers to land in fans and rows and stacks; then were gathered up, to fall again, over and over, rhythmically, almost hypnotically. I watched this game, fascinated. It looked like a kind of pick-up-sticks or counting exercise. I couldn't figure it out.

Chien materialized at my elbow. Sometimes he seemed to have an uncanny ability to pick up my thoughts.

"Old man read *I Ching*," he said. "Read message

from gods in patterns sticks make when they counted out."

"He tell your fortune," he added brightly.

I wasn't sure I wanted to know.

How much of our fortunes do we make ourselves? If the old man told me we wouldn't make it back to base, would I give up trying? And if he told me we *would* make it, would I stop taking the proper precautions and get us caught instead?

"He tell good fortune," Chien said encouragingly. Meaning he told only good, happy fortunes, or meaning he was a competent, accurate interpreter of the future?

The old man looked over at me now, a deep, penetrating look. His eyes were black as ink and bottomless, with no highlights to show they reflected back the world, only took it in and drowned it in mystery.

I mentally shook myself. This was silly. The *I Ching* was only an old man's game, as meaningless a trick as the snake charmer's art in the bazaar. Then I remembered that the snake charmer had been awfully realistic.

The old man motioned me over, slowly, like a tree limb swaying in a stiff breeze. I walked to his table, Chien at my side. The fellow motioned for me to sit in the chair opposite his. He muttered something in a voice that sounded like the wind soughing in the trees.

"He say gods to speak to you."

"All right." I made myself as calm as possible. May as well see what the old fellow had to say.

He looked at me, or into me, with those bottomless eyes. He picked up the stalks, divided them into two piles, passed them through his hands, and laid them out on the table in a pattern of parallel shorter and longer lines. Sighing, he picked them up and went through the ritual again. This time they ended up in, as far as I could see, the same pattern. A third time, and still they fell into the same configuration.

The old man muttered in his windy voice.

Chien interpreted. "He say, 'Lake over thunder.' Very powerful."

The old man muttered something else, staring down at the sticks.

"Light on water," Chien said. "Much power in air, like lightning."

"But what does that mean?" I asked.

The old man put his gnarled hand on mine, with a touch like a long-buried root, hard and damp and secret. Again he spoke in his windy voice.

"Light on water, very bright but maybe—" Chien's English failed him. "Maybe it go away fast. . . ." He blinked his eyes and shook his head to illustrate someone suddenly not seeing something.

"It disappears." I suggested.

"Okay, it disappear, not there."

The old man gripped my hand fiercely. This time his voice came like a storm in thick branches.

Chien's eyes were wide. "Very powerful, he say, but must be careful."

The old fellow released my hand and gathered up his sticks. The reading was over.

I shook myself, mentally. I felt as though the old man had cast a spell on me. What did he mean, "very powerful, but maybe disappear"? That I would disappear into the South China rice paddies, or into a Japanese prison camp, never to be seen again?

"Lake over thunder." I pictured Kunming Lake, deep blue, shimmering in the summer sun, bottomless like the old man's eyes, and the airplanes that had gone down forever into her secret depths. Planes that made a sound like thunder when they rose into the sky. Lake now closed over silent thunder.

Well, he couldn't mean that. My plane was already down, on dry land. Probably he meant nothing. He was just a well-meaning, superstitious old man.

I smiled at him as I got up from the table. "Sheh-sheh." Thank you. He did not smile back.

Now afternoon was sliding into evening. The tea house was in shadow. Finches darted in and out under the sloping eaves, twittering busily at the coming night. The village men went home to their working wives. Lin lit a pair of oil lamps and set them in the window.

"Keep away night spirits," Chien explained.

Weng lounged in the doorway, leaning up against the frame, staring into the deepening gloom toward the home of Lin and thoughts of his lovely daughter.

The woman I had seen that morning, herding her ducks, returned with only the guide stick, evidently having had a successful day at the market.

A child ran up the street, singing something in a high, clear voice, then turned a corner and was lost to sight and sound.

The sky turned purple and Venus, the evening star, appeared. Lake over thunder. Everything appears and disappears and appears again in time. Maybe that's the way the world is.

I joined Dalton and Horton at the back of the tea house, where they were lying on a bench half-asleep.

"Hey, buddy," Horton said, getting up and clapping me on the back as though he hadn't seen me in a week. "How you doin'?"

"Horton here's getting kind of stir crazy," Dalton said.

"No, I'm not. I'm just wonderin' when we're gonna get out of here."

"In the morning," I said.

"*When* in the mornin'? How?" Horton persisted.

I realized that I didn't have any idea, and what's more, I hadn't asked. I had left it to the villagers, or fate, or the *I Ching* to take care of the problem. Not a very wise idea.

"I think we'd better find out the details," I said.

Weng and Chien were, for once, nowhere in sight, so there was no one to ask. We were alone with Lin and no common language between us. I wondered where the boys had gone.

"Weng?" I said inquiringly to our host, but he just nodded and smiled. "Chien?" I tried. More nodding and smiling. I pantomimed the heights of the boys, repeating their names. I wasn't getting through.

"That Weng's probably off pinin' in front of that little girl's front door," Horton said.

But no, here he came, dragging in from the night with his face even longer than it had been before. Chien was right behind him.

"Where've you two fellows been?" I asked.

"Get ready for morning," Chien said.

"When I never see Lin's daughter again," his brother added mournfully. He looked so much like a lovesick hound dog that I had a hard time suppressing a laugh.

"When exactly are we leaving?" Dalton asked.

"Early," Weng replied. "Before sun rises on girl I will never see again."

"How are we goin' to get out?" That was Horton.

"Better you not to know."

"Why not?" I heard the faintest thread of alarm in Horton's voice. I felt the same thread run through my own mind.

"Weng, I think you ought to tell us."

He sighed deeply. "Okay, but you tell no one."

Again I suppressed a laugh, or a frown of frustration. Who was there for us to tell?

"We won't tell a soul," I said. Dalton and Horton nodded in agreement.

Weng sighed again. "Villagers take you in water."

The thread of alarm tangled into a knot in the pit of my stomach. "In water." I pictured water closing over my mouth, my nose, my head. Lake over thunder. Water over me.

"Wait and see," Chien said happily. "You like."

In the waning hours of the night, when the tea house was closed up, the oil lamps blown out and the stove embers burned down to glimmering sparks. I was awakened by the sound of the door creaking open.

Even in the dim light, I could see immediately that it was Lin because of his characteristic gesture. He stepped in the door and pushed back his hair from his face. He went to the boys and shook them awake, carrying on a whispered conversation with them.

Now they came to us pilots. "Time to go," Chien said excitedly as if we were off on a picnic excursion. Weng glumly hefted his pack, too depressed to say anything.

I looked around to make sure we hadn't missed anything. Wherever we were going, it wouldn't do to leave any clues behind. I had my pack, Dalton, Horton and the boys had theirs; Dalton had his stick. We had left no clothing, no canteens, nothing to show we had ever been in this tiny refuge. Except for one thing. Looking at Weng, I saw that he had left his heart behind.

We stepped out into the gold and pearl of early morning, Chien dancing ahead, Lin nervously brushing his hair aside, Weng bereft.

And suddenly, coming up the street toward us was

the old fortune teller, supported on one side by Lin's daughter. The morning sun caught in her hair and reflected back like burnished metal. She was carrying something in one hand, but when she got close to us she hid it behind her back. Now she stopped in front of us, and bowed to her father.

Lin said something to her. It was obvious that he was trying to be angry with her for coming out unbidden, but that he could never lose patience with her. She was a beautiful girl and he was a doting parent. However, he tried again, speaking rapidly and with many gestures.

She replied sweetly in her soft voice, and looked from him to us to Weng. This was too much for Weng. He stared at the ground. Then she said something else.

"She say you very brave men," Chien interpreted. "She say Kuan Yin to watch out for you."

The old man muttered something in his wind in the trees voice. He motioned to the girl.

"He say," Chien said, "he notice Captain's hands hurt from stick."

Dalton looked down at his hands as if he had never noticed how raw and sore they were.

"Village make gift for you." The girl brought out the object she had concealed behind her back and presented it to Dalton. It was a crutch, seemingly carved from the same gnarled wood as the old man's hands and padded at the top with a square of rich, red silk.

Dalton was speechless for a moment. Then, "It— it's beautiful," he said. *"Sheh-sheh."*

The girl smiled shyly, and the old man bowed his head once, contemplating Dalton with those bottomless eyes.

Weng had turned away. I think the sight of the red

silk, apparently taken from the girl's wedding trous-seau, had undone him.

Then, as soft as water trickling off a lily pad, the girl said, "Weng?"

He turned back as though struck by fire.

She said something, ever so softly, in Chinese, something the rest of us weren't meant to hear even if we could have understood the language. From her pocket she drew a scrap of red silk, tied into a knot so that it looked like a flying bird. She placed it in the boy's palm. Then, without another glance, she and the old man turned and walked back up the village street.

Weng stared down at the red silk bird, his face completely blank and somehow very white. Then he turned, his face suffused with light, and set off ahead of us, shoulders thrown back proudly.

We walked out of the village gates as quickly and quietly as we had gone in. The sun was still low on the horizon, flushing the rice paddies and duck ponds of the countryside with pink light.

Down a slight slope and along a reedy marsh. And now here was the river, silver and slow-moving, lined with long grasses and bordered by a slender footpath.

Lin stopped us behind a willow thicket a hundred feet from the river. He whispered something to the boys and Chien said, "We wait here."

Lin went ahead to where a boat rested on the water. *Boat*, however, was a rather generous term for the object that sat before us. A long, thin prow, like a mosquito's sucking apparatus, was all that was visible beneath an immense, squared-off stack of hay which took up the entirety of the narrow, ten-foot vessel. Perched on the side of the load of hay was the boat-man, his face invisible beneath his wide-brimmed coolie hat. He maneuvered his boat closer to shore with a long paddle, and jumped down to talk to Lin.

The two men conversed for a good couple minutes, glancing around furtively as they talked. When they were done, Lin motioned to us to come ahead.

"Why, what's going on?" Horton asked.

"You ride in boat," Chien said.

"We can't ride on top of that," Dalton said. "Everyone we pass will see us."

"You ride *in* boat," Chien repeated.

The boatman, standing knee deep in the river, was poking at his hay load with a long pole. I suddenly understood.

"We're not riding inside the hay, are we?" I asked.

"You like," Chien replied.

I didn't see how I could like it very well. There would barely be room for all three of us pilots inside such a tiny vessel, and it would be hot and scratchy and cramped.

But it was ingenious. Traveling upriver was by far the fastest route back home, but dangerous for us on foot because it was also the most heavily trafficked. This way, however, we could travel by daylight, on the river and as invisible as Lin's night spirits.

I formed my face into a smile. "I like."

The boys jumped in the water with both feet, then clambered up on top of the haystack, grinning like lords of the hill. Then Horton climbed inside the load of hay, coughing and sneezing and grumbling, but in a moment he simply disappeared from view. It was really rather neat.

Now Dalton sloughed into the river. I hated to think what kind of water-borne germs were eating their way into his leg wound already, but there was no other way. The boatman had got his vessel as close as possible to shore. Dalton handed his crutch into the hole in the hay and clumsily slid in after it.

My turn. I too splashed into the river, trying not to think of the germs working their merry way within my leg wounds, was hauled aboard by Dalton and Horton (I couldn't pull myself in because of my injured hand), and then I too disappeared from sight. In the light and then gone. Lake over thunder.

CHAPTER FOURTEEN

Upriver Undercover

Inside the hayrick it was dim, and dark, and close, but not altogether unpleasant. Someone had cleverly hollowed out a space just large enough for the three of us to lie there, cheek by jowl, flat on our backs, and breathe without having the hay collapse back into our faces. There was no room to sit up, and we dared not try to make room, for fear of sending our grassy cave tumbling down about our ears.

The hay was a tawny gold, the color of the hills on my grandfather's ranch in midsummer, and tiny particles of it floated down before my eyes, like dust motes in the sun. That was all I had time to register before the light was shut out by someone—the boatman?—blocking up the hole with a thick chunk of hay. There was the smooth sensation of movement as the boat was pushed off from the shore, and we were away.

I pictured Lin hurrying away from the riverbank, not looking back, nervously brushing the hair from his face, scurrying out of the sunlight back to the dim safety of the tea house.

Courage takes strange forms, I thought. Who would

ever have guessed that Lin, apparently afraid of his own shadow, out of all the men of his village would be the one to engineer a rescue and an escape for foreigners he had never even met and would never see again?

In the dark cocoon of the hayrick I offered up a prayer of thanks to whatever gods were listening, thanks for Lin and the people of his village, and the boatman perched above us on his pile of hay.

I had caught only a glimpse of the boatman as we hurried aboard. Stick-thin as the rice paddy workers, dressed in the same faded and shrunk blue cottons, a coolie hat shading his face, he was only a quick impression, a mere sketch, of youth and strength and flashing white teeth. Nothing else. I knew no more about him than I had about Lin.

I could only wonder why he was doing this for us. A sense of adventure? A wrong to be righted? A bribe to be paid? We would probably never know.

I shifted uncomfortably on the straw and stared up into blackness. Beneath me, I could feel the boat moving, in long, gliding strokes punctuated by the push of the oar against the shallow river bottom. The water was still and silent, but tiny waves created by our wake lapped against the hull, echoing up faintly into the hay. It was almost restful. Almost.

I didn't like being unable to see. It was almost like when we had been holed up in the rock cleft, this feeling of being blinded, trapped, caught in a vise. It wasn't claustrophobia, just a frustration at being unable to move freely; I felt helpless.

Still, I told myself, this was different from the rock cleft. Here, we had the boatman to be our eyes and ears. And Weng and Chien were sitting up there with him—two more pairs of eyes to be alert for the slightest danger. I ought to just relax and take this time for what it was—the opportunity to lie back, rest body and brain, and let someone else steer our course for a while.

I forced my muscles to loosen, my eyes to stop straining into the invisible hay overhead, my ears to be lulled by the glissando of the water.

I felt like a pharoah, entombed in a straw sarcophagus, being ferried down the river Styx to the vast and sunless underworld.

"It's okay," I told myself. *"Relax."*

Think about Dalton and Horton.

I knew they weren't claustrophobic, since, as pilots, they were confined to small cockpits every time they went up. However, there's a big difference between sitting up in a glass bubble, the world spread before you, your controls at your command, and being pinned flat in a dark box with no way to see where you are and no control over your destination.

I turned my head to judge my companions' emotional state, but no light filtered through the thick layers of hay and I could see nothing. From Dalton, on my right, I heard thin, shallow breathing—from anxiety or from exertion? Exertion, for he groaned faintly, involuntarily, and then as if to dismiss it he whispered, "Just like taking the 'A' train, huh?" His leg must have been giving him a lot of pain.

I knew because my own leg hurt and my injured cheek, where it had somehow scraped against the hay as I was pulled in, throbbed with a steady fire.

I heard a faint rustling as Horton tried to make himself comfortable, then nothing more from him. We had all wordlessly agreed that it was best to keep even whispering to a minimum, since we couldn't know where we were or who might be listening.

Up above, I could hear a bright thread of chatter, drifting down through the straw, spinning out over the water. Chien. Then a silence and a few quiet words in reply. Weng. I pictured him, perched on the hay alongside the boatman, balancing the bit of scarlet from Lin's daughter on his palm as softly as a soap bubble, smiling absently into the sun.

Another thread of chatter. A push on the oar and another glissando of the water. A smooth, clear sensation, like floating on glass. The darkness seemed to float, too, rising above my face, inches high, and higher, far above me, until it was as high as the night sky and salted with stars.

A cool breeze whispered out of my memory, ruffling my hair with a playful touch, until I drew on my cap, eluding it, and turned toward my plane.

Night patrol.

Three bandits had been spotted, heading toward Kunming. Flying dark, no running lights, no cockpit lights. But we knew they were coming. And we were going up to intercept them.

"Just escort them out of the area," the Colonel had said. "Don't fire on them." Unless they fire on you first. It was an unwritten rule, like the Code of the West, that you didn't shoot at night. The sanctity of the dark hours was to be preserved.

Most likely, the bandits had no intention of firing on us either. Their mission was probably two-fold: (a) scare us, keep us off our guard, disrupt our sleep so we'd be less effective by day; and (b) recon, spy out whatever they could while we were caught unaware.

But this time we weren't unaware, and George Keran and I were being sent aloft to catch them at their own game.

The night wind tugged at my cap as I started across the runway. I glanced down at my watch. Midnight. The witching hour, when the creatures of the dark took to the air. Soon I would be transformed into a night rider myself, skimming across the face of the moon in search of the enemy.

I hurried across the field to the revetment where Belle waited, prepped by her ever-vigilant ground crew and ready to roll.

The base lay in darkness. The ground crew had done their work quickly and invisibly, God knew how, working without lights so the Japs wouldn't know we were alert to them. All around us the revetments, the barracks, the tool sheds and maintenance bays and briefing shacks, mess halls, hostels and hospital wore a mantle of black. George had gone off to his own revetment on the other side of the field, and it was as though I was the only moving object in the night.

When I reached Belle, Hanks, the ground crew sergeant, stood up from where he had been crouched in her shadow. An unlit cigarette bobbed on his lower lip. "She's ready."

I clambered up over her wing and into the cockpit and Hanks lowered the canopy, closing out the night wind. I fastened the leather mike strap around my neck, although we wouldn't be using it tonight, did a quick check of the gauges—as much of them as I could see in the dim light of a quarter moon—and gave Hanks the high sign. He gave the propeller a powerful turn, and we were off. Forward on the throttle, bumping over the loose dirt of the auxiliary runway, nosing onto the smooth, hard-packed main runway.

Here came George, approaching from the opposite side, swinging into line beside Belle and me. In tandem, in perfect sync, we picked up speed, roaring down the runway, hands pushing on the throttle, till we reached the magic speed of 125 miles per hour and our wheels left the ground. Airborne into the night.

Searching for bandits. They were headed this way,

coming from the south, from Hong Kong. But where would they appear, and when? I scanned the sky, watching, waiting.

To the west, a crescent moon hung like a pearl pendant on a velvet gown. Above, a scattering of stars shimmered in the wind, diamonds blurred by a breath. In the east, a sudden movement, a wing caught in reflected moonlight. My hand tightened on the stick. But it was only an owl, on a night patrol of its own, soaring above the brush in search of a late supper.

I put Belle into a banking turn, describing the first lap of a ten-mile circle above the base. George was ten miles distant from me, starting at the opposite edge of the turn.

Around we went, and over, sweeping the night with bare eyes, with binoculars, with the fighter pilot's invisible antennas, stretched out beyond the cockpit into the unknown.

A patch of cloud passed over the moon, covering it like a veil. The dark night grew darker. And suddenly I knew where they were. Zeros at eleven o'clock, dead ahead. I couldn't see them yet, but I knew they were there. I could feel them.

I dipped down low, grazing the trees at a hundred feet, so low that they'd never guess I was there. I hoped George had gotten the same invisible signal, that he too was lying low. I wanted to surprise them.

An elm tree sprang up out of the night. I pulled up on the stick, sharply, out of its grasp, then leveled back down to a steady hundred.

The cloud peeled away from the face of the moon.

There they were. Three bandits, outlined against the bright lunar light, flying abreast at about a thousand feet. I waited until they were almost directly above me, at eleven o'clock high, then pulled back on the stick and shot up into their midst, hoping to appear between them like a bat out of hell, a hellion out of nowhere.

It worked. I came zooming up from the ground, aiming straight for the center meatball, and all three bandits scattered like buckshot, so fast I could feel the pilots' hands shaking on their sticks. They turned tail and disappeared into the southern sky. I grinned to myself in the dark. I'd have to remember that trick.

I circled around a bit, enjoying the feel of the night to myself, the twinkle of the stars beyond a film of cloud.

Then I caught a different twinkle. Moonlight on a wing. A meatball. Here they came again. A burst of bullets spewed out of the lead plane. Tracers arced into the night like a meteor shower.

I dove down toward the trees, out of the way, out of their line of sight. The stars poured past in liquid lines and the ground rose up in a wave. There was that damned elm again. Up on the stick, fast. Bank sharp and climb. I was going to get those guys.

Five hundred feet, a thousand. My finger poised on the gun button. There they were, hiding behind a trail of cloud. I dove again, soared up, came in behind them, raining bullets. Two of the planes scattered again. The third dove down and came up, straight at me. Where was George?

Another burst of bullets from the third guy, tracers flying past Belle's canopy like confetti on fire.

Obviously this guy didn't care about the unspoken rule of not shooting at night. His companions hung back, peering out of the clouds. They were going to catch hell when they got back. If they got back with this meatball intact. He was asking for it.

I let him chase me into the moon, hoping to blind him for a moment. Then I had an idea I was going to try. If it didn't work, I'd be dead. Literally. The Zero followed like a cat after a mouse. Straight into the moon. I throttled back and dropped down like a rock. Down to the elm rising too high from the ground.

The bandit followed hot on my trail, dropping as swiftly as I had, like a stone. But he didn't know the elm was there. I got down to two hundred feet, and he was still on my tail. A hundred and fifty. The elm would be coming up any second. He'd keep dropping, and I'd soar back up, out of the way, in the nick of time. The elm would get him for me.

But in a curious way I hated to do that to this guy. He was good, as good as I hoped I was. And he had guts. While his companions were hiding in the cloud cover like frightened kittens, he was out here making mincemeat of me. Alone in enemy territory. I almost hated to consign him to the elm's ensnaring arms. But I wanted the kill for the record. It would help to make me an ace.

Ten seconds to decide.

I dropped down to a hundred feet, letting him stay on my tail. Five seconds.

And it occurred to me that he could have been shooting at me all this time. He could have had his finger jammed on the trigger all the way down and all the way across. But he hadn't. Either he was out of bullets—and he hadn't used that many yet—or his gun was jammed, or he didn't want to kill me any more than I wanted to kill him. He was only after the excitement of the chase. Or his gun was jammed and would unjam any moment. Let him go or not?

Three seconds to decide.

Two.

A hundred yards away I could make out the spreading branches of the elm, visible only because I already knew they were there.

I banked around the elm. If I had soared up, he

would have hit the tree, expecting me to hold my course. This way, he'd still be on my tail, and he'd miss the tree. If his reaction time was fast enough. I'd left him a three-second leeway.

I allowed myself a glimpse in my rearview mirror, half expecting to see a burst of flame, a bright orange glare as he collided with the elm. But there was only night sky and dark ground, and then, high above, a waggle of wings as he soared aloft and south toward home. His companions snuck out of the clouds and followed him away.

I keyed my mike. "George?" I called. "Let's call it a night. Nobody out here to chase."

As we flew back toward Kunming, a comfortable glow rode with me. I supposed I ought to feel badly for not having cracked up that bandit, but after all, I was only following orders. Escorting him out of our territory. Scaring him away rather than firing on him. Although somehow I doubted that I had scared him any more than he had scared me. Instead we had each developed a respect for the other. And if everyone felt that way, we wouldn't be in this war in the first place. I thought about that pilot and the glow stayed with me. Maybe someday the whole world could share it.

Another night patrol, another midnight. Bandits had been buzzing the base for three weeks straight, keeping us up at nights, firing on fuel dumps and ammo supplies, not doing a lot of damage but enough to keep us overextended and nerve-frazzled, putting out fires and listening, always listening, for the sounds of enemy engines in the night sky.

Now we had searchlights set up around the base, raking the sky with their hypnotic gaze, sweeping back and forth, over and under, constantly grazing the clouds for signs of Zeros.

Tonight, we were going up too, as we had done so many nights recently, in the hopes of catching the Japs at their own game, spiking them on a light beam and cutting them down in a hail of bullets. Then we could get some rest.

Five of us took off down the runway, Bill and George and John Chennault, me, and a new guy named Wade. We lifted off into the familiar night, softened to gray by the diffusion from the searchlights, and climbed to 1,500 feet. Our orders were to sit in the sky all night, if need be, until we caught the bandits and sent them spinning earthward. For they would surely be back tonight.

I looked at my watch. Ten o'clock. Sometimes the bandits didn't come until three. It would be a long night. I set Belle on a heading of 060 degrees, swinging to the east, and settled back. It was cold, colder up here than down on the ground.

I had a heated flying suit, a quilted affair of heavy cotton and electrical wiring (which plugged into the plane's instrument panel) that looked like an industrial-strength set of long johns, but I hadn't worn it since last winter when, halfway to Kweilin, it had shorted out and nearly electrocuted me in my cockpit. Uncle Sam had given me a replacement, of course, but I preferred to leave it in my footlocker.

So I sat and shivered in my leather jacket, trying to convince myself that the heat from Belle's engine was seeping up from her floorboards into my own bones.

I looked out into the night. I didn't like the feel of this mission. I never minded striking out on a search-and-destroy sortie, looking to bag a couple Zeros. But riding around up here in the glare of the searchlights made me feel like a sitting duck.

I clapped my hands together for warmth and wished

I had a cup of coffee. I pictured its steam drifting through the cockpit, carrying with it the camaraderie of the mess hall and the quick energy of a caffeine rush.

I peered out into the night again, but there was nothing to see but the white glare from the searchlights. Below, a copse of trees flickered to life and died into darkness as the searchlight drew across and away. The other guys were off on their own headings, out of my line of sight and sound. We were on strict radio silence.

My watch said eleven P.M. What would happen if the whole squadron of Zeros was just beyond those trees, waiting for the next sweep of the searchlight, waiting for it to illuminate me, buzzing slowly back and forth here like a drugged fly?

"Snap out of it," I admonished myself. "You're only spooked because you're tired. You've been at this too many nights already. Find something else to think about."

But what else was there? Thoughts of Ovella, snug and warm and sweet in our bed back home, only made me depressed. The future was too tenuous to contemplate. The past was over and done with. Whatever mistakes I had made I regretted every time I took to the sky nowadays; it seemed my life flashed before my eyes each time I went up. I had caught a hint of the same undercurrent of stress, or fear, running through the other guys in my squadron; they let it slip in little things they said and a lot of things they didn't say.

Well, we'd catch those damnable bandits tonight, and it would be over for a while. We could rest.

Or they'd catch us.

My hands were still shaking, from the cold, of course. I pulled something from my breast pocket. A Bible, government issue, one to every pilot, with a cardboard back cover and a metal front. Some of the guys joked that if the holy word didn't protect you from stray bullets, at least the metal jacket, carried stragically over your heart in your pocket, would.

I had thumbed through this Bible so many times the pages were worn thin. I had never been religiously oriented, except in a quiet, private sort of way, but up here, in the cold, dark night, waiting for gunfire to come and get me, I found the Bible to be a roadmap to a more peaceful world.

By the glare of the searchlights, I sat in the cockpit and read of Joshua and Gideon, of Samson and Saul and David, warriors all, but also men, real men who had lived through worse than I had and found their way.

I still dearly would have loved a cup of coffee, but I felt better. I replaced the Bible in my pocket and gave Belle a pat. We'd make it together, she and I. Her engine throbbed in agreement.

And underneath her throaty hum, I heard a different throb, higher, whinier, more distant. Zeros.

Now the Zeros came into view, five of them at about 500 feet, hesitating at the edge of the light, then diving through, at just the moment when the beams intersected, so that they could evade the greater sweep of the two lights. They were like moths, helplessly attracted to a lamplight that would burn them, but they had snuck through.

I put Belle into a dive and we too soared into the light, finger heavy on the gun button, tracers arcing palely in the glare.

Two of them got onto my tail, chasing me out of the light into the blackness beyond Kunming. But my buddies were onto them, Bill and Wade and George, screaming down out of the night, guns blazing. The Zeros fell to earth.

I banked sharply and we went after the other three bandits. I had vengeance on my mind, just like the Bible heroes of old. We fired and soared and dove and fired again, hitting one Zero so that smoke poured from its engine, bleeding into the light, and sending the other two high-tailing for home.

Three out of five crashed up or banged up. They'd think twice before making night raids on us again. We hoped.

And hopeful, warmed with the flush of success, we turned back to Kunming and a well-deserved night's sleep.

CHAPTER FIFTEEN

Terror on the Water

I flew back to Kunming triumphant but weary, aching in every bone. Belle's throaty hum vibrated in my ears, my elbows, my knees. My eyes burned. Lord, I was tired.

The searchlights were still tracking the sky, making gray day out of midnight. Kunming Lake, under my left wing, gleamed in a vast pool of ink, ready to suck in the unwary.

I forced my concentration to remain steady, eyes on the night outside the canopy, on the altimeter and air speed indicator, for we were almost to the base and about to descend, on oil pressure and fuel gauge and compass heading. But the lake beckoned, dark and still and deep.

Deep within the hayrick I shuddered. The lake had seemed malevolent that night. The old man's words echoed across the long months between then and now, "lake over thunder." I turned my head in to the straw and closed my eyes. Best to stop thinking about it. It didn't mean anything.

The boat glided on over the water, stroke and skim, stroke and skim. Beneath the shallow hull, fish darted in its wake, diving for the river flotsam stirred up by our passing. Perhaps a snake slithered in the reeds close to shore, searching for his own delicacies. An owl slumbered in the trees that lined the banks and a quartet of thrushes wheeled overhead. I could see it all in my mind's eye, restful, peaceful, soothing.

Stroke and skim, stroke and skim, gliding downriver toward home. Gliding into the sun on water wings . . .

The boat jerked to a stop, rhythm abruptly broken. I could hear voices up above, the bright thread that was Chien's, the slow, short tones of Weng and a light, almost musical voice that must surely belong to the boatman. The boat was poled in toward the shore. I heard the scrape of the reeds along the hull.

And now another voice, deep and demanding. I strained to catch the words, although I would not have been able to understand them anyway.

Dalton had fallen into a doze, judging by his slow, even breathing. Now he came awake, stifling another involuntary groan. The deep voice spoke again, louder, and I felt Dalton's body go rigid next to mine.

Who was it? Why had we stopped? Had we been discovered? Why didn't the boys say something, anything that would give us a clue down here to what was going on?

The voice of reason, deep within me, said they couldn't say one word to help us out. The very act of speaking in English would give us all away.

The boat rocked as someone stepped on or off, I couldn't tell which. The voices ceased as abruptly as they had started. There was a dull splash, like a body falling into, or being dumped into, the lake—the river—we were on the river, I reminded myself. On the river and nothing bad was going to happen. We were simply having an adventure, like Huckleberry Finn.

I didn't believe it.

The voices started up again, only Chien's was missing. Chien. Where was he? They couldn't have thrown him overboard, the water was too shallow. He'd simply get up and walk away. Wouldn't he?

I couldn't keep lying here, silent as in a tomb, still as a shroud, and not do anything. My nerves were stretched to breaking point. My muscles twitched with barely restrained movement. But I had to lie still, not move, remain disappeared. I didn't *know* that anything awful had been done to Chien; didn't know the splash was him. It would be safer for us all for me to stay where I was.

The boat rocked vehemently under a firm tread. Again, I couldn't tell whether it was stepping on or off. A spate of demands from the deep voice, and we pushed off again. Stroke and skim, stroke and skim . . . only this time not peaceful at all. Where was Chien?

Though I strained my ears, I heard nothing but the lap of the water against the hull. A sudden, horrible thought. Perhaps the deep voice had taken his place, an enemy sympathizer just waiting for us to emerge from our hiding spot.

I made myself breathe in time to the oar strokes. Stroke and skim, inhale and exhale, stroke and skim, inhale and exhale . . .

An eternity passed. If there were fish frolicking under the hull I had forgotten them. All I saw was Chien's tattered body, floating face down in the water. If birds soared in the sun, I didn't know it. I only saw the stinking hole of a Japanese prison camp.

Beside me, Dalton still lay stiff with fear. Horton I

could neither see nor hear, but I assumed the same awful thoughts were passing through his head, too.

Eternity rolled around again.

And then the boat skimmed to a stop. There were the reeds scraping against the hull. The boat tipped to one side as its weight load shifted.

Sunlight poured in through a hole in our straw cave. I blinked in the sudden light. A face filled the hole. The light was so bright I couldn't make out the features. I felt as though I couldn't breathe and look at the same time.

The face pulled back and creased into a smile. The boatman. He said something in his melodious voice and reached in a hand to help me out.

I was so stiff from the hours of lying flat on my back that I could hardly crawl out of the small opening. I half-jumped, half-fell into the shallow water, my bad leg dragging behind me. Dalton could not get out at all; his leg had completely seized up. Horton had to climb over him, splash out into the water, then turn back and carry him to shore.

Weng was standing on the bank, waiting for us, his expression no more nor less serious than usual. Chien was nowhere to be seen.

"You hide in bush," he whispered, indicating a thicket of wild honeysuckle about fifty feet away. "Fast."

Horton, still carrying Dalton piggyback, headed for the bushes. The boatman had already leaped back aboard his craft and was rapidly poling downriver. I held up a hand as I turned away and he waved in return, a quick flash of his palm and a quick smile; then he was gone. That was the last we saw of him.

I followed the guys into the brush, Weng at my heels.

"Where's Chien?" I asked.

Weng put his finger to his lips in the traditional signal of warning, but I didn't care. I was becoming really worried about the boy.

"Is he all right?" I whispered.

"He get fruit."

The water torture technique again. Since the Chinese language has only the present tense, its speakers often carry this same trait over into English, either refusing to, or being unable to, distinguish between past, present and future. I had no idea whether Weng was telling me Chien was fine and was just now collecting fruit from some mysterious source, or whether he meant his brother had gone at the time of the ominous splash to get fruit and had never come back.

"When did he go?"

By this time we were within the shelter of the honeysuckle. We crouched down beneath its fragrant branches. We were wet and muddy and cold, for the day had turned chill.

"Soon."

I believe I was turning red with frustration.

"What are y'all yellin' about?" Horton asked, picking up our whispered tone.

"I'm trying to find out what happened to Chien."

"Yeah, where is that li'l fella?"

"Get fruit," Weng said.

Dalton sat shivering miserably, his face pinched and white. He leaned in toward the rest of us. "Something happen to Chien?"

"Get fruit," we all chorused.

I decided to start over again. "Weng, where is your brother right at this minute?"

"This minute?"

"*Yes.*"

"He here."

I whirled around, almost throwing myself off balance. Chien was standing right behind me, arms full of produce, grinning delightedly.

Weng, uncharacteristically, beamed. "See, you no need to worry."

"Right." Why argue? I was just glad to see the boy.

Chien handed his treasure to us and crawled into the thicket. "Much fruit. You like?"

There were oranges the size of tangerines, one for each of us, a thick-skinned, bright green thing that looked like a cross between a pineapple and an artichoke, called a jack fruit, and a handful of pale green berries.

"Gooseberries," Horton said.

"*Longan,*" Chien corrected.

Longan is the Chinese word for dragon, and the berries are supposed to represent dragons' eyes. And since dragons bring luck in China, a longan is a great treat.

"Either way, my ol' granny could make a great pie out of 'em." Horton sighed at the memory.

We cut up the jack fruit with the help of Horton's pocket knife, dividing the soft, pale butter center into wedges, one per person. The tiny oranges were shared around, and then the *longans,* two berries each.

Dark gray clouds scudded across the sky, trailing vapor streamers like unraveled wool. A drop of rain spattered on a honeysuckle leaf, and another on the ground beside me. The air was filled with the scent of damp earth and fresh water, and charged with the energy of rain borne on the wind.

We tore into our makeshift meal with gusto, having lost the capacity to worry about germ-grown fruit some days back. Beggars can't be choosers, and we were too hungry now to care. Orange juice dribbled down chins and was licked back up. The exotic jack fruit went down like backyard apples. The *longans* disappeared without a trace, except when Chien made everybody stop and look at them for a moment.

"Very lucky," he said solemnly.

"Lucky," we all murmured, and the berries were made a memory.

The citrus juice still burned my cheek like fire and every time I swallowed I tasted blood, but I doggedly ate on, forcing down each bite before I had time to stop and think about the next. I needed to keep up my strength, and it wasn't imagination that told me my clothes were looser on me now than when I started this journey. I was losing weight, too fast.

I pushed this thought aside and ate my lucky berries. Best to think about something else. I asked the boys what had happened on the boat.

It was a somewhat garbled tale, but apparently a man had hailed the boatman over, wanting to buy some fish from him. The boatman had explained that he was going downriver to sell his hay, and had no fish. The man would not take that for an answer, had boarded the boat, slipped and fallen in the water (there was only the narrow prow on which to stand), then had waded back to shore where he stood and hollered threats until the boatman pulled away. That was the entire episode.

We three pilots sat looking at one another. The word uppermost in our minds was *spy*. Why else would this mystery man have insisted on boarding a boat which anyone could see had no room for any cargo but straw?

"I suppose there could be loonies anywhere," Horton said.

I agreed, doubtfully. Dalton only looked whiter, and colder. There was nothing to do but carry on and be careful.

The boys seemed to see nothing unusual or worrisome in the event and their instincts had always been right. So far, I reminded myself.

"And where man go I see many fruit," Chien added, so we would know there was a happy ending to the tale. "Jump off boat, run and—"

"Get fruit," we all chimed in.

So Chien had run all the way downstream with his hands full of fresh food, to meet up with us when the boat disgorged us here. It couldn't have been that far, perhaps two miles, an easy trip in daylight along the well-worn path beside the reeds.

I got out my compass and map and tried to figure our position. The boat had taken us no more than five miles by my estimation. Five short miles, but accomplished in the daytime. And five miles was as much ground as we usually covered in a whole night's walk. If we could hitch other boat rides, we could get twice as far in each single twenty-four-hour period. We could get home that much faster.

Weng had said the boatman dropped us off just before he reached the market town he was headed for. That told us two things: (1) any other boat ride would not be much longer, for the spaces between villages were small; and (2) with a market town—larger and more prone to outsiders than the little villages we had so far visited—so close we would have to stay well hidden until nightfall. No more boat rides today.

There was no moon tonight, just a dirty gray sky that slowly turned sooty black. We buried the orange peels beneath a honeysuckle branch, collected our gear, and crawled out of the thicket. The night was very dark. We could smell the river and hear a frog plop on a lily pad, but it showed not even a glimmer. The path was soft and sandy under our feet, but we might have been walking on water, so little of it could we see.

Dalton had his crutch out, and I caught the ghost of a smile as he slipped it under his shoulder. I heard his hand caress the fine wood and the little exhale of satisfaction as the padded silk tucked into his arm.

We had gone only a few yards when I had the thought that if it was too dark for anyone to see us, it was also too dark for us to see anyone else who might be coming along this well-trod path. We were not that far from the town.

"I think we ought to head inland, away from the water," I whispered into the night toward my companions. I remembered from the map a tributary about four miles east that cut back along the river. If we could find our way to the stream, we could work back along it, in a less populous area, to the river.

"It's easier staying along the river," Dalton said, the closest he had come to complaining about his leg.

"Who do y'all think we're gonna bump into out here? Frankenstein?" came from Horton.

I told them whom I thought we might bump into, and we all agreed to take the harder way, into the brush.

And harder it was. There was no path that we could discern, and we frequently walked straight into tree branches, tripped over rocks or stumbled over dips in the ground. We took to walking single file, switching the lead position every quarter mile, so only one person at a time risked being poked in the eye or breaking an ankle. The rest simply avoided what he had discovered the hard way.

After about two hours we came upon a tiny valley, a bowl about fifty feet wide, carved into a hillside, and we sank down for a much-needed rest.

At that instant the moon broke out of the clouds,

sailing gloriously aloft on tatters of gray wool, as bright and gaudy as a neon sign. The valley came alive with ferns and grasses, dewdrops and silent, sleeping finches, a spiderweb draped, shimmering, across a rock, and a diamond thread of water cascading out of a cleft.

Within this fairy tale landscape the five of us looked ragged and grubby and coarse. But fortunately no one was looking at us. We simply stared, drinking in the scenery as if it were nectar until the moon wrapped her cloudy veil around herself and disappeared again, leaving us in the dark with the memory of something beyond day.

We struggled to our feet and set off again, up out of the valley and down toward the stream on the map. Dalton picked up his crutch and again I saw a hint of a smile as his arm rested on the shiny silk.

The moon never entirely left us after the valley, peeping in and out among the clouds, and the going was easier. About a mile further on, we came upon a farmhouse nestled in another valley. Beyond it was the stream we had sought.

The boys decided to go down and reconnoiter the farm. The rest of us would wait here, hidden behind a grove of pines. They crept away, stealthy as two cats, and returned shortly, fingers to their lips, beckoning to us to come ahead. They performed an exaggerated tiptoe, letting us know that extreme caution was called for.

We left the pine-scented safety of the trees and stepped out into a clearing between grove and farmhouse. Just then the moon threw off her cloak again, dancing across the sky in a brilliant, stage-struck limelight.

A door screeched open in the house and someone yelled, a curse by the sound of it. We were struck silent, caught in the light in the clearing with our shadows stretched out full in front of us. No one moved. No one breathed.

The door screeched shut; someone yelled again and was silent. The moon gathered her clothes about her, trailing beams of light like a stripper dripping sequined plumes.

The boys motioned ahead and we walked on toward the farm. I wondered why we were moving toward what seemed to be a dangerous situation, but I was so tired my thoughts weren't straight. I could only trust the boys.

We stepped into shadows and then out. In the moonlight, the silk of Dalton's crutch gleamed richly, a bright, glowing red that cried for attention. We were within yards of the farm. The boys motioned again, absolute caution. The silk shone in the moonlight like fired rubies. Slowly, reluctantly, Dalton bent down, grabbed a handful of dirt, and rubbed it into the precious fabric until it was as dull and dirty as the rest of us. It would no longer call out to anyone. He tucked it back under his arm, and we continued on to the farm.

We spent the night not in the farmhouse, but in a dank and dingy outhouse or shed, jam-packed with old buckets and baskets, all encrusted with dirt, containers whose use I did not want to know. Some fairly clean straw had been spread on the bare ground in the center of this collection of junk, and we bedded down on it, being now all too well acquainted with hay, I thought.

Apparently two brothers and their wives occupied the house and worked the farm together. One of them was anxious to help us, eager to please, but the other had a violent temper and was not the least inclined to assist anybody. He was the one we had been tiptoeing around.

I gathered all this from the nice one, who came creeping in at daybreak, bringing us a breakfast of bean curd and rice cakes, prepared by his wife. Of course, he didn't speak English, but he was only too happy to unburden his family problems on Chien, who passed them on to me.

I was frankly frightened. "His brother can go to town and tell everyone we're here."

"Brother not know we here," Chien said placidly.

"How can he not know—we're right outside his door!"

"Brother not see."

"All he has to do is look."

"Brother cannot look. He not see."

"Oh." The brother was blind.

"But he can hear," I whispered.

"That's why we be quiet." Chien finished his bean curd in peaceful silence.

Poor Dalton looked at his muddied silk in dismay, its glamour stained for a man who wouldn't have seen it anyway.

"You'd only have had to dirty it up today or tonight," I said. It was true.

Under the noisy cover of the two wives banging together pots and pans (to feed the ducks, Chien said), the nice brother led us out of his unhappy farm and down to the stream. His neighbor was going to market and would take us aboard his boat.

"Did he ask this neighbor?" Horton asked suspiciously.

"Neighbor will do it," Chien said.

"How does he know that?"

Chien conferred with our farmer. Then he turned to Dalton. "Neighbor afraid of brother, too."

The blind brother must pack a mighty punch in this region.

The neighbor's boat was exactly like the one we had ridden in yesterday. The straw was not hollowed out as well, since the neighbor had had less warning, and we were more cramped for space, but otherwise the trip was the same. With one exception.

This time we knew what to expect. And so, although we were scrunched together like sardines in an itchy can, we lay and listened to the waves lapping against the hull, enjoying the gliding rhythm of the oar in the stream.

I felt myself growing sleepy, for it was stuffy inside the hay and we were breathing in as much carbon dioxide as oxygen. The hay smelled sweet. I remembered tossing big pitchforks of it off the truck on Granddad's farm, working up a sweat and then dozing in the shade of the old pecan tree. I drifted into dreams, teetering on the edge of oblivion.

The boat slid to a stop. The scrape of reeds against the hull. Nothing, I reassured myself hazily, just somebody wanting to buy fruit. Back to sleep.

Dimly, I heard voices—Chien's, Weng's, the neighbor's. And another voice, harsh, guttural, choppy. I knew that sound. At once I was wide awake, heart pounding like a hammer. That was the sound of spoken Japanese.

Now there was another Japanese voice and another. And another. My God, we were surrounded! The bile rose in my throat and I almost choked. Lay still. *Lay still,* I commanded myself. *Don't move.* With the tiny part of my mind that was still functioning rationally, I sent out a mental signal to Dalton and Horton. Stay calm. Don't move.

There was a series of splashes, then a bump and a

jolt, as if the Japs were in the water, moving around the boat, or moving it around. *Don't make a sound.*

Someone laughed, a harsh screech like a seagull's cry.

The hay next to my head rustled. Thinly, over the water, and the thud of my heart, I heard the pounding of booted feet. An army.

I knew the Japanese had fragmentation armies, groups of twenty to fifty men, combing the countryside in lines, making seventy-five-mile sweeps for stragglers such as Dalton and Horton and myself. I knew they were all around us. I knew we were bound to run into them sooner or later. But I had fervently prayed that our one incident, back near the Hong Kong coast, had been it. We had paid our dues. We wouldn't be forced up against them again. I was wrong. And now there was no way out.

CHAPTER SIXTEEN

Laughter on the River

The booted feet stood on that bank forever, stamping around, barking in their harsh tongue, while the hay rustled next to my head and my blood pounded in my ears.

Finally, around it all, I heard another sound, the bright thread that was Chien's voice, chattering loud and louder. Don't antagonize them, I thought. Don't call attention to yourself. Then I realized what he was doing—calling attention away from us.

Was it working? I strained my ears but I couldn't tell. The sounds from the shore seemed to have quieted, dimmed a little, now fallen silent. Did that mean the Japs had gone away?

They couldn't have left; it was too providential. And too fast. It takes longer than the seconds that had elapsed for an entire army to reassemble and turn away. Then why were they so quiet?

Now I couldn't hear Chien anymore either. In fact, I couldn't hear anything or anybody. What was going on up there?

A high, sweet note pierced the air, filtering down

through the thick hay like a silver needle, brighter even than Chien's chatter. A pipe. Someone was piping a tune on a reed pipe.

Dead silence from the shore.

Another burst of chatter from Chien.

More silence. Then harsh laughter, a splash, and we glided away. Thank God it was over.

Or was it? Like before, I couldn't be sure the boys and the boatman were the only topside passengers on our little craft. I tried to reason it out. The hay was not all that stable. There was room for the farmer to perch on the side of his load of straw, and apparently room enough for the boys to cling to the top. (I assumed that's where they sat, I had never seen them do it.) But could the slippery, fresh hay support another person without collapsing? I didn't know.

There was no way to know if we carried an enemy passenger until we reached our destination, five miles downstream. In the meantime, it was sit tight and don't move.

I tried to relax, tried going back in time to Granddad's ranch . . . but it didn't work. I was too keyed up, my nerves stretched tight, ready to snap like high-tension wires . . .

Afternoon sunlight lay in weak puddles on the floor of the briefing room. Tension swirled in the air as thick as the smoke curling up from a dozen cigarettes, as grating as a fingernail scratched across a chalkboard.

It was always like this after a mission. All the anxieties held so carefully in check during flight were released in debriefing, poured out into the room in a tidal wave of suddenly unleashed stress.

The Air Force tried to prevent it. After each mission we were handed a drink concocted of four parts alcohol, I think, to one part Lord knew what else, presumably vitamins and minerals. It was supposed to calm the frayed nerves of fighter pilots. I never knew whether it worked or not; all I knew was that it tasted vile and was so strong I was sure I'd burst into flames if anyone lit a match within five feet of me. I always handed mine to the next guy in line, and I soon discovered that all the guys who drank too much were always right behind me.

At one point I was found out. The Colonel took me aside, all starched shirt and indignation. "Look here, Captain. This beverage has been developed specifically to help settle your nerves. You need to drink it down, son."

"Yes, sir." I stood holding a cup of the stuff, away from me.

"Well, Captain?"

"Sir." I had hoped he would walk away before I had to dispose of it, but he just stood there, staring at me.

"Believe me, son, it's for your own good."

He wasn't going anywhere. I lifted the stuff to my lips and poured it down, trying not to taste it. My eyes smarted and my throat burned. I forced a smile.

"It sure is, sir."

After that I was careful to pass my cup to the next guy only when the Colonel had his back turned.

At any rate, the drink had no effect on the debriefing fireworks. Everyone wanted to be an ace, and the arguments over who received what kill frequently reached screaming proportions.

This afternoon we had come in from a knock-down, drag-out dogfight over Hanoi, in French Indochina. It was a long flight there, carefully gauging your fuel, maximizing every drop for the lifeblood it was. Humidity rose up from the jungle into Belle's cockpit, staining my flight suit and masking my face with salty beads of sweat. The heat was enervating, sapping the strength from my muscles and leaving only the nerves, stretched taut, waiting for action.

And suddenly, there it was. We were over Hanoi and there were the Zeros, a full squadron of them, dead ahead. The sweat froze on my face. Belle and I were zooming. Three hundred miles per hour, and more. I had one of them, no—two—in my gunsight, but I could go for only one at a time. Blood pumping, I was working by feel, flying by the seat of the pants, not thinking, just doing, all the long hours of practice coming into play.

You don't hold an airplane level unless you're on someone's tail. I had these guys face to face. A hundred yards closer and I could have seen their almond eyes behind their goggles. You try to roll the plane to get a wider sweep. Belle spun through the sky, carrying me with her, rocketing from horizon to horizon. Don't worry about where you're going. Use tunnel vision to watch that enemy plane. Watch them both.

Our gunsights had lights now, a glowing red dot to fix on the target. I had one lined up smack in the light. I hit the trigger; squeezed it off. Got my burst off, held it, got off another burst. Smoke poured from the Zero. I lined up the other one. Red dot right on him. Squeezed him off. The first one fought for control; he was diving—he regained altitude—dove again. I squeezed off another round. Smoke billowed from the second Zero. It spun down, spiraling down and down, crashing right into the first.

The whole thing was over in two minutes. Sweat poured down my face, dribbled into my collar, twisted my hair into tight curls that stuck to my forehead. All around, the sky was filled with smoke and debris, and sunny, puffy clouds.

We turned for home, praying our fuel would last, praying our ammo would last if we needed it on the long flight back. Praying we wouldn't need it.

By the time we reached Kunming and the briefing room, the long hours of anxiety showed only too clearly, in sweat-stained khakis and stubbly faces, in shrill voices and accusing fingers.

"I got three meatballs," one guy announced belligerently.

"The hell you did," another one yelled, knocking over a chair as he leaped to his feet. "Two of 'em were Pete's."

"I said they were mine." Fire darted from bloodshot eyes.

"We told you, I got two of 'em," Pete hollered.

"Which two are you yellin' about?" I called irritably into the fray. "*I* got two myself."

"Yeah," Bill Griffith added on my behalf.

"I don't know what their names were," Pete yelled. "They were right over that lake thing."

"That lake—that was only one meatball and it was mine," somebody else bellowed, slamming his fist into the back of the chair in front of him.

"Gentlemen, gentlemen." That was the major designated as debriefing officer. He could hardly be heard above the din. He stood up, his face turning red. "*Quiet. Please. Men.*"

The room volume lowered to a slow simmer, with little knots of dissent still bubbling here and there. The Major sat down again. "We'll take this one step at a time. I'll ask the questions and you may respond in turn."

With the Major at the helm and his secretary, a

tubby corporal, taking notes, we went back over the mission, minute by minute. But it still wasn't calm and collected. There were cliques who rooted for one pilot or another and attributed to him more kills than he might actually have accomplished. Sometimes pilots claimed kills for themselves that didn't exist.

The two Zeros I had hit this afternoon were reported by three other guys as deflection shots. Sometimes it was hard to tell who got a hit because of the angles of the guns, but I knew what I had done. It was depressing to have it refuted.

The Major was judge and jury. When the debriefing was over, he gathered up his corporal and all their notes and left, to evaluate the evidence and assign kills.

The next afternoon the results were posted. Pete was assigned a quarter kill, and three other fellows shared in the other quarters. Two other guys got a kill each. Mine were reported as probables.

"Maybe we can get it changed later," Bill said, clapping me on the back sympathetically.

"Maybe." But I didn't think so.

Nighttime in the city of Kunming. We had gone into town on a pass, Bill's attempt to cheer me up. "I'll buy you dinner," he said. "I'll even buy you a girl."

We both laughed, but it wasn't really funny. It was pitifully easy to purchase a pleasure girl in Kunming. Small boys roamed the streets, stopping every soldier they saw. "You likee my sister? No mama, no papa, no per diem, no flight pay. You likee my sister." And if you so much as nodded, they'd push the poor girl right at you, if she was there, or grab your hand in their grubby one and pull you away down the street toward her.

Of course, Uncle Sam did his best to train you away

from nodding yes. We had been told in a hundred lectures, "If you want to play the game, you have to pay the price."

Just walking through the city was enough to warn me away. Lepers, missing fingers or noses, stood in the gutters next to spittle-flecked men with bent and brittle rib cages. Tuberculosis, syphilis, rickets, diphtheria, malaria—who knew what these ravaged people were carrying? God only knew what germs one would encounter on intimate contact.

I felt so sorry for them I could hardly bear to think about them, and there was nothing I could do. But we were out here to have fun, I reminded myself, to cheer up, not get more depressed.

In many ways, Kunming resembled any modern city, with wide boulevards and big buildings housing shops and offices. The focal point was the main square, featuring a three-story, semicircular office structure with drapes in the windows and a cinema on the street level.

The square bustled with people, slinky satin-haired girls in vibrantly colored cheongsams, the skin-tight, slit-skirted dress of the modern Chinese woman; tiny old women in black trousers, hobbling on bound feet; peasants in coolie hats; businessmen in Western-style suits; boys in tatters; soldiers and sailors and airmen in khakis and whites.

At night, lights gave the square and its denizens a garish glow. Red and yellow—the lucky colors of China—competed in looping neon with white bulbs strung over shop windows and spotlights trained over doorways. Candlelight flickered in the restaurants and occasionally MPs passed by, beaming flashlights into dark corners.

Bill and I cut across the center of the square, heading for an Air Force–authorized restaurant set on one side. Two small boys darted out from under a cart. "Shine your shoes?"

"No, thanks."

"Cheap, only one quarter, good job."

"No, not tonight."

"You need shine. Shoes very dirty."

In the end we let them do it. It was easier to nod yes than to say no, and to be thankful they were offering shoeshines instead of sisters.

At last we gained the restaurant, set on stilts high above the street in an effort to separate American noses from the smells of the world below. It didn't work, but we ate there anyway. There was nowhere in all of China you could go to escape the smell, so you just tried, after a while, to ignore it.

We ate a passable meal of chicken and rice—always rice, even in the mess hall now—and tiny carrots, washed down with plum wine. The waiter tried his best to please, the cigarette girl smiled winsomely, the cook yelled orders from the kitchen in a voice like water tumbling over rocks. All in all, not an unpleasant evening. I felt the tension begin to drain away, washed out by the city sights and sounds.

We started back through the crowded streets, idly window shopping, sticking close together, "like we were on a date or something," Bill said, sighing for the girl I was not. But the Air Force had a standing rule that you didn't walk the streets of Kunming alone. There was always the potential of someone shooting at you, simply because you were an American; or the less glamorous potential of getting lost, for the streets wound in a confusion of alleys and lanes and backways that were difficult or impossible to figure out.

We peered in through dingy windows at the ginseng shop, where the brown and arthritic-looking roots of all sizes and shapes were displayed on long counters, to be purchased by the pound and taken home to be made into elixirs and teas that promised longevity.

We gazed in at shops that sold ivory and jade and pearls, guarded by coral figurines of Kuan Yin and Confucius, and approved by avuncular brass Buddhas.

Here was the fortune teller's tiny shop, its walls plastered with charts for astrology and *I Ching* and *feng shui,* used to determine the proper sites for homes and businesses.

And the tea merchant's storefront, perhaps the most fragrant spot in Kunming, with its essences of orange pekoe, imperial and souchong blacks, its delicate greens, its jasmine and cinnamon and chrysanthemum.

Or perhaps the most fragrant spot was the brass-mongers, with its cheap and gaudy elephants and goddesses and tea trays; and its filigreed incense holders wafting the scent of sandalwood to the smoky ceiling.

Here was the grocery store, where we sometimes went to buy the canned goods that weren't available in our little canteen on base. You could always find some tinned meat or vegetables, set in dusty rows on a back shelf, but there was nothing like the variety you could count on in American markets.

Of course you could barter, and you could bargain; the black market was big, but I stayed away from that. There were, however, things you could legitimately sell to the Chinese and make a little spending money.

Like cigarettes. Not just any smokes, but Lucky Strike greens. Lucky Strikes had a green packet and green bands around each cigarette. The Chinese took the packets, soaked them in hot water and transformed the liquid into an emerald dye they used to paint pictures on silk scarves and handkerchiefs, beautiful dragons and flowers and birds. Of course when you wet the scarf or hanky the dye bled away and the pictures dissolved, but the artists made enough off them to pay premium for the cigarettes.

Lucky Strike's advertising slogan was "Lucky Strike goes to war." And here they were, in China, earning pay for the soldiers they were so popular with.

You could also sell a bottle of iodine, sent from the States, for five dollars American. This, too, was used as dye for painting on silk.

Here was the shop that sold those painted scarves, along with cheongsams and sandals and silk shirts. I wondered if Ovella would like one. I supposed it was silly, sending her something to wear she could never wash, but they were beautifully done.

I stepped inside the shop, still open at ten in the evening. "Look at this one, Bill, the dragon—"

I stopped short as the lights went out. In this store and in every shop on the street, every building in the city. A three-ball alert, gongs clanging, MPs running through the town rounding up soldiers, civilians running for cover. A three-ball alert meant the Japs were coming, were virtually on top of the city already.

Bill and I ran out into the street, peering into the night for possible transportation back to base.

Another fellow burst out of the shop next door, ran right into us, caromed off and asked breathlessly, "Where do we go? What do we do?"

"Get to your squadron," we answered briefly, for the place was a mad melee of running bodies.

A weapons carrier lumbered along, its driver steering in the dark with no headlights, stopping to collect any pilots he bumped into.

"Hey!" I yelled, for it was too dark for him to see anybody or anything. "Two—right here."

The driver slammed to a stop and we jumped in. Our new friend jumped in alongside us. Now there were nine or ten of us in the carrier. The city was in total blackout. We could recognize each other by voice, by the faintest glimmer of a crooked smile or a remembered gesture. But our new friend was a stranger to us all.

The truck left the city and lumbered out onto the country road, gears grinding, engine laboring under the load. We might have been on the road to Hell, riding into pitch-black terror, for the Japs were due any second and their bombs could easily hit us before we ever reached the base.

So much for my stress reduction evening. I felt my shoulder muscles tense up, my neck contract in an instinctive effort to protect my head, my breath quicken. The rest of the guys tensed up, too, muttering private incantations to themselves to keep them safe.

Our mystery man piped up again. "Who are all you guys?"

"Fighter pilots, who'd you think?" somebody answered brusquely.

"*All* of you?" our friend said, completely confused. "Aren't you one of us?"

"No," he answered, still confused, "I'm a transport pilot."

In the windy back of the weapons carrier, in the dead of night, on our way to battle, we all laughed and laughed and laughed. It seemed the funniest thing in the world.

We all introduced ourselves and our new friend gave us his name. "Jackie Coogan, fellas."

Well, that was even more entertaining. A real movie star in the midst of our squadron and he was as regular as any other Joe, more regular because he didn't even know who he was with or where he was supposed to be.

We laughed again, and Jackie laughed right along with us. The stress factor had been reduced after all.

Was that a laugh I heard up above, filtering through the straw? Or was it just the memory of that dark night? I strained my ears. It *was* laughter, bright and high and clear. Chien.

The boat slid to a stop again. The straw was pulled away, and Chien's face appeared, wreathed in smiles.

"Okay to come out now." He laughed again.

Dalton and Horton and I snaked our way out of the hay, splashing into the water, and like the day before, making quickly for the shore and the shelter of a grove of bamboo while the boatman rowed away without a backward glance.

Once we reached the safety of the trees, I turned to Weng and Chien. "All right, guys, what's so funny?" For they—even Weng—were still giggling.

"Japanese all around boat. Very scary," Chien said.

"That's not funny." Horton wrung out a sopping trouser leg.

"Very frightening," Weng said, stifling a smile.

"Want to know what we hide in hay," Chien continued.

"What did you tell them?" Dalton's face was as white, or whiter, than yesterday.

The boys laughed again, hilariously.

"We say," here they were convulsed with laughter, "we say not hide anyone. We say look if you want."

Chien's eyes suddenly grew wide, his mouth went slack and his face bleached almost to the color of Dalton's. "And they look." A tear trembled at the corner of his eye. He blinked and it was gone.

And I understood. There had been nothing at all funny about the incident with the Jap army. Just as there had been nothing funny about Jackie Coogan losing his way among us. Laughter was a release, like a steam valve on a pressure cooker.

The boys were laughing instead of crying. They had been through so much. But I could not let them lose face by showing my own emotion, demonstrating sympathy or pity.

"Well, you managed to get rid of them," I said.

"Not us," Weng said. "Farmer. He play his flute for them."

"And they liked that, did they?" Horton asked, wringing out his socks.

"No," Chien said, deadpan. "They think it awful noise. They tell us go away so not have to hear more."

Now *that* was funny. We all sat beneath the spreading willows, soaking wet and shivering, and laughed and laughed and laughed.

CHAPTER SEVENTEEN

The House
of the Lantern

After a time the laughter died off, to be replaced by the chill of exhaustion. We all sat and looked at each other as though we'd never seen ourselves before. There were the three of us pilots: gaunt, unshaven, unwashed, dressed in too-small, tattered clothes. Already Dalton and Horton were thinner than when we had found them; Dalton was beginning to look like a skeleton and his leg, crusted with blood, stuck out at an awkward angle.

I didn't know what I looked like—I had avoided any glimpses of my reflection in still water for fear of spooking myself—but my appearance couldn't have been any better than Dalton's. Worse probably, for I had not only a leg but a hand and a whole side of my face stiff with dried blood and soggy bits of bandage.

The boys, thin and small to begin with, were physically undamaged, but their ordeal showed mentally in the dark smudges under their eyes and the shadows that moved beneath their ivory skin.

I looked at my companions; then I looked away. Something was stuck in my throat and my eyes blurred. This was ridiculous. I was *not* going to give in to simple exhaustion. Somewhere deep within myself, beneath the fear and fatigue and pain, lay a well of strength I knew I could tap into. We would make it back home; I would see to it.

I shook my canteen. I knew it was empty, but it was something to do. "Come on, boys, let's fill this thing up."

Chien took the metal container. "You stay here, hide. I fill this thang for you." So now he was picking up my Texas drawl. It sounded funny transposed into a high, thin Chinese voice, but I was too tired to smile.

"No point in fillin' it," Horton said. "We can't boil the water here, so we can't drink it."

We were too close to the river, too close to a well-traveled path to risk building a fire.

"Maybe if we headed inland a ways," he went on.

Dalton, rising like an automaton at the suggestion, fumbled for his crutch. He grabbed it, levered himself to his feet, and then fell, as it slipped from his grasp, with a thud that must have been excruciating.

"I think we ought to stay right here for a while," I said. We would have to. We were all at a point where movement was only dangerous; we were too tired to think rationally about where we were going or what we were doing. We would hole up here in the willows and rest.

When dusk fell on our little group some five hours later, we were still huddled together, shivering, pale and cold. The hours of sitting on the damp ground of the willow grove had done us no good at all. The chill had sunk into our bones, made our teeth chatter, seeped into our thoughts.

Before it was even fully dark, we started out, along the river, towards some sort of shelter where we could build a fire and get warm. What we were doing was risky, sticking to the banks where any traveling peasants or soldiers were likely to venture, but it was the fastest, smoothest path and we planned to stay on it only until we got past a maze of brambly thickets that rose between the river and the higher ground.

But the brambles, some sort of wild rose whose petals were limp and faded, stretched on and on. Tendrils of fog crept in, weaving about our feet, obscuring the ground and making us stumble even on the soft, sandy path. The moon skimmed just above the horizon, a faint glimmer of phosphorescence like a lantern on a ghost ship far out at sea.

I set my sights on it, not thinking, not feeling, just walking, walking toward that thin disk of diffused light. But I never caught up to it; it always stayed just ahead of me, just out of my grasp. Walking, walking into the moon.

And then I noticed it was growing larger. We were getting closer to the moon. I didn't tell the others; I didn't have the energy required for speech. But I quickened my pace. We were walking into the moon.

Now it had stopped growing larger, but it was brighter. Instead of a lantern on a ghost ship, it was a lantern on a real ship.

Could it be a lantern? I peered into the distant darkness, wishing I had the binoculars I kept stashed in Belle's cockpit. The light glowed warm and bright, flickering every now and then like a candle flame in a breeze. Definitely a lantern.

But why? There was nothing out here, and no one, for in all our hours of trudging along we had, mercifully, encountered neither the sight nor the sound of a single soul.

None of my companions said anything about the light. I wondered vaguely whether I was seeing things, but I couldn't think that it would matter at this point, so I kept watching and walking.

There was nothing else to do except ignore the sharp pain in my face and hand, the sticky rivulets of blood trickling down my skin, and the faint groans from Dalton as he stumbled over stones with his bad leg.

A village. It was a village up ahead, slumbering darkly in the dark night, and a lantern was lit in the house closest to the river, set in the window to welcome weary travelers.

Weng and Chien went ahead to reconnoiter the situation, but I knew it would be all right. The light was meant for us.

The house of the lantern belonged to a doctor, a fellow of about thirty with crisply brushed hair and a crisp, professional manner to match.

Light spilled out into the night as he opened the door and ushered us inside. His horn-rimmed glasses twinkled in the lamplight, contrasting with the grave look in his eyes. He spoke softly to the boys in Chinese, seating us all on a low divan strewn with cushions and pillows.

After so many days of sitting on nothing more comfortable than a straw mat or hard wooden bench, I felt I was sinking into pure cloud fluff. The doctor, whose name was Sung, was the proprietor of Heaven.

"He say he wait for us tonight," Chien translated.

"But he didn't know we were coming," I protested.

"He know," Chien said.

Maybe this *was* Heaven; maybe we were dead and the doctor was God—otherwise how could he possibly know we were arriving?

"Boatman tell him he give us ride."

Of course. I must get a grip on myself and stop being so fanciful.

Dr. Sung's house was on nowhere near a celestial scale, but it was, unlike all its counterparts we had so far seen, light and clean and comfortably furnished. The room we were in had a floor of thick straw mats on which were set the divan, a wicker peacock chair, and a Western-style armchair covered with red chintz. There was a candle lamp on a low wooden table and another in the window. Another table held kitchen equipment, and a kettle of water, hissing gently, sat on a brick stove.

The doctor bent down and examined Dalton's leg, frowning and pushing his glasses up on his nose. He rubbed his hands together briskly. Then he looked at my face and hand, peeling the bandages away carefully and shaking his head at what he saw.

Strangely, this did not worry me. I was glad to be in the hands of a competent medical man, someone who could put to rest my fears about gangrene, and I was secure in the knowledge that he could patch me up effectively. He would sew up my wounds, set Dalton's leg, and we'd be good as new, strong and healthy for the journey home, which would now be so much easier.

Dr. Sung went to the stove, poured some water into a white ceramic dish and carried it over to where we sat. He spoke in his soft voice to Chien and the boy translated.

"Please to sit on other chairs. Doctor want to see Captain's leg." He indicated Dalton.

The divan was cleared of its pillows and Dalton was instructed to stretch out on it. Sung ripped Dalton's thin cotton trouser leg above the knee; then he applied the steaming water with a gauze pad. Dalton blanched to the roots of his hair and grabbed the side of the divan with knuckles that showed white.

Maybe this was not going to be so wonderful after all, I thought.

The doctor continued sponging at Dalton's leg until the water in the basin was as red as the blood it had been cleaning. Then he drew a paper packet from inside his cotton tunic, tore it open, and sprinkled the contents over the leg. Pale beige powder drifted down like tainted snow.

"I thought sulfa was white," I whispered to Horton.

The doctor turned and looked at me, then said something to Chien. Chien translated. "Not sulfa, special plants." Dr. Sung continued working on Dalton, splinting his leg with gauze and clean sticks he brought from the kitchen, while Chien translated further.

"Not have sulfa in village. Must go to cities, pay much money. Doctor not have money. People not have money."

Weng suddenly spoke up, his old self for the first time since meeting and leaving Lin's daughter. "Medicine good," he said authoritatively. "You take. Not worry."

"Okay," I said, sinking back in the armchair, but I did worry.

Dalton's turn as patient was over. The leg was splinted and bound, neatly and cleanly. The bloody trouser leg had been cut away. The whole thing looked a hundred percent better.

Dalton sat up shakily and I asked him how he felt. He swung his leg over the side of the divan and a perplexed look came over his face. "Not bad," he said, as though he couldn't believe it. "Not bad at all."

The doctor motioned to me. *Your turn*—I didn't need to understand Chinese to know what he said. I helped Dalton over to the armchair and took his place on the divan. Sung went over to the stove and did something with the kettle of boiling water. I hoped he was washing his hands; I couldn't see from the angle I was at. Of course he's washing, I chided myself. He knows modern medical procedure—you can see that by the way he fixed up Dalton.

He brought over a clean basin of hot water and I gulped. Here we go.

It wasn't that bad. After the first shock of steaming heat against my skin, I was able to lay back and let him sponge away the grime, and I hoped, the germs from my face, hand, and leg. I felt better just being cleaner. Then he sprinkled on the beige powder and bandaged over everything with clean gauze.

"Sheh-sheh," I said, jumping up from the divan. A buzz like a hundred angry hornets filled my head and the room spun. Oh boy. I sat back down.

The doctor came back from his kitchen area—how did he get over there and back in an eyeblink?—with a cup of steaming liquid. He handed it to me, murmuring in his soft voice, and I drank it down.

"Ginseng," Chien translated. "Much magic for you. Now you sleep."

I lay down. I was aware of Dalton being given a cup of tea and being led into the other room, but only vaguely. I hadn't slept soundly in all the other places we'd spent these past nights, hadn't dared to, for a fugitive must always keep an eye open and an ear cocked for danger. But here I felt safe. The boys would watch out for me; the doctor would watch over me. My head buzzed and I drifted off.

A kaleidoscope of colors swirled beneath my eyelids, pinks and blues and yellows . . . tinny music reverberated over loudspeakers . . . the shrieks of girls on the ferris wheel . . . the delectable scents of popcorn and cotton candy . . . the county fair.

What was I doing at the fair? This was wartime. Fairs were for fun. But we had fun in China sometimes, didn't we?

Night in the mess hall. Burlap sacking hung over the windows. Inside it was pitch black and quiet except for the hoots and whispers of the guys gathered on wooden benches. Here was the steady click, click, click as the film reel spun through the projector and an ivory glow lit up the screen. Movie time.

We never saw anything current. The most recent picture we got was two or three years old. Guys who had just come to Kunming had already seen them in the States, but for those of us who had been in China a long time already, they were new. We didn't know the difference.

Our favorites were, of course, anything to do with flying. Errol Flynn was a swell *Dive Bomber,* Tyrone Power, a *Yank in the RAF,* had it much cushier than we did—he got the girl, didn't he? And then there was John Wayne in *Flying Tigers.* It wasn't terribly accurate, but it was about us, and it made us feel like heroes.

It was exciting to sit in the silvered darkness and see yourself portrayed by the Duke as a fearless tough guy. If only we had a girl to share it with, someone soft and sweet to clutch your arm in the dogfight scenes, be scared or impressed, or giggle at a funny line. Or kiss you during the slow parts.

Sitting in the mess hall with a bunch of guys in combat boots was not the same as taking Ovella to the pictures on a Saturday night. There were no red plush seats, no velvet ropes in the lobby, no ushers in pillbox hats, no popcorn or Necco wafers or Jujubes.

Candy was strictly rationed on the base, along with gum, cigarettes, and Coke, and there wasn't much variety in the candy bars you could get with your weekly allotment. But I didn't smoke, so I would trade my carton of cigarettes for Baby Ruth bars or chewing gum.

Or there was the black market. Anything you could buy in the PX or get sent from the States you could sell on the black market. The most valuable gift you could receive from friends back home was a Parker 51 fountain pen set, because it was made with gold. Whatever price had been paid for it in the States you could increase by five in China. A carton of cigarettes that cost sixty-nine cents in the PX sold for ten dollars American on the black market. You could sell anything but Gillette razor blades. You couldn't give away a razor blade in China; the Chinese didn't believe in shaving as most of them had little need to.

The black marketeers weren't hard to find. They were just there, and everyone knew it. They came into the base on legitimate business, selling food or picking up laundry; some of them worked on the base as military employees.

Sometimes the black market was funny. Or we made it funny. If we hadn't tried for laughs, we'd have gone cuckoo sitting around waiting for the next bombing raid to finish us off.

Like the time somebody got the idea, "Let's holler 'MP raid,' and shake the place up a little." They made up dummy MP bands, slipped them over their arms and ran into our hostel.

A couple pilots were in their room, canvas mattress covers full of Parker 51s, cigarette cartons, canned goods, iodine, transacting business with a wiry little Chinese guy in a fedora. He was just handing over his American bills when the phony MPs charged in, hollering, "Raid!" The black market contact dropped everything and ran, leaving the pilots with the goods they had just sold and all the money. It didn't work out quite the way the fake MPs had planned it, but everybody got a good laugh out of it. Everybody but the black market man.

You could get into serious trouble dealing in the black market. General Chennault tried to slow it down because there was too much American money circulating in China. A program was instituted where everyone on base bought Chinese war bonds instead of goods to sell on the black market. But there were other ways you could make a dollar.

Summer night outside the maintenance bay. The cricket orchestra was in full swing. A moth dive-bombed in and out of the dim glow of a single light bulb trained against the back wall. A breeze rustled in the trees and flicked at the cards spread on the bare ground. A poker game was in session and Tony Gerardi was winning. Tony always won.

I was on standby tonight. Nerves too taut to sleep, I had wandered out to the revetment, watching the moon, gauging the weather conditions, planning in every detail the flight I might or might not have to make. Tony had come along, spiffy in his khakis even at ten in the evening, black hair fashionably slicked back, and found me staring up at the sky.

"Watcha doin' out here all alone, kid?" he asked in thick Brooklyn accents. Tony was thirty-seven, and therefore qualified to call me a kid.

"Nothin' much."

"Then come on. You need to liven up a little." He grabbed me by the arm and started marching me off.

"But I'm on standby."

225

"We're only around the corner here. They'll findja."

"All right."

No need to ask where we were going. Tony was in a poker or dice game every night. The wonder of it was that there was anybody left on base to play with him. His reputation followed him everywhere.

Tony was a career gambler; he was also a career Air Force man, a ground radio operator who did an excellent job. He loved radio and Morse code, but he also loved gambling.

Sometimes he would come along, as he had done tonight, when I was on standby and I'd sit and watch him play, in restrooms or shower rooms or outdoors where a light had been left burning. The location moved, but always there was a game. Everyone liked Tony too much not to play with him.

I couldn't figure out why in the world he had joined the service when he could have lived more than comfortably on his earnings as a gambler. "I had to join the Air Force," he said. "I was too well known in New York."

He almost became too well known in Kunming. He made more money than he was allowed to send home. I helped him out, taking big stacks of bills and mailing them, under my name, to his sisters back in Brooklyn.

Tony was as much fun as movies in the mess hall. More fun, because Tony, for all his gambling, was an honest, solid friend. Not a ghostly image on a cloth screen, but a flesh-and-bone person to come along on anxious nights and take you out of yourself, away from chilling thoughts of bombs and bullets to the warm glow of queens and jacks beneath a sixty-watt bulb.

*   *   *

Another yellow glow, another evening, another place on the base. The Officers Club, and Tokyo Rose on the radio. We had an old shortwave set, a massive Zenith Transoceanic, battery-powered because of the shortage of electricity. Tokyo Rose came in loud and clear.

We derived a lot of entertainment from her, sitting in the battered old armchairs, listening to her tell lies. She'd announce in her perfect American diction, with the barest undercurrent of Japan in her tone, "Captain Smith, while you're risking your life for your loved ones at home, your wife is out with your best friend. How does that make you feel, Captain Smith?"

We'd hoot and laugh. Captain Smith, or Rogers, or whomever she had picked on that night—for she sometimes used real names—was immune to her poison. We knew it was lies.

More chilling was when she announced the names of those who had been shot down in the day's combat. Sometimes she had the names of the men almost before we did. And sometimes she'd claim that their wives were out with other men, too. Then it wasn't so funny.

In between announcements Tokyo Rose played music, popular tunes that reminded you of home. Some evenings it was pleasant, listening to dance tunes, humming along with Benny Goodman or Glenn Miller, picturing yourself whirling around the room with a beautiful girl in your arms. And some nights it tore you up inside, hearing the songs you associated with your wife or your girlfriend, and knowing she was on the other side of the world.

But mostly Tokyo Rose was funny, a piece of propaganda to fight against. We could believe that if the Japs were stupid enough to think we'd fall for that drivel, they'd be stupid enough in combat to make winning easy.

I could hear those dance tunes even now, Lionel Hampton and His Orchestra playing "Stardust," the shimmery sounds of the xylophone echoing like shooting stars in the night. And I felt the clear, cool radiance of the stars against my hot forehead.

It was Dr. Sung, I think, placing his hand on my brow. Or maybe it was someone more glamorous. Maybe it was Ann Sheridan.

CHAPTER EIGHTEEN

Kunming Canteen

Ann Sheridan was coming to Kunming. Not only was she a famous movie actress, but she was from Texas, just like so many of us pilots. That elevated her above the ranks in our eyes. She had graduated from North Texas State Teachers College and was a true, dedicated actress. We all loved her.

When George Raft fell for her in the movie about the truck drivers, or when she worked with Dennis Morgan and Jack Carson in the one about the Lockheed assembly plant, we were all there too, right alongside her. With her fair skin and blond hair, she was a vision of loveliness. And now she was coming here on a USO tour. We were thrilled.

The big day dawned damp and gray. By mid-morning it was drizzling; by noon it had turned to rain, cold and sullen. But the show would go on. One of the bombers was pulled from its revetment and a platform was set in its place to serve as a stage. The men on base who were not on duty surged over the area, sitting on top of the revetment, leaning against it, crowding the stage. There were howls and wolf whistles, practice ones presumably, for Ann had not yet appeared.

Jerry Bartone, a pilot from my squadron, and I squeezed in among several chunky tech sergeants at the top of the revetment. From here we had an unobstructed view of the proceedings.

A couple guys in khakis rigged up a tarpaulin over the stage. A couple more guys set up a microphone. They all clambered down again. The rain slowed to a fine mist.

Another fellow in khakis walked up onstage and the audience began a polite applause. It was Melvyn Douglas, the movie actor, who was also a major in the Air Force and the entertainment officer for Kunming. He stood before the microphone, looking as urbane and sophisticated as if he were at a Hollywood party.

"Men," he announced, and the microphone squealed angrily, "men, I know you're all here under duress—"

Laughter from the audience.

"And I know you'd all rather be anywhere else on this fine afternoon—"

Another big laugh.

"But I know you'll all be gentlemen and give a great big, warm Kunming welcome to—Miss Ann Sheridan!"

Wild applause.

Ann climbed purposefully up onto the stage, given a helping hand by Major Douglas and every other guy within reach. She stepped up to the microphone.

"Hi, fellas." The mike didn't squeal at her. But a hundred guys did.

I glanced at Jerry out of the corner of my eye. He

was a quiet guy so he wasn't saying anything, but he had a smile a mile wide on his face. I guess I did too.

Ann looked every bit as lovely as she did in the movies. Long, tapering fingernails enameled a bright red; blonde hair waving midway down her back; that sharp smile and trim figure—wow.

She put on quite a show, singing and dancing, backed up by three starlets from Hollywood who had come along on the tour. They were pretty, too, but they weren't Ann Sheridan.

When it was over, Major Douglas announced that there would be a photo session with Miss Sheridan in front of the mess hall. More yells and wolf whistles, and Ann jumped nimbly off the stage. The guys surged after her, including Jerry and me.

Somewhere between the revetment and the mess hall, she had found time to change. Instead of the sequined dress, she was wearing a no-nonsense cotton skirt and blouse. The beautiful blonde hair was caught up in a snood of some kind of fuzzy wool, giving her the appearance of having a head full of frizz. A cigarette dangled from her lips. Over her snapping, lively eyes she wore sunglasses. In the rain?

But she allowed us all to snap photo after photo of her—getting out of the weapons carrier, standing in front of the weapons carrier, walking to the mess hall, sitting down in the mess hall.

And then she began to gripe. She didn't like the restroom facilities. They were outdoors, and cold and dirty. We felt lucky to have restrooms at all. In China, our crude outhouses were a great innovation. She griped about the shower conditions, again outdoors and cold and stingy in water supply. The Chinese didn't have those either. She didn't like the food—

well, neither did we, but we ate it anyway. Her mouth turned down and her nose turned up, and the girl we had idolized suddenly turned into a woman we never dreamed existed.

Ann Sheridan went down about three hundred percent in our eyes. She had had a tailor-made audience in China, hers for the taking, and she had alienated us all. She took the unpleasant conditions we had been laboring under for months and years, knocking ourselves out for the war effort, striving mightily to convince ourselves that things were not so bad; and she made them, and therefore us, look cheap and mean and distasteful. She was a tremendous disappointment.

The USO people apparently felt the same way, for soon afterward she was yanked out of the tour program and sent back to Hollywood, where there were real bathrooms and tile showers with lots of hot water and exquisite, chef-prepared food.

Fortunately, she was the exception to the rule. Other USO shows came to Kunming, other entertainers touring the twenty bases scattered throughout China, and they were all gracious and charming and kind.

Only the weather was not accommodating. It was always cool and overcast, drizzling or outright raining. But it didn't matter.

Jinx Falkenberg, the tennis star, visited Kunming, accompanied by a covey of girl and guy tennis players. We thought of Jinx as the All-American Girl, and she was.

She walked out on the makeshift stage in a little halter top and tennis shorts, her wavy dark hair held back by a white ribbon, and we all applauded like crazy. No wolf whistles this time, though, for Jinx was like everyone's kid sister.

She and her troupe put on an excellent exhibition match, as well as doing some singing and dancing. Jinx was an actress, too, and when she looked out over the microphone at us with that mischievous smile, we all beamed like approving big brothers. She was swell.

Paulette Goddard was something else entirely. When she walked out on stage in what appeared to be nothing more than a black negligee, we all went wild, each of us imagining ourselves with the glamour girl in our arms. What enthusiasm! It took Major Douglas a good five minutes to get everybody calmed down enough to introduce the rest of the show.

Paulette was a knockout, her curvaceous figure accented by crisply curling hair, wide-set eyes and creamy skin. She was on center stage every minute and was every inch the lady.

When she left the base, trailing perfume and powder and bug-eyed corporals, she took with her all our hearts. We were all in love with her.

Then there was Ben Blue, a little guy in a too-small hat and a too-big suit over a plain white t-shirt. A wisecracking face and the filthiest mouth that had ever stepped onto our stage.

But Ben, just like in his movies, was a consummate actor and a great comedian. He had a group of kids from Hollywood with him, starlets and a couple fellows, and they put on a wonderful show. A lot of us didn't quite understand his vulgarity, but his warmth and honesty shone through. He really cared about us and it showed. So we laughed in all the right places and applauded in all the right places, and in the end it was hard to tell who had a better time, him or us.

* * *

Perhaps the people who gave the most were the unknowns, the little bands of singers and actresses who had not made it big in Hollywood and maybe never would, girls with silky hair swinging in the wind, pink cheeks, bright eyes and high, sweet voices, who poured their hearts out to us through their shows.

Sometimes their stage was a platform set up in a spare revetment; sometimes it was only the back of a weapons carrier. But they always jumped right up and sang and danced with all the verve of Ziegfeld's best. They often put on four shows within a couple of days, to give every guy in Kunming and the surrounding bases a chance to attend, and their energy at the end of the fourth show was as high as at the beginning of the first.

They showered us with attention, lavishing hugs and kisses, giggles and adoring glances with gay abandon. They climbed up into the cockpits of our planes, admiring the look and feel of them, allowing us to be proud of our equipment and ourselves.

They ate in the mess halls with us, walked around the base, slept in the same kind of candle-lit hostels, posed for pictures, smiled in flowered dresses in the rain or severe tailored USO suits in the wind.

There were almost no women stationed in Kunming, in all of China for that matter. A few of the nurses were girls, but most were male medics. General Chennault had a very few secretaries hidden away in command headquarters, but we never saw them. The Chinese girls were strictly off limits.

So when the USO girls came to Kunming it was like being visited by Venus, Aphrodite and Betty Grable, with a dash of your mother or your sister thrown in for memories of home.

To be able to sit in the mess hall across from someone wearing lipstick and nail polish, powder and perfume, all soft and sweet, was heaven itself. And to have that heavenly person take an interest in your plane, well, that was even better.

We were so cut off from the States, from the normal flow of radio and newspapers and newsreels, from street corner conversation, that it was difficult to know if the people cared, or even knew, what we were doing out here. The USO girls reassured us that our friends and family did care deeply and were grateful.

And they, especially the bigger stars who got the media attention, were our voices back home. They were the ones who told the press how we were faring and how we felt, what conditions were like in China and what we were doing for the war effort.

Stars & Stripes, the military newspaper, helped too. It was gratifying to be able to read about our own exploits and those of our comrades in other parts of the world, and to find that our efforts were not only appreciated but commended.

We got mail, of course, but it wasn't the same. It was difficult to put down on paper how you felt, to write objectively about yourself and your pals. And you could never be sure how much would get through. A lot of mail was censored and a lot of it never reached its destination.

Mail coming to us from the States was very sporadic. Air letters were fairly frequent, but packages were always behind schedule. A box mailed to you in October full of Christmas goodies might not arrive until February. And if your mom or girlfriend hadn't read the ladies' magazine articles on baking and packing cookies that shipped well, you'd end up with nothing but crumbs.

Mail call was the highlight of the day or week or month, whenever the bags came in. There was always somebody wandering around in tears, the recipient of a Dear John letter, somebody leaping around yelling with joy because his wife had a baby; somebody standing around dejectedly because he hadn't got any mail for the fourth time in a row. We shared our letters and snapshots and cookies with the poor guy, and he was appreciative, but it wasn't the same.

And that's why the USO shows were so important, so well received. Everybody got attention. Each guy got a warm kiss from red lips. A cool hand on his forehead . . .

The memories faded away, dreams sliding into daylight. It wasn't Ann Sheridan's hand, or Paulette Goddard's, or even Ben Blue's. The hand was Dr. Sung's. I opened my eyes to find him gazing down at me, brown eyes still grave behind the horn-rimmed glasses.

He murmured something, a question perhaps, but I didn't understand. I looked around for the boys. They were asleep on the floor, curled up by the stove, although there were pillows and rugs near the divan. Probably the stove, with its plumes of radiating heat, was a novelty not to be ignored.

The doctor repeated his question. I assumed he was asking how I was, so I smiled and nodded and said, "Fine," trying not to talk too loud as people do when communicating with foreigners. *I* was the foreigner here.

Sung smiled and nodded in turn, pouring out a string of syllables in his soft voice, and pointing toward the door. He wanted me to leave? No, that wasn't it, for he pointed at himself now and then at the door, motioning toward me and the divan with a flowing hand. He held up his thumb and forefinger, measuring a space of half an inch, then turned and walked out the door.

That was it. He was leaving, for a short time, but

would return. I was to stay here and rest. The door closed behind him.

I rose cautiously. The buzzing in my head was gone, but I was surprised to find I was soaked with sweat. The weather wasn't all that warm.

I went and peered into the other room. Dalton was out cold, and so was Horton. Now what? I sat down again, feeling like a houseguest caught on a Sunday morning before the hosts are awake.

Daylight streamed in through the window set deep in the front wall. The bamboo shade had been pulled high to take advantage of the light.

I was too restless to sit. I got up again and looked out the window. It faced south, toward the river and the way we had come, away from where I assumed the rest of the village was, behind us. It seemed an odd configuration, to have your home looking away from all your neighbors, your patients, who would have to walk all the way around to reach you in time of need, away from the heart of town and the center of things.

Perhaps it was due to *feng shui*. *Feng shui* is the mystical Chinese art of placing people and their buildings in the proper spatial relationships for harmony with nature and, of course, for good luck.

There were men throughout China, in every village and town, fortune-tellers who specialized in determining on which site a home should be built, in which walls the windows and doors should be placed and which direction they should face so the life force could flow through the most easily.

Feng shui means "wind and water alignment" and the optimum direction is from the south. In that case, the doctor's little house was ideally situated. Not only did he face south, but he had the river at his feet. Wind, water and sun—the perfect combination.

Something sparkled in the sun, up at the eaves—a

tiny mirror tacked to the curving roof at the corner. Another item to generate good luck. There was probably another one at the opposite corner. Their reflective surfaces repelled bad luck.

Was it good, I wondered, to have a physician who believed in all this superstitious nonsense? He was obviously Western-trained; perhaps he kept up with the mirrors and the *feng shui* for the benefit of his patients.

And what, I asked myself, gave me the right to label any of it nonsense? There were many more things in heaven and earth than I had knowledge of. The Chinese were an ancient race who had been around for more centuries than any other civilization in history. It was entirely possible that they knew things the Western world, still in its youth, could only scoff at.

Besides, I liked the thought of a life force, God perhaps, flowing peacefully through the house of the lantern, sweeping the anxiety, pain and grime out of my body, airing out my soul and cleansing my spirit. I glanced up at the twinkling mirror and smiled into the sun.

But the life force apparently didn't flow that fast, because after I had stood at the window a few minutes more, I began to worry again. It wasn't smart to stand in full view of anyone walking by. Perhaps someone had already seen me and I hadn't noticed. Maybe I should close the bamboo shade, and maybe if I did, someone would notice that it was normally open. My head started to buzz again.

"Okay, buddy, get a grip on it," I commanded myself. If Dr. Sung thought it was okay to leave things the way they were, then that's what I would do. He knew his village better than I did. I sat back down on the divan, sweat dewing my forehead.

The kettle rattled on the stove. The boys were up, scavenging for something to eat.

"Morning." Chien turned and smiled at me.

"You awake," Weng said, stating the obvious. He found a plate of bean cakes and offered it to his brother and to me.

"We should wait," I said. "Those aren't ours."

"Doctor not mind."

"Probably not, but they're not ours to take."

Both boys looked at me reproachfully. How do you think we've managed so far, their faces seemed to say. Again, I preferred not to think about it.

Weng offered me the plate again. "I'll wait," I said.

Chien put out his hand, then, after another glance at me and one at Weng, retracted it. "I wait too."

Weng sighed, as though at some incredibly citified dandies. He put the plate back on the shelf where he had found it.

At that moment Dr. Sung walked in the door. I started guiltily, although I hadn't done anything amiss. The boys eyed him with wide, innocent eyes.

The doctor went to the stove, perked up the fire under the kettle, and took out a plate of cakes. He offered it to the boys. Weng took two, throwing me a glance which clearly said, "I told you so."

Chien held out a cake to me, but Dr. Sung put it back on the plate, reprimanding gently in his soft voice. Apparently something else was planned for me.

Tea. A steaming cup was placed in my hands, so hot it almost scalded to touch.

"Ginseng?" I asked.

The doctor must have understood the word, for he poured out something for Chien to translate.

"Not ginseng. Special plants."

"What kind?"

"Not know English. Magic plants. Good for sick person."

Magic. Too bad it wasn't sulfa, or that new stuff, penicillin.

Chien was still struggling for words. "Flower that smell good, big and white."

A picture popped into my head. "Chrysanthemums." Somehow I knew exactly what he meant. I sipped gingerly at the hot liquid. The flowers might smell good, but the tea tasted awful, grainy and glutinous.

"Chrysanthemum," Chien repeated, committing it to memory. "And magic."

Magic. Why not? What did I have to lose? I drank the tea down.

Dr. Sung removed the bandages from my face and hand, sprinkled the wounds with more of the pale beige powder, and covered them up again.

"You rest now," he said through Chien.

"I'm fine," I protested, but I lay back down obediently. Truthfully, I felt sort of strange. Maybe it was the beige powder and maybe it was the magic tea, but I didn't feel like going anywhere. My eyes closed of their own volition. I felt myself drifting off, beyond the doctor's house, beyond the village and the river, back to Kunming in the dead of winter.

Christmas morning. The sun rose hazily, piercing through the elm trees that grew outside my window. I lay and stretched lazily, anticipating the Christmas dinner to come. It had been rumored that we'd have real turkey and gravy, real mashed potatoes, real pumpkin pie. It was likely just a rumor, but it was something to think about.

It was cold outside, but Mr. Swee, our houseboy, had a fire going in the coal stove and it would soon warm up in here. Might as well get up and stand in front of it. I pushed the khaki blanket back, my feet hit the icy plank floor, and the phone rang.

Trouble. The phone only rang when they wanted you to go up on a mission. I sighed and reached for the receiver. "Captain Sperry speaking."

It was the O.D.—the Officer of the Day. He sounded infinitely weary, and a little frightened. "Get together eight more pilots. You're on standby. We could have a Pearl Harbor situation here any minute now."

My mind immediately clouded over with fear, but I pushed it aside. "Roger." I hung up, threw on my clothes and got together eight fellows from my squadron, the cream of the crop.

We had a briefing and a quick breakfast and by eight forty-five had collected our parachutes, survival belts and a driver to take us out to our revetments.

My crew, as always, had my Texas Belle ready and waiting. I was ready and waiting. My eight buddies and their crews, at their revetments, were ready and waiting. Waiting, endlessly waiting.

The skies were clear. The sun shone. Dew sparkled on the grasses that lined the runway. And somewhere, in the distance, destruction was on its way.

Hanks and his corporal and I spent the hours talking desultorily, wondering what our families were doing on Christmas morning, discussing the movie we'd seen at the mess hall last week, making small talk. Our mouths were going, but we weren't really listening to each other, only to the sounds that weren't yet audible in the sky, the angry hum of Zeros on the move.

Operations got word that the Japs had been spotted someplace down the line, and we were put on plane alert. This meant we were to sit in our aircraft, ready to taxi as soon as the bandits were sighted.

I had just put my binoculars in Belle's cockpit and

was climbing in myself, when all hell broke loose. The warning gongs clanged with a deafening din, and the roar of low-flying aircraft filled the air. The Japs were right on top of us, slipping in at treetop level, nineteen Twin Betties, loaded with deadly banana cluster bombs that would fragment on ground contact.

CHAPTER NINETEEN

Across the Top
of the World

I rallied my eight guys together and we roared down the runway, hands heavy on the throttle, hearts in our throats, eyes on the sky. Pushing for 140 miles per hour, the speed needed for our P-51 Mustang wheels to leave the ground.

The Japs were at treetop level, heading for the heart of our base. Here they came, black shadows over the barracks, the mess hall, the aircraft maintenance bay. Bombs cascaded from their bellies, sparkling silver like Christmas tinsel.

Eleven fifty-five A.M. They thought we were in the mess hall, eating Christmas dinner. Calmly, methodically, they turned and headed for home.

One hundred fifty miles per hour. Back on the stick. We were airborne. I spared a split second glance back at the base. Thanks to Japanese quality control only ten percent of the bombs had gone off. The base was intact. Undetonated shells littered the ground, glinted off the tops of buildings, souvenirs of the bandits' holiday visit.

We were gaining altitude, going for the ceiling. Back

on the stick. Wheels retracted. Even before they snapped into the wells, we were pulling Gs, climbing at 200 miles per hour, charging up into the sky. Gravity clutched at us, flattening our faces, sitting on our chests like a set of weights. We kept climbing, tiger sharks going after fresh meat.

The Japs were at full throttle, about 240 miles per hour, pouring on all the speed they could muster. We caught up to them at 2,000 feet, hopefully scaring the holiday cheer right out of them. Now we came in behind with our ammo full out, six .50-caliber machine guns blazing on each P-51, four .50-caliber guns flaming from the P-40s.

There was a Betty right in front of me. I jammed down hard on the gun button, spraying bullets. Red-hot tracers arced across the sky, connected with the bandit. The fuel tank blossomed into a fireball and the Betty went down like a rock.

Forward on the throttle and I closed in on another one, maneuvering through a sky full of bright orange flames. Explosions wracked the air, creating waves of turbulence that bounced Belle and me around like gravel in a shaken cup.

The Japanese pilot knew I was on his tail. He knew he couldn't shake me. I was faster than he was, and I was gaining rapidly. He did the only thing he could. He dove, straight for the ground, hoping, I'm sure, to pull up at the last second and lose me. I stayed on his tail, hurtling toward the earth, planning the split second when I too would pull up and away. I had my finger on the gun button. When he pulled out, I'd be right behind him, spraying bullets. A copse of elms rose up dead in front of the Betty. He yanked back on his stick. I yanked back on mine. He was too late, going too fast. He hit the trees at full speed, shearing off the tops, limbs and leaves flying everywhere, and exploded in a hot yellow glare.

I didn't look back, couldn't; I was fighting the stick to get up and way before the fireball caught my wing. Now I was hurtling again, up instead of down, the earth falling away as Belle climbed into the blue.

Suddenly there was another bandit smack in the middle of my canopy, about a hundred feet up. I banked right and climbed another hundred feet, planning to come down on him, guns blazing. I was already lining him up in my gunsight. *He* banked left, dove, and another Betty was right in front of me, tracers spewing from its turrets. I climbed, quickly, as if trying only to get away, then screamed down on both of them, chasing the first one into my wingman's sights and the other into the ground where it blew into a thousand dull metal bits.

I pulled up again. There, at three o'clock, another Betty ambling along, apparently unaware of the destruction all around it. I fastened onto it like a magnet.

Out of the corner of my eye I saw two of my guys, Hank Tubbs and J. C. Dixon, high above me at about 16,000 feet. I concentrated on the slow-moving Betty, pouring a round of hot lead into it.

Tubbs and Dixon went into a dive fifty yards in front of me, making a pass at the same Betty, putting themselves directly in my path. Their P-40s were much slower than my P-51. They couldn't get out of the way in time and I couldn't slow down fast enough. We were on a collision course. I pulled hard to the left, praying I'd miss them, and almost rammed into my wing man, who was covering me.

But we got the Betty. It went down in a smoking spiral and we went after another two bandits, this time in different directions. Two more explosions, two more smoking spirals. To my left, a drifting trail of sparks where a third bandit had fallen from the sky. On my right, a dirty brown smudge lingered where a fourth Jap had gone up in flames.

And that was it. Nothing else in the sky but us. All nineteen bandits were gone, either shot down by our guns or smashed into treetops trying to get back into Burma. None of them had got more than sixty miles out of Kunming. I checked my watch. The show had lasted forty-five minutes. We still might make Christmas dinner.

We flew home, weak with relief, giddy with accomplishment. The dusty tarmac of the main runway rose up to meet us, as comfortable as an old quilt. We were back, all nine of us.

Three of the guys, Bill Cummings, Tom Bartlet and Thad Burns, had been injured by Japanese gunfire. Some of the planes were riddled with bullet holes. But the Christmas bandits had been chased away, and we were safe.

The injured men were taken to the hospital. The rest of us went in to a debriefing.

We had all outdone ourselves. Our ace ratings were growing fast. I was given credit for one kill and two probables. Tom, Thad, J. C. Dixon and Bill Baxter each got two kills and a number of probables. Cy Packard and Bill Cummings received one kill each and they also got, along with Ted White, one probable each. Hank Tubbs got three kills. He also got one hell of a chewing out from me and two other pilots for doing such crazy flying.

We were late for Christmas dinner, breezing in just as the cooks were clearing the last dishes from the serving line. But they had heard about our exploits that day and they set the stuff back out for us.

As far as food, we had missed nothing. Instead of turkey and all the trimmings, there was chicken and dumplings (emaciated Chinese chickens), pineapple from Australia (the kind that always smelled moldy), some kind of Chinese salad, the ingredients of which were difficult to determine, wonderful fresh bread and cookies flown in from India, and tea. Tea enough to drown in.

Then there was the appreciation of Uncle Sam. Each of us was awarded the Distinguished Flying Cross, and our injured fellows also got the Purple Heart. It was a Christmas to remember, the most exciting any of us had ever had.

Day slid into night. Our hearts still pounded with the thrill of the chase. The mess hall was closing up. The cooks were tired. We begged from them the last loaf of bread and a tin of Spam and retired to my hostel.

The moon rose luminous over the maintenance bay, the one the Japs had tried to shell. A star rose in the east, shining out over Bethlehem and Burma and Kunming alike. Outside the hostel the night was cold, clear and serene.

Inside, it was still flame-lit day as we relived yet again the events of the afternoon, washing down Spam sandwiches with 110-proof rice wine.

Mr. Swee had kept the coal stove going for us. The floors were swept of the dirt that always seeped in, and the beds had been made.

Mr. Swee's left arm hung limp where the Japanese, at some point in his past, had cut out the muscle from forearm to shoulder. But he was the best houseboy of any in the hostels, cheerful and kind and efficient. He kept the place clean and warm, ironed our clothes, shined our shoes, gave us somebody to come home to. He had no family left in the world except a cousin who worked at the post office in San Francisco, and his fondest dream was to get to California and make a new home in the city by the bay.

I always felt sorry for Mr. Swee. But pity was not the proper thing to give, so instead we gave him our cast-off clothing, our worn G.I. boots and our friendship.

And tonight we gave him a glass of white lightning. Mr. Swee drunk was funny. Lights danced in his sad black eyes. He whirled around the room, humming a high-pitched Chinese melody. He clapped my officer's cap on his head and did a wicked imitation of "American captains." He told jokes. They were all in Chinese, so we didn't understand them, but he laughed so uproariously that we had to laugh too. I began to see what he might have been like if the Japanese hadn't invaded his land.

But we'd shown them today. We drank one more toast to ourselves. It burned going down like the fiery embers of the bandits. The kerosene lamp glowed and the candles gleamed, the star shone outside the burlaped windows, and the world inside our hostel was at peace.

Lord, that stuff burned. I hadn't remembered that it was that strong. It wasn't so much my throat that was scorched, it was the inside of my mouth. And while rice wine never tasted like rice, fortunately, it shouldn't taste like blood either.

The sweetish salinity of it lay on my tongue like warm thin ice. I struggled to my feet. Someone pushed me back against the cushions. I opened my eyes. It was . . . I didn't recognize him for a moment . . . then lucidity returned. Dr. Sung, with Chien peering over his shoulder.

"You rest, need sleep," Chien said, worry staining his small face.

"I've *been* sleeping."

"Not enough," Weng said, from over the doctor's other shoulder.

I strained for a glimpse out the window. The late afternoon sun was already dissolving into the western hills. Time to be on the road again.

"I'm fine," I protested, pushing back a faded cotton rug that had been thrown over my legs. "We've got to get moving."

The memory of that Christmas dogfight was still vivid in my mind, and the urgency we had felt as we roared down the runway had been transferred from my dreaming to my waking thoughts. The Japanese were ruthless. We had to get going.

"Where's Dalton? Where's Horton?" I sat up, despite the doctor's objections.

"They in other room," Chien said. "You rest."

"It's getting dark. Time to go." I rose unsteadily.

Dr. Sung shook his head, voicing obvious warnings, gesturing toward his back room.

"Dalton's leg is worse? He shouldn't be moved, is that it?"

"No, you're the one who's in rough shape, buddy." Horton's tall frame filled the tiny doorway. "Sung here says you shouldn't go anywhere till he's properly doctored you up."

"That's silly. Dalton's the one with the bum leg."

"Yeah, but it's all splinted up," Dalton called from the back room. "You're the one who's still bleeding."

I tasted blood on my tongue. "Yeah?" These guys were scaring me, although I didn't want to admit it to them or myself. "Well, maybe we'll stay just for one more night." I sat down again. Dr. Sung smiled and nodded, murmuring soothingly.

Chien nodded and smiled. Weng nodded. Horton plunked down in the armchair. "I wonder if he's got any of that tea house liquor."

I never found out whether he had tea house liquor or not, for he rubbed some kind of greenish salve— "magic plants," Chien said—into my cheek, dosed me with another cup of magic tea, and soon I was off again . . . soaring over China.

I was on my way to India to pick up a new P-51 and leave the one I was in for overhaul. I liked going to India. The base at Chabua had the best food in the entire CBI Theater, and it had a bakery. Already I could smell the bread, taste the pastry. My mouth watered.

Everything we had in China, all our food, our supplies, our planes, every drop of gasoline came in over the Hump from Chabua to Kunming. Most of it was delivered in the big transport planes, C-47s, but occasionally one of us fighter pilots would be dispatched to pick up a new P-51 or escort a group of new guys in their Mustangs across to China.

The Hump was treacherous. It stretched from the border of China and Burma, across the Himalayas, shown on the map as the inverted funnel-shaped tip of Burma, to Chabua. The Hump could kill, in sudden, severe downdrafts, in ice on your wings, or with blinding fog banks.

But I wasn't thinking about that. I was enjoying the green and gold plateau of Yunnan shimmering below me, embroidered with the blue threads of streams and rivers, the reds and browns of towns and villages, sequined here and there with lakes and ponds. *Yunnan* means "South of the Clouds" in Chinese, and this day not even a puff of white marred the turquoise sky.

The P-51—not Belle, for she would never desert me

long enough for an overhaul—hummed companionably, smelling faintly of smoke and hot oil. She was enjoying the trip, too.

Below was the base of the mountains, *shan* in Chinese, rising in waves from the plateau. Out of habit, I checked my charts.

One of the things General Chennault taught us was to memorize the landmarks of China from the air. He taught us to keep an eye on our maps, too, but you could not rely solely on charts to tell you where you were. China is one of the hardest countries in the world to navigate over; so many features look the same. With rivers everywhere and thousands of little tributaries, you had to be careful you didn't take a fork, thinking it was the Yangtze, and find out too late it was really the Salween. The only safe way to navigate was by maps *and* visual identification.

The General had us memorize all the mountains. We knew where all the enemy bases were. We knew where our bases were. We were frequently on radio silence, and if you got into trouble and needed to land fast, you couldn't break that silence to call and ask directions.

I was on radio silence now, not because I expected any bandits, but because there was nobody to talk to. No one was up here but me.

The silence was beautiful, almost majestic as I climbed up, up along the hills into the mountains that formed the Hump. Grasses waved in the breeze, visible from the sky as variations in greens, like velvet brushed against the grain. Wildflowers, their colors barely discernible, flickered like spots before my eyes.

And suddenly, here were the Himalayas, jagged rock encrusted with ice, thrusting abruptly into the sky. I was at 15,000 feet, and the peaks were just below me. I climbed to 16,000 and still they were only a thousand feet short of my belly. It doesn't really matter how much distance you put between you and them, I told myself wryly. If you get into trouble there's nowhere to go but down.

The peaks were getting higher. I climbed to 17,000 feet, 18,000, higher, leveling out at 20,000. The fog began to swirl in, obscuring the peaks, then mysteriously clearing, revealing tiny snow-filled valleys. I would catch just a glimpse, a hint, before the clouds blotted them out again.

It was cold and growing colder. I had on thick wool underwear, a fleece-lined flying suit and my trusty A-2 leather combat jacket. I never wore the electric suit after it shorted out on me, contenting myself with the warmth from the plane's engine. The cockpit was small and the engine heated it fairly well, but frigid air still seeped in through the floor joints and under the canopy.

Now the fog was as dense as a wall. I couldn't see a thing. I may as well have been flying in cotton coated with thick gray paint. Even the sound of the plane was muted. It was eerie.

My ADF, automatic direction finder, was dead. The mountains had blocked off the radio signal. I checked my magnetic compass. It still pointed west southwest, but if it was off somehow I'd never know until I smacked into the side of a mountain. I checked the little whiskey compass, so-called because it was filled with alcohol. It pointed the same way, so I could assume I was still on course.

I flew on into the void. Planes went down frequently in the Himalayas, and I had never heard of anyone who went down ever walking out. If you went down over the Hump you were lost forever.

I checked both compasses again. The whiskey compass had a tendency to get knocked out of whack by turbulence. Thank God I hadn't run into that.

Suddenly the clouds disappeared as if they were cobwebs brushed away by a celestial hand. Except for a few wispy tendrils clinging to the peaks, the sky was crystal clear. Ice sparkled on the peaks, so bright it hurt my eyes. Snow lay, pristine and shining, in the valleys. For five minutes I flew above beauty the likes of which I had never seen.

Then the clouds poured back in, billowing in and out like curtains in a breeze, and we hit a downdraft.

The bottom dropped out of the world. I was flying at 20,000 feet and suddenly I wasn't at that altitude any more. The plane dropped 1,500 feet in the blink of an eye. Another five hundred feet down and I'd hit a mountain.

The slower planes, transports and bombers, got into a lot of trouble when they hit downdrafts. But a fighter, having twice the speed, had a better chance of recovery.

I grabbed the stick and pulled back hard. The nose lifted. I banked left, aiming around the side of the peak, pulled back on the stick. We rose, up, up, higher, higher . . . we cleared the mountain. I started breathing again.

Now there was a lot of turbulence. We bounced and jounced around, the jagged peaks jumping about in front of me like circus performers. I would have to watch carefully to make sure we didn't start drifting. I set a visual point just ahead of me, picking one peak, and when we passed it another, and kept it right in front of me. If it started drifting to left or right, the winds were buffeting me off course.

I checked my watch. One hour into the Hump, one hour to go. Two hundred more miles of trailing cloud and twisting turbulence. Two hundred miles over some of the most desolate terrain in the world.

But at last it neared an end. The peaks were getting lower. Not softer or less jagged, but lower. They were still capped with snow and surrounded by mists, still a dangerous place to go down in. There were headhunters in the valleys and barbarians in the folds of the mountains. Still no place to lose an engine.

The mountains grudgingly gave way to foothills, green and waving and lush. The icy cockpit grew pleasantly warm then hot and humid. I stripped off my jacket, wishing there was enough room to take off the flying suit and long johns. The foothills tapered down to a long, flat plain filled with trees and shrubs. The base loomed ahead. Chabua.

I touched down on the long flat runway, light as a feather, taxied in smoothly, parked where the crewman pointed, raised the canopy and jumped out. Pretty good flying, if I said so myself.

First stop was the hut I was assigned to, to take off those stifling clothes. Second was the bakery. I had a Coke and a slice of cherry pie. The cherries were tinned, I was sure, but the pastry was fresh. We never had pie in China; we never even had cherries. This was worth the trip.

There were two British officers in the bakery, having a cup of tea and watching me wolf down the pie.

"I don't see why you Yanks should find anything so marvelous about pie," one of them said petulantly. "*You* can bloody well get all the sweets you want any time."

This of course was entirely untrue, but it probably looked that way to him. All of our bases in India were in joint use with the British, so their people saw a lot of us. And one of the things they saw was that we were allotted rations of candy bars, Coke and chewing gum, while they received no "sweets" allotment at all. It must have seemed horribly unfair.

We got along well with the British, bantering back and forth when we met them at clubs or rest camps. I always wanted to try out their light, speedy little Spitfires, but I never got the chance. Probably the top brass of both countries would have had us up on charges if we tried it, so it was a good thing the opportunity never came up.

In the afternoon I went out to the airfield to meet Torrance Groves, another pilot from Kunming who had just come in over the Hump, and we spent the rest of the day kicking around the base, shooting the breeze with transport and bomber pilots, listening to their war stories and telling them ours.

The transport pilots were the unsung heroes of the CBI Theater, flying back and forth, mission after mission, day after day, across the Hump and back. Their planes were slower and unwieldy, unarmed and usually unprotected by escorts. It took them four hours one way, a full half day sweating out dangerous conditions, and all they got at the end of a mission was a return trip.

Another group of transport pilots flew the milk run, the routes by which I arrived in China, from India to Africa or South America and back.

"It's not fair," they'd complain. "You fighter guys fly ten or twelve missions and get a decoration. All we ever do is fly back and forth and we never get any medals."

They were ribbing us, having a little fun at our expense. They didn't expect to be taken seriously, and I laughed them off, on the outside. On the inside,

I was proud of every word I heard. We fighter pilots worked hard for the rewards we got.

While we were wandering around on the airfield, trouble was brewing in the sky. Thunderheads were building in the west, purple shading to black. The air was thick with humidity and hummed with electricity. A monsoon was on the horizon.

CHAPTER TWENTY

Monsoon Season

The storm hit at dawn the next morning.

I was already awake—it was too oppressive to sleep. I sat cross-legged on the floor of the little hut assigned to us, similar to the one we had had when I first arrived in Kunming, and watched the monsoon roll in.

First the sun rose, a lemon yellow blur behind the wall of clouds, disappearing almost as quickly as it appeared. The clouds had diffused themselves, overnight, from the angry purple of a fresh bruise to a dull gunmetal gray that lay oppressively over everything. But you didn't need eyes to know the storm was approaching; you could feel it. There was a tension in the air, a heavy vibrancy that clung to your nerve endings like a lingering headache.

I didn't understand how Torrance and our other roommate, a bomber pilot named Wade, could sleep through this. They lay sprawled on the thin cots, dead to the world.

Outside the hut, everything was still. No birds sang in the trees. No one walked on the dirt paths crisscrossing the huts. The monkeys you sometimes heard chattering from the deep woods at the outskirts of the base were silent.

The storm sat on the horizon, ten miles distant, static, while the sky crackled with tension, unnaturally silent. Nothing moved. The air was still.

And then the rain fell, a silvered curtain of water, dense as a waterfall. It was if someone had flicked a switch. One moment the air was clear; in the next a torrential downpour had invaded the world. It thudded on the thatched roof of the hut like an army of booted feet, sent up sprays of mud from the path, drummed on the leaves of the banana trees outside the window like Gene Krupa gone crazy.

Torrance and Wade leaped out of bed.

"What in hell's goin' on out there?" Torrance yelled, pulling on his trousers.

"Monsoon," I said quietly, awestruck by the fierceness of the storm.

"What?" Torrance yelled, hopping around looking for his boots.

"What'd you say?" Wade hollered.

"Monsoon!" I hollered back. You had to yell to be heard above the din of the rain.

Torrance had woken up enough to appreciate the sound effects. "A storm," he yelled disgustedly. "Doesn't it know we're tryin' to sleep?"

Nobody bothered to answer. He sat down on the cot. "I'm hungry," he hollered, jumping up again. "Let's go get some breakfast."

"Out there?" This came from Wade, incredulous.

We all stared out the window. The rain sluiced down, as thick as if someone were up on the roof, pouring over fifty-gallon drums of water. Anyone stepping out into it would be immediately soaked to the skin.

"Sure, why not? I'm dressed." Torrance found his other boot and rammed his bare foot into it.

"It's not going to let up," I yelled. I had heard that monsoons often lasted for days. We had to go out sometime. No one was going to bring us breakfast through this torrent, and if we didn't go after it ourselves, sooner or later we'd starve.

The second we stepped out the door we were drenched. Mud caked our boots to the ankle and splattered knee-high on our slacks. Our freshly pressed khakis were plastered in wet folds to our wet skin and water dripped into our eyes from our streaming hair.

The rain was warm and the air steamy. By the time we had covered the quarter mile to the mess hall I thought we would have done just as well to go out wearing nothing at all; at least our clothes would have stayed dry.

The mess hall gave the appearance of catering to a large party of drowned rats, every man in the place (except the cooks) leaving a trail of water wherever he stepped. Rainwater puddled on the wooden floor and dribbled in little streams from table to table. The windows were opaque with running water, and tendrils of vapor collected above the serving line.

But the food was good. Fresh eggs instead of powdered, fresh milk and orange juice and bacon. And no rice anywhere on the menu. I dried off my face with a paper napkin and dug in.

By the time we got back to our hut we were, if possible, wetter than when we had started out. We dug a dry set of khakis from our B-4 bags and hung the wet stuff up to dry. Then we sat and watched the rain.

* * *

For nine days we sat and watched the rain. In nine days it never let up once. Twenty-four hours a day, sixty minutes an hour, the rain thrummed on the roof, throbbed on the foliage, pounded on the airfield.

There was no possibility of getting into the air, flying away from the torrent. In the first place, visibility was nil; in the second, the sheer force of the rain was enough to knock your instruments so far out of whack you'd never get back on course.

So we sat and watched the rain.

The clothes we had hung to dry never did. The air was so hot and humid that they merely steamed to a clammy dampness before we were forced to put them on again to replace the ones that got drenched on our trips to the mess hall.

There was nowhere to go except the mess hall. Everything else was too far to go in the rain or not open because of the rain. We had a pack of cards, but not being gamblers, the thrill of the game wore off in the middle of the third day. There were no other games, no radio, no books. We were bored stiff.

Somewhere around the fifty or sixth day of enforced idleness, we decided to clean our .45s, just for something to do. We got out the pistols, the metal-stained cleaning rags, the extra bullets. We passed a pleasant half hour cleaning and polishing. That was it. In half an hour we had used up the one remaining pastime in our little shack.

Wade and I put our guns back in their holsters and the holsters in the B-4 bags. We sat and stared at the rain. Torrance had his bag at his feet. He kept twirling his gun around on his finger, aiming out the window, at the cot, at a spider on the wall. He twirled it again. It slipped out of his grasp. His finger caught on the trigger and pulled. A tremendous *crack,* and he had shot a hole right through his B-4 bag. It ruined all his dress clothes and scared the three of us half to death.

It was the most entertaining thing that had happened since the monsoon started.

At last the rains let up. I collected the new plane and filed a flight plan for the Hump. From Chabua back to Kunming we usually took the lower route, across the smaller peaks, but the rain had got to me. I was tired of sitting around safe and bored. I filed a plan for the higher route, right over the top of the roof of the world. The guys in the operations shack looked at me like I was crazy, but they didn't say no. Maybe they were used to stir-crazy people; they sat out those monsoons year in and year out.

Once you left Chabua you had to gain altitude fairly quickly. There were the foothills, and then the Himalayas, rising like a giant's castle keep in the foreground.

I climbed to 16,000 feet. I could see my shadow far below me, skimming over the lower peaks, a gray-blue dragonfly against the lighter rock. Wisps of cloud curled between plane and shadow. The air grew cold. I pulled on my jacket, still climbing. Thick wads of cotton cloud puffed in and out of the peaks. I could smell the snow they carried.

Still climbing. Twenty thousand feet. Japanese Zeros sometimes hid in the clouds on the edge of the Hump, lying in wait for the unwary, especially the unarmed transports.

A lot of Air Transport Command pilots carried pistols so they had *something* to fight back with. I had heard stories in which ATC guys had fired at bandits, but I had no idea if they were true. I couldn't see how you actually hit one from the distance between you.

I never saw a bandit on the Hump. Other people did. It was almost like a fairy tale, with invisible monsters lurking in the mists. And the mists were such that you could well believe it.

We did have planes shot at going over the Hump. Frequently, when a new group was coming in, several of us would fly over and intercept, just to let them know they had an escort and to let any Japs know there were experienced pilots around.

We'd go on radio communications, chattering back and forth constantly, so the bandits, if they knew our frequencies, would realize there were more of us than of them up here. The bandits were always loners, hot shots looking for an ace rating, no more than one or two at a time, and most of the time our chatter was all it took to keep them at bay. They knew the dangers of the Hump as well as we did.

Now I was alone, unescorted. Still climbing. Twenty-two thousand feet. I peered through the thickening clouds. I didn't *see* any bandits. But the cloud cover was getting heavier.

I broke through it, still climbing. Twenty-five thousand feet. The sun shining down above me, each radiant beam picked out in iridescent thread. Nothing but clouds below me. A solid, impenetrable floor of puffy white stained rose and gold by the sun. Somewhere to the north was Mount Everest, too distant in far-off Tibet to be seen. Everything else was below me, below the clouds.

Somewhere down there were snow-filled valleys and sleek exotic snow leopards, howling blizzards, thickly fleeced yaks, orange-silk-clad lamas and intricate prayer wheels, perhaps even the elusive and mystical Shangri-La.

But they were all below, far below me, in a land that was hidden from sight.

I rode above the clouds, alert for wind shear, ice on the wings, downdrafts, or any of the other myriad dangers the Hump offered, but there were none. It was the smoothest flight across I had ever had, a journey tinged with the glow of the sun, the serenity of the clouds, touched perhaps by the magic of Shangri-La drifting up from below.

Magic. Now why did that sound familiar? I wasn't a fanciful person. Why was the thought of magic echoing through my head?

"Magic plants." Chien. What was he doing up here in the clouds? I was alone, drifting in the purity of the sky. Wasn't I?

And why did I feel so dizzy? I had managed to hold out the whole time we were in the brush. Why fall apart just because we reached a doctor? I was frustrated with myself, angry at my body for giving in. Better to drift . . . drift among the clouds.

The clouds were gone. The sky was clear. I knew where I was. On a bombing run into French Indochina.

The Japanese were all over that territory, moving men and materials from China down to the sea and back. There were hundreds of little bridges in the area. We'd fly in and bomb them. The Japanese would rebuild. We'd bomb again. They'd rebuild. At times it seemed almost like a game. We were aiming at inanimate targets, not people. And bridges can't shoot back. Or so I thought.

In China the war was frightening. In French Indochina, we almost had fun. We fighter pilots got cocky, blowing up bridges, and we began to seek out other targets on our own.

There were Japanese trains carrying supplies from Hanoi to the sea. We knew they were the enemy from intelligence reports, and even though we hadn't been told to hit them, sometimes we did.

And sometimes we got in hot water for our over-enthusiasm.

Returning from a bridge-busting mission, we flew over a hospital emblazoned with a big red cross. But when we got out our binoculars we could see that it wasn't a medical area. A large pen next to the main building housed cattle. Stacks of oil drums and wooden crates lay nestled under canvas tarps. Tiny raven-haired men scurried back and forth. Their build and the hue of their uniforms said they weren't French. They had to be Japanese and this was obviously a materials staging area.

We took a gamble. Our flight leader gave the green light and we strafed the place to bits. The cattle rammed through the pen and disappeared into the brush; men dove for cover. The buildings were reduced to rubble.

We flew home proud of the work we had done. We had blown up an important staging area we thought no one else knew about. We were wrong.

Intelligence knew all about it, but they had been planning to let the Japs load everything on their ships and then take the whole thing at once. We all got a chewing out. We were to stick to bridge-busting, which kept the Japanese isolated.

This afternoon I was headed into the interior, just south of Hanoi, to drop a single 500-pound bomb on a bridge over a small tributary, and then return to base. Two of my buddies were flying alongside, headed for bridges a few miles to the east and west.

About ten miles from the bridge I was to bust, they peeled off, banking away to left and right. I headed due south.

There was the bridge, dead ahead, a ten-foot-wide,

thirty-foot-long concrete structure over a pretty, placid green stream. Easy. I thought.

I came in low, at 200 feet, aiming for the bridge at a 20-degree angle so when I dropped the bomb the concussion would hit in the center of the structure and not somewhere off in the stream, as would occur if I came in at a wider angle. I pulled the release lever and banked sharply away from the bridge so I wouldn't be hit by flying debris.

A spray of bullets pierced the exposed belly of the plane, ricocheting around inside the cockpit, rattling like rocks in a bingo cage, startling the daylights out of me. Not until that moment did I notice the gun emplacement half-hidden under a wing of the bridge, nor the man on the bicycle furiously peddling away as the bridge blew to bits.

Now there was shrapnel banging around inside the cockpit. I didn't have time to worry about it. The plane had been hit in the oil system. The engine seized. I couldn't hold altitude.

Dense brush all around. Pockets of jungle. The plane was dropping fast. Two miles to the west was an open field surrounded by rice paddies. Come on, I coaxed the plane, come on. We can make it. Only a mile. Another hundred yards. Keep your nose up. Fifty feet. We can make it.

The earth rose up to meet us. We slammed to a bone-jarring stop. My head rammed into the instrument panel. Everything went black.

I was only out for two or three minutes. When I came to, I was sitting in only part of a plane. The front had been sheared away from the cockpit section where the engine cowling attached to the main fuselage and was lying on the ground in front of me. The rear of the plane, just past the cockpit, was also separated from the midsection of the plane and was lying about ten feet behind.

I climbed out shakily, brushing blood out of my eyes, and surveyed the damage. There was no way I was going to fly out. There was shrapnel in my legs. I could feel it, but I could walk so I didn't worry about it.

I was much more concerned about the possibility of being captured. The French in Indochina blew hot and cold about Americans and I was terrified that I'd be turned in by those with anti-American sentiments.

I forced myself to calm down and examine my surroundings. I was in a small valley surrounded by low hills. A hundred yards to the north a gradual slope rose into a foothill. In the other three directions were working rice paddies. Between me and them was the open field in which I had landed, about an acre of bare ground strewn with rocks. There were farmers in the rice paddies, even now looking in my direction. If they decided to come investigate it would take them no more than fifteen minutes, even threading back and forth between the paddies.

From the sky came the buzz of aircraft. I shaded my eyes and looked up. Tiger shark's teeth and a waggle of wings. It was my buddies, circling overhead like hawks, protecting me from enemy air fire. Thank God they were there.

I waved to let them know I was all right, then turned back to my more immediate surroundings. They would radio for help and watch over me until it came.

I brushed blood out of my eyes impatiently. They could protect me from air fire, but a ground sniper could get to me before they even saw him.

We had been taught little whistling tunes that would be recognized by the French Underground. I practiced two or three of them, watching the hills for signs of life.

The peasants in the rice paddies were still watching me, warily, I thought, trying to decide if they should advance.

I stayed with the plane, as we had been taught to do in a situation like this. My position had been reported and someone would be along sooner or later to pick me up. I knew they would because it was not a heavily Japanese infested area, and the ground was flat enough and wide enough for a rescue plane to land. The only question was, when would they come for me? How long?

I whistled my little tunes, trying to appear jaunty, although I was shaking as much from fright as from shock. No one came, from the ground or from the air. My legs were getting weak. I sat down in the lee of the plane. Blood dripped into my eyes. I stood up again. I was too anxious to sit.

I forced myself to think about something else.

The time General Beebe had selected me to fly cover for the B-24 carrying the bomb from the Ashland Grade School.

The children in Ashland, Kentucky, had raised the money to build the 500 pounder and sent it to Washington with a request that their school name be painted on the weapon. Washington followed through and a bomb was sent to China that read clearly across the face, "To Tojo, From Ashland Grade School."

The kids were proud of their contribution to the war effort. I was proud to be chosen to fly cover on a mission with the heart of young America behind it.

I brushed more blood out of my eyes. I could feel it caking on my brows.

Think about something else.

How about the time I met Pearl Buck, the woman

who had made China come alive for me so many years before I ever saw it myself? Or the German nuns I found in the countryside, working so hard for peace and harmony in their little Chinese missions while all around were death and destruction?

Think about something else.

Remember the time we performed the victory roll over the main runway, only fifty feet off the deck? We got chewed out for half an hour afterward for stunt flying. But it was worth it. Wasn't it? Would there ever be any other victory rolls?

I practiced my whistles again, looking around the hills.

Now the sound of another plane in the sky, a lighter, higher buzz, like a hummingbird among hawks. I looked up. My buddies were still there, still circling, but now they were making way for the bird dog, the little rescue plane.

Here they came, nose down, making a perfect three-point landing, taxiing in over the rough ground. They came to a stop within five feet of me and pilot and medic both jumped out.

"Need a lift?"

CHAPTER TWENTY-ONE

Secret Message

Did I need a lift?

"If you're headed my way," I answered, hoping they couldn't hear the shakiness in my voice.

"I think we might manage it," the pilot said casually. He was a tall, craggy-featured guy in his thirties who looked perfectly capable of flying his little plane in or out of just about anywhere.

"First let's look at that bump on your head." The medic, a younger fellow with red-gold hair and sandy eyebrows, was already unpacking his medical kit, pulling out rolls of bandaging, adhesive tape, a bottle of iodine. He dipped a gauze pad in alcohol and started dabbing at my forehead.

The farmers were trickling in from the rice paddies, curiosity having overcome fear. Soon a small crowd of men, women and children was gathered about me, my rescuers and my broken flying machine, staring with wide almond eyes, rustling and chatting among themselves like spectators at an odd pageant.

The alcohol burned on my forehead, my face, deep

into my cheek. The almond eyes moved in closer and closer, grabbing at my hand and making it burn . . .

I awoke with a jolt, disoriented in time and space. Was I on the ground or in the air? I felt as if I was floating, but no comforting cockpit surrounded me. In the dangerous territory outside of Hanoi or back safely in Kunming?

Gradually the fragments of memory fell into place like the pieces of a puzzle. I remembered being bundled up in the netting of the bird dog's hammock-like stretcher and flown back to base. Getting stitched up in the hospital in Kunming. Being awarded the Purple Heart. Displaying it proudly on the top of my footlocker. Flying out on other missions . . .

And I remembered where I was now. Not being airlifted out of French Indochina, nor safely back on base. No one was going to fly into Dr. Sung's small house and rescue me. No one even knew where I was. I'd have to make it back on my own. I'd have to leave now.

The boys. How could I have forgotten the boys and Dalton and Horton? We'd all have to leave now.

I jumped up from the divan. The little cottage was empty. Where was everybody? We had to get going. I went to the window. There they all were, just coming up the little dirt path, arms full of kindling for the stove. Night was falling—already?—and the sun's afterglow washed the sky with dull orange.

"You wake up," Chien said as soon as he came in the door. "Good. We have good food tonight."

"No time for supper. We've got to get going."

"We gotta eat," Horton said.

That was true. No point in leaving without filling our stomachs. No telling when we'd eat again. But the thought of food brought on a wave of nausea. I sank down on the divan.

"You guys go ahead. I'll just get our stuff together." In a minute. I didn't feel like moving.

The doctor dropped his kindling next to the stove, rinsed his hands in the simmering kettle and bent to examine me. I could see the concern in his eyes. Chien translated for him.

"He say you not get up. Rest."

"Tell him thanks, but we've got to leave tonight."

The doctor started shaking his head and murmuring protestations before Chien had even finished translating my words.

"He say—" Chien began.

"I know, but we've been here too long already."

"But he say you too sick to go." Chien's small face was pinched with worry again.

"I'm fine." I jumped up to demonstrate my fitness. A tidal wave of nausea washed over me.

"I think the doctor's right," Dalton said over my shoulder. "You don't look too hot."

"We safe here," Weng added.

"All right. We'll stay. But just tonight. Tomorrow we go." I gave in easily, for in truth I didn't think I'd make it very far tonight.

I woke abruptly in the middle of the night. *Lake over thunder*. The old fortune-teller's words echoed in the dark, still air. A sliver of moonlight shone in through the window, a silver arrow aimed at the foot of the divan.

Lake over thunder. Power, he had said. Deep within myself lay the power to make it back to Allied lines. Submerged beneath the turbulent waters of injury and anxiety was a thunderbolt of energy that could be tapped into, my own personal power source. I would call it forth, like King Arthur pulling the sword Excalibur from the lake. I could feel it already. I closed my eyes and slept.

By morning I felt much stronger. I wasn't sure how much was due to Dr. Sung's herbs and how much to my vision in the night, but I was grateful for the man's medical skills and for his hospitality.

"But we really have to be on our way," I explained through Chien.

Dr. Sung protested vehemently. "He say you not ready yet," Chien said. "Too sick. Must stay here. He afraid for you."

"Sheh-sheh," I said to the doctor. "Thank you. But it's been three days already. We must go."

Sung took off his glasses, polishing them absently with the hem of his tunic, focusing all his attention on me. He sighed and shrugged in a gesture that clearly said, "Suit yourself, but don't blame me when you find out you're wrong." Then he smiled and held out his hand. I shook it warmly. Dalton and Horton did the same.

I wished I had something to give the doctor in return for his kindness and concern. A handshake didn't seem enough, but I had nothing else. *"Sheh-sheh,"* I repeated inadequately. *"Sheh-sheh."*

The doctor bowed once and watched us gravely out the door.

We planned to go through the village and out along the rice paddies. Although it was broad daylight, Dr. Sung had assured us that this was the safest course and that his people would watch out for us.

The dirt path was damp with early morning dew. In the distance we could see farmers straggling out to the paddies, hoes slung over their shoulders. We veered to the right, into the gap between two shacks leaning drunkenly toward each other, and the doctor's house disappeared from view. We were in the village proper now, as one whiff from the gutters attested.

Footsteps padded up behind us. The sound of someone panting for breath. I whirled around.

It was Dr. Sung. He wheezed out something in Chinese, his eyes still serious behind the twinkling spectacles.

"He have idea," Chien said. "Help you."

"Good idea," Weng added.

"Well, what is it?" Horton asked, kicking at a rock in the path and sending up a cloud of foul-smelling dust.

"Ride in . . ." Chien hesitated. "Not know American for it."

"Boat," Dalton suggested.

"I know *boat*." Chien was miffed.

"Besides, we're headin' away from the river," Horton said. "A truck."

"Farmers not have truck," Weng said.

This was true.

"Then what is it?" I asked. I wasn't sure I was in the mood for any surprises.

The brothers looked at each other and shrugged. "You see," Chien said. "Come."

There wasn't any point standing in the street playing guessing games. We followed the doctor. Through the winding lanes of the little village, out across a grassy field and into the nearest rice paddy.

The farmer, clad in the baggiest pair of shorts and tunic I had yet seen, his coolie hat shading his face, was guiding a water buffalo through the knee-deep water. The animal pulled a wooden plow, attached to the yoke with lengths of chain. A bamboo muzzle covered its snout. Long, flattened horns curved in toward the creature's back, ending in sharp points.

"Now you see," Chien announced gleefully.

"We're gonna ride on *that?*" Dalton asked doubtfully.

"Not me." That was Horton, rooted firmly to the spot.

Dr. Sung hailed the farmer and carried on a rapid conversation with him. The farmer, face invisible in the shadow of his hat, turned from his beast toward us and back. Then he tilted back his head, smiled a gap-toothed grin, and motioned us forward.

"Go ahead, Chien." I gave him a little push forward.

"No." His brother stopped him with a hand on his shoulder. "Only room for two. You ride." He indicated Dalton and me. "We walk."

That Dalton should ride was fair enough. It would save stress on his broken leg. But I'd rather have one of the boys go with him than me. I was fine. But Dr. Sung insisted, and soon I found myself hoisted onto the water buffalo's broad back with Dalton hanging on behind me.

We waved good-bye to the doctor, who allowed himself a faint smile, and with another round of *shehshehs* we were off. At a snail's pace. Water buffaloes do not move rapidly.

The boys and Horton walked along beside our beast of burden. The farmer still guided his plow from behind. It was rather pleasant. I felt that from a distance we'd blend in with the rest of the farmers in the fields, so I didn't have to worry about being spotted. The sun bounced off the animal's coarse black hair and sparkled in the water of the paddies. The plodding pace was soothing, interrupted only by the clank and bump of the plow as we humped over the dike between the fields.

It ended all too soon. In an hour we had reached the limits of the farmer's paddies. We slid regretfully off the buffalo's back onto the dike separating the farmer's last field from his neighbor's.

As soon as we stood up it became obvious that we were not Chinese rice farmers. Our height was the immediate giveaway. The neighbor, his wife and teenage daughter rushed over from where they had been planting seedlings to stare open-mouthed at us.

Our farmer told how he had ridden us across his fields on his water buffalo. The neighbor farmer spoke excitedly, as did his wife. His daughter just stared. The neighbor hurried away. His wife and daughter reluctantly returned to their seedlings. The neighbor came back, leading his water buffalo and plow. We were ushered aboard. Another hour passed pleasantly as we sloshed through his fields.

When we reached the end of his paddies, he thanked us. He seemed to consider it a privilege to be allowed to ferry us along.

"No," I said to him, *"sheh-sheh."* I pointed to myself and then him. *"I* thank *you."*

He smiled, nodded and bowed. *"Sheh-sheh."*

After that, we walked. For hours. Through the rice paddies and around them, across the dikes, between one farmer's fields and the next. There were people scattered across the silvery paddies, ivory figurines in the distance, bent double as they tended the bright green shoots.

As we approached they'd turn and look at us, sometimes staring wordlessly, sometimes with a smile and a nod or a string of words to the boys. Although they stared, they never seemed surprised to see American giants traipsing across their land. I finally realized it was because word of our presence was traveling ahead of us, tumbling from the lips of one farmer to those of his neighbor like dominoes falling across the fields.

I only hoped we blended in, for if the Chinese could pass the word along to each other, they could also pass it only too easily, wittingly or not, to the Japanese.

Sometime in the early afternoon we reached a spot where the rice paddies ended abruptly at a line of hills. We left the camouflage of the fields behind and started climbing.

The hill sloped gently, but it was heavy work, especially for Dalton, whose arm was now rubbed raw by the friction of the crutch. And we were too exposed. Nothing moved on the bare, scrub-covered slope but us. We needed a place to hide until dark.

We found it easily enough, a rocky table set into the hillside, screened by a row of wild plums. Supper and shelter, all in one. There was even a trickle of water running down the rocks to drink from.

We decided to drink it straight; whatever germs were going to attack us would already have done so with everything we'd eaten and sloshed through so far. Lighting a fire to boil water was too big a risk. We put our lips to the clear liquid and drank. It tasted pure and sweet.

We ate the wild plums. The sun set. Night took the reins, with a thin crescent moon to light the way. Another river lay on the other side of the hills, leading us closer to home. All we had to do was walk. It was going to be easy.

I stepped beyond the screen of trees. Something crinkled under my foot. A crumpled square of waxy paper. I picked it up, squinting at it in the faint moonlight, although I knew what it was. A Japanese army food wrapper.

The even tenor of the night turned ominous. A chill ran down my spine.

We couldn't stay here, and we couldn't walk blindly into the night, into the arms of the enemy. Go or stay? I tried to think logically. They must be beyond us somewhere, either ahead or behind, but with space and time between us. Otherwise we would have heard them. If they were still on the hill and we waited until daylight we'd be easily spotted. Best to move out now. I prayed that I was right.

We walked all that night and on into the day, until we reached the river bank and beyond.

The world became a blur of rice paddies and river banks, mottled greens and grays and silvers, muddled up with the muddy brown of villages. Sharp blacks and shadows at night, moonlight fading into sunlight filtered through anxiety and fatigue.

I lost track of time, the days piling haphazardly one upon another, then tumbling together so that it was hard to remember events in sequence.

There was a day when we rode in a sampan, hidden in a tiny cabin that reeked of fish, the cabin in turn hidden beneath bales of hay. The sampan was pulled along the still stream's bank by a man on the shore, hauling on a rope attached to the prow.

And a day spent in a village where everyone bickered and babbled at the top of their lungs. The Japanese fragmentation armies were a scant mile away and the people were terrified of being caught with us in their midst and too afraid for us to turn us out.

A night when the moon was as bright as day, illuminating every leaf on every tree with a brilliant glare that made it impossible to move in secrecy. An entire night lost to travel, waiting in the brush for another night and a dimmer moon.

We learned that it was best to stick to the rice paddies, walking in the day when we could, where we were disguised among the farmers in their cotton shirts and shorts, our round-eyed faces hidden like theirs under the wide-brimmed coolie hats.

The Japanese, realizing that in their uniforms they stood out from the peasants, stuck to the hills and desolate valleys during the days, striking into the tilled fields and villages mostly at night like marauding bandits in a Bible story.

And now in every village we passed, the word spread like wildfire that the Japanese were close. A mile away, two miles, ten. Around the next bend, across the river, in the caves outside of town.

We were exhausted all the time. And thirsty. The constant stress was causing dehydration. It was difficult to think rationally, to make logical decisions, to decide to stay in a village or pass on its outskirts, move at night or during the day.

We spent an entire day and night perched in the lee of a secluded stream bank, too tired to think what to do next.

I spread out our map, now worn and creased, on the damp earth and examined the fine scorings of hills and rivers.

We were getting close to Allied lines. But so were the Japanese. We had crossed through their ranks, missing them by miles, or minutes, over and over in the past few days. How much longer would our luck hold out?

Somewhere in the next village, or the next one, someone had a telephone. Someone was willing to call Kweilin and tell them we were here.

It was a risk. If the Japanese picked up the call, we

were as good as dead where we stood. But we were close, not more than a hundred miles from home. They might be able to come in and pick us up. We took the risk.

We told Weng our serial numbers. He memorized them, and went away with the head man of the village to the telephone. I never saw it. How the call was routed from village to town to Kweilin I never understood. It was the townspeople's secret and they either didn't understand my questions or didn't want to answer. But the call went through. Our base in Kweilin knew where we were.

But they weren't coming to get us.

"Japanese," Weng explained. "Too much danger for your Americans to come. Maybe later."

So we were still on our own. Still in enemy territory.

Walking and watching and waiting. Hoping today they'd pick us up. Tonight. Praying it would be the Americans and not the Japanese. Three days went by, or four or five.

Another village, another day. Or was it night? The moon was so bright I couldn't tell. The little alley where we sat was washed with light. As always, the people of the village hung about in the doorways, staring at us with wide eyes, surrounding us with wonder.

A fellow about my age, in black silk trousers and tunic, came up to Weng, whispered something in his ear and drew him away down the alley. They melted into the shadows like cats.

A half hour went by. An hour. Weng returned. He had a curious look on his face, a suppressed tension, as though he had clamped down hard on some barely containable emotion.

"What is it?" I asked, anxiety flickering into my own face.

Weng shook his head, a gesture meaning, not here, not now.

Dalton and Horton picked up on the tension. "What's wrong?" they asked in unison.

Weng refused to say a word.

Chien was strangely quiet, looking into the distance, kicking his feet against the wall.

The moon set. The people faded into their homes at last, to sleep before tomorrow's labor.

Weng turned to me. "Bend in river," he said.

My heart leaped into my throat. I knew what he meant.

"Your people meet you at bend in river."

CHAPTER TWENTY-TWO

Rescue

At last we were to be rescued. I was so excited I could hardly breathe. And yet, now that we were so close to the end of our ordeal I was almost more frightened than I had been at the beginning. So much could go wrong so easily. The Japanese were still within a few miles of us, weaving in and out along the Allied borders. The same secret intelligence that had engineered our rescue could just as easily maneuver our capture with one false move, one word to the wrong person.

But that's human nature, I told myself, to worry that the gods will frown on good fortune. Kuan Yin had been kind to us so far. Why should she let us down now?

Dalton and Horton weren't concerned, or didn't seem to be.

"Let's just hope we get to the rendezvous point in the mornin'," Horton said, "so we can get back to base in time for a decent meal."

"And a shower," Dalton said. "I can't stand the smell of myself any more."

"You can't," Horton said. "Take pity on the rest of us."

And the boys laughed, and they all went into the small house that had been allotted to us, and went to sleep.

I couldn't. I spent the night propped against the wall in the alley, staring up at the stars, listening to the crickets, the lucky orchestra of China, waiting for dawn.

Before the sun was even on the horizon, when the sky was barely tinged with pink, I woke my group.

"Get your gear," I whispered. "Time to be on our way."

I had studied the memory of the map in my head all night. The river was at least ten miles from this village, a two-day walk. I thought that with luck we might make it in one day.

Our silk-clad message courier had told us where to meet our people but not when. I was assuming that they knew how long it would take us to reach the rendezvous point, and that they would wait if we were late. But all this was assumption. Our safest bet was to lay on all possible speed. We would have to hurry.

There were rice paddies beyond the village. We could travel during daylight. Kuan Yin was smiling on us.

The day passed in an agony of mud-slick dikes, knee-deep lotus ponds, a patchwork of greens and browns to be navigated around and through and over. Twice Dalton slipped, lost his footing on the narrow levees and fell into the foul water. I turned the ankle of my good leg, and fell in myself. We didn't have time to stop and examine our bruises. We got up and kept walking.

We didn't eat. We had no food with us and there was no time to stop and scavenge. The village water in our canteens ran out at midday. We slogged through the rice paddies, like the man in "The Rime of the Ancient Mariner," surrounded by water but with none fit to drink.

The rice paddies petered out into brush-covered hills. The sun began a slow descent behind the hills, burning big and orange as flame as it slipped away. The day was gone. We were only halfway to the river.

"We've got to keep moving," I told the group. "We can't risk missing the rendezvous."

"Sure," Dalton said.

"We don't have anythin' better to do," Horton added.

Weng and Chien were already fifty feet ahead of us.

We kept walking, every eye alert for the Japanese, every ear tuned for disturbances in the brush.

The moon rose, shining distantly through a film of cloud. The stars winked in and out of a soft mist.

An owl hooted and we all jumped. A frog croaked somewhere off to the left.

"Water," Weng said.

We veered left. Glimmering in the moonlight, a hundred yards away, was a tiny pond as clear and round as a vanity mirror. We splashed the cool water down our parched throats like wine. The frog dove into the depths and disappeared.

We turned back to our course. Walking and watching and listening.

Something crackled under my foot. Another Japanese food wrapper? My heart pounded. But when I bent down to look, it was only a dry leaf.

The soft mist thickened, blotting out the stars. The moon disappeared. We were left to navigate the brush in darkness. Fortunately, the hillside growth was all scrubby and no more than knee-high. A lot of it we could walk over, and the rest we simply walked into, then around. Higher brush or trees, which could knock you flat if you walked into them, didn't grow here for whatever strange reason. Maybe due to the foresight of Kuan Yin.

But it was slow going. You can't walk fast over ground you know is going to trip you up at every step, and we had to hold down our pace for Dalton, who had more difficulty than the rest of us, maneuvering around on one leg. I became more concerned by the minute that we wouldn't reach the river bend in time.

The hours seemed to drag fitfully and fly like the wind. Time was out of control. Night ruled the world and it would never be light enough to see, or day would dawn all too fast.

We walked on. Bumping over shrubs. Banging into something thorny. Tripping over rocks.

A downhill slope. Slow down, don't tumble all the way down among the rocks. The river must be near. I thought I could smell fresh water.

Downhill, slowly, take your time. Don't break an ankle.

False dawn. The pitch-black night grew lighter, an opaque gray that coated the world with pearly luminescence.

We could just make out the silhouette of the thorny things. I hadn't noticed before that they smelled like jasmine.

A delicate smudge in the east. The barest hint of soft shell-pink. The sun was rising.

The first rays sang into the sky just as we hit the bottom of the slope. We were going to make it. Ahead was the river, glassy and greenish-blue, snaking across the valley.

I got out my map, laid it on the damp ground. The

river curved in and out all along the area we were in, but there was only one spot where it twisted back in on itself in a deep bend. That was the rendezvous point, and it was still about three miles distant.

"Think we can make it?" Dalton peered over my shoulder.

"Sure," I said heartily. I was almost too tired to talk. I hoped I sounded believable.

"We get there easy," Chien piped up.

Easy. If he could make it, and cheerfully, so could I. I folded up the map and put it in my pocket. "Let's go."

There were rice paddies lining the river bank. We stuck close to the shore, weaving in and out among the willows and honeysuckle, hoping that by association we'd still appear to be rice farmers. Threading through the paddies was just too time-consuming.

Gradually the river narrowed to a stream and then a creek. We had left the paddies behind. Sand and mica-flecked rocks, wild plum and mulberry lined the banks. The sun was at midpoint in the sky. Noon.

A thick copse of trees, hiding a bend in the creek. A deep bend. We were here at last. Our pace quickened; we broke into the limping approximation of a run. Rescue was a hundred yards ahead.

We threw ourselves into the shadow of the trees, panting and grinning. No one was there.

We looked around in bewilderment, disappointment etched clearly in each face, too let down to talk.

"Maybe we're early," Dalton said at last.

"Maybe they have flat tire," Chien suggested, always ready to look on the brighter side.

Maybe. A hundred things could have happened. They could have run into the Japanese and been slaughtered. They could have waited for us all night, or all morning, and given up and gone home. The courier could have misinformed us about the rendezvous spot. He could have misunderstood. Or he could have deliberately given us false information, led us into a trap.

Our fate was in the hands of Kuan Yin now, as I supposed it had always been. I offered up a silent prayer and sank down in the sand beneath the trees.

"We'll just have to wait."

"And watch." The thought of a trap had occurred to Horton, too.

We waited. And watched. A lizard scurried among the tree trunks, intent on his own urgent business. A thrush poured out his emotions to the sky, then fell silent. The sun drifted toward the horizon. Darkness was only an hour away. We were alone.

I began to wonder what we should do when night fell. How much longer should we wait? Perhaps we should give up the idea of a rendezvous and just keep walking. We couldn't be more than 75 miles from Kweilin. I was calculating how many more days of walking it would take when I heard it.

A distant dull rumble, so low it was almost inaudible. A low, insistent grinding sound. A sound I hadn't heard in so long I'd almost forgotten it. Gears. A truck.

I didn't actually believe I heard it. But now it was louder, closer. Unmistakable. They were coming!

I stood up. Dalton stood up, and Horton, and the boys. We stepped out of the ring of trees. The sun slanted down in golden rays, and in their nimbus, as if in a halo, was a big, heavy, lumbering olive drab American military truck. The most beautiful sight in the world.

Dalton was waving his crutch and cheering. Horton was jumping up and down, yelling. Someone else was making an awful lot of noise. It was me. I was so happy I didn't know what I was doing, cheering and yelling, waving my arms.

The truck drew closer, only a hundred yards away. The guys in it were yelling and waving, too. Grinning from ear to ear.

We stumbled toward them. A grinding of brakes and the truck creaked to a stop. The guys, five of them, jumped out, ran to us, embraced us as if we were brothers.

Joy spurted up inside me, hurtling to the surface like an oil well about to blow. I couldn't speak—I was afraid I'd burst into tears.

I don't know whether Dalton and Horton said anything or not. I was struggling too hard to control myself to notice. The guys from the truck clapped us all on the back, talking enough for all of us. I don't know what they said. The sound of their voices was enough.

They helped us to the truck. My legs were shaking so bad I could hardly walk. I put my good hand out to be pulled up to safety, to home, and I noticed something was missing.

Chien's gleeful babble had been strangely silent during our joyous welcome. He and Weng had never said a word.

I turned around. The brothers were standing alone, off to the side of the truck, watching with wide eyes as our comrades embraced us.

How must they feel? They had done so much for us, for me. I wouldn't be here without them. Now I was among my people, going home. And they were alone among strangers, with no home to go to.

"Wait a minute," I said to the guy who was helping me up. "I want you to meet some fine people."

I walked over to the boys, put an arm around each of them. "Come on," I said, *"we're* going home."

EPILOGUE

The two-hour trip back to Kweilin was gloriously uneventful.

The big truck, a sort of modified weapons carrier, was mounted with two .30-caliber machine guns, one in the rear and one on the front. There were two gunners, two medical corpsmen and the driver. I had never felt so protected in my life.

Dalton and I were laid on stretchers on the floor of the truck; the boys and Horton rode on benches built into the side. The truck bounced and jounced over the uneven, unpaved ground. The gears ground and the engine rumbled. It was heaven.

In Kweilin—home!—we were given a full medical examination, then hot showers, clean clothes, warm food, and an intensive debriefing.

We had been missing for twenty-three days, had traveled at least 300 miles, and had made it back safely to Allied lines. Intelligence wanted to know how we had done it.

The doctors were there, to make sure the intelligence officers didn't get too carried away with themselves, and we were led through a questioning session that was almost an interrogation.

Who did we talk to? Where did we go? When did we travel? What did we eat? How did we get it? Where did we get the clothes we were wearing? How did we avoid the Japanese? They had more questions than we had answers. I was exhausted, my brain was fuzzy, refusing to coordinate with my mouth.

Finally the questions stopped. I was taken to a hospital room with cool, clean sheets and a soft, warm bed. I slept.

I didn't have to keep one eye open, one ear cocked for the enemy. I was safe. I was home.

In the night, I awoke abruptly, sweat pouring down my face. You're home, I told myself. Go back to sleep. I lay and listened to the silence. It would take time to trust the night.

After five days in the tiny quonset-hut hospital at Kweilin I was airlifted to the 92nd Station Hospital in Kunming.

My cheek was sewn up and my hand and my leg. There was plenty to eat and drink, although my diet was limited. I had lost sixty pounds and the doctors felt that too much food too quickly would make me ill. That was okay.

What I didn't like was the shots. Before my ordeal, I hadn't had an injection in over a year. Each time we had routine immunizations on base, I had bribed the corpsmen to sign off the little card. I hated shots and I didn't think I needed them.

Now I was being made to pay. The doctors pumped us full of vaccines for every disease we could possibly have picked up, and probably half a dozen more. I was a human pin cushion.

Other than that I was treated well. I rested, read magazines, read my mail. I wrote to Ovella. My buddies came to see me. And the boys paid me three visits.

Their visits were short. It was difficult for them to get into the hospital and past the red tape, and the doctors wanted our meetings kept brief to protect me from possible anxiety or excitement. But I asked to see Weng and Chien, and they were allowed in.

The first time the boys came, they stood beside my bed, staring at me with big solemn eyes. They had been given shirts and slacks and shoes by the military, all just a little too large, hanging awkwardly on their small frames. They looked terrified.

I gazed around the room, at the burn victims swathed in bandages, the guys with concussions and broken bones wrapped in tape and gauze, the doctors with their authoritative air, the corpsmen bustling around. "Haven't you fellas ever been inside a hospital before?"

They looked at me. Weng drew himself up. "Sure," he answered. "You not remember Dr. Sung?"

I looked back at them. Chien started to giggle. Weng broke into a slow smile. "Of course, it maybe not same thing exactly."

I laughed, and the ice was broken. As always, the boys cheered me up and I cheered them. But there was not too much else to say, or else there was too much left unspoken.

The boys were working at the Officers Club in a capacity I didn't quite understand, probably as dishwashers or busboys. They lived in the Chinese quarters on the base along with the houseboys and kitchen help. They seemed as safe and as happy as could be expected. But as when we had first met, a curtain was drawing down between their lives and mine, one which my eyes and my questions could not pierce.

The next visit was the same—cheerful, short, and mostly silent. The boys were safe and still together; I was learning to relax again.

At the end of November I realized I would soon be leaving China and the boys for good. I asked the chaplain to arrange a final visit.

Here were the boys again, in civilian slacks and sweaters that still fit a little oddly. Still smiling and cheerful and quiet.

I wondered what would happen to them. I knew they had been paid for returning me to the Americans. The money they received would be enough to keep them comfortably for a long time—if things remained the way they were. If the Japanese overran the territory it would be a different story.

There were German nuns in and around Kunming who might take over the boys' welfare; they were missionaries and that was one of their good works. Or they might be taken in by a group of pilots, as the fellows in my hostel had cared for Mr. Swee. And they had jobs; they were living among their own people. They *had* to be all right.

The late morning sun slanted across the wall. A white-clad nurse hovered over the three of us, prompting the visit to a close.

Inwardly, I sent up a fervent prayer to Kuan Yin. "Take care of my boys. Let them be all right."

Outwardly, I smiled and laid a hand on Weng's thin arm. "See you Stateside," I said. I sent up another prayer to Kuan Yin. "Let it be so."

A few days later, I was flown to the big American hospital in Calcutta.

Horton had disappeared into the military machinery, off at another base on another mission. The boys had received some press coverage for helping me back to safety, and I understood that one of the American pictorial magazines had unofficially adopted them and would send them to school in the States. I hoped it was true.

Dalton, who was recovering smoothly at another hospital in Kunming, was driven down to see me off, in among a crowd of well-wishers. My pals.

My stretcher was carried up the steps of the plane. Dalton raised a hand in farewell. I raised mine in return. That was the last I saw of any of my traveling companions.

The last I saw of them in the flesh. In spirit I saw them often— Dalton's wan smile, Horton's lightning laughter, the boys . . . especially I saw the boys and the strange, strong threads that had bound us together from the start.

When I met Weng and Chien they had no destination in mind other than escape from the terror and destruction of their former lives. They had no people to go to, no relatives to look to as a safe haven at the end of the road.

Yet they had bravely faced that road, alone in an atmosphere of terror. And when they found me, they had taken me along on the road, sharing their shining spirits as well as food and water and shelter.

I thought back to the hours I had spent in their company, watching the wind sough in the trees, the sun and moon drift across the sky, the shadows fall like leaves upon rice paddies and lotus ponds and tiny bamboo huts.

I remembered dark days when we read and re-read my little Testament, the boys listening with rapt attention as I thumbed through the worn pages. Days when we huddled together, lonely, cold and scared, memorizing the Twenty-Third Psalm for its message of deliverance. Hours of blackness suddenly brightened by Weng's quick wit or Chien's guileless chatter.

The boys were listeners more than talkers, but their voices rang out true and clear in their actions—in the love they had for each other and for me.

When I reflected on our journey I saw that they were leaning on me to lead them into freedom while I was leaning on them. They could have gone on without me—I doubted I'd be here on this stretcher, in the arms of the Air Force, without them. I gave them moral support; they gave me that and much more.

Perhaps, during that arduous journey, I was their haven as they were mine, a resting place for the spirit along the road. Wherever they were today, and tomorrow, I hoped they were safe and sound and happy. I hoped they had found their lasting haven.

My stretcher was lifted into the cabin of the plane, placed in a rack against the wall. The heavy metal door clanged shut.

Over the Hump to India. Chabua to Calcutta. Lots of Brits in the hospital. White sheets, olive drab blankets. Two more weeks building back my strength. Orders transferring me to the base hospital in Miami. I would see Ovella again.

The night before we left for home, we were taken to a USO club in town and treated to a meal of real American food. Linen on the tables, glowing candles, flowers. Waiters in suits.

It reminded me of the evening I spent in Kunming with Bill Griffith. The night of the red ball alert. A night of fear and confusion, like much of my time in China.

293

Yet I would miss China. The beauty of the land, the kindness of her people, the strange, exotic sights and sounds and smells. The thrill and pride of helping to defend her, soaring over the peaks and valleys, rivers and mountains, mist and cloud and bright, piercing sun. I would fly again, but not as a Flying Tiger. I would miss it.